Digital Image Processing Handbook

Digital Image Processing Handbook

Edited by **Niceto Salazar**

CLANRYE INTERNATIONAL

New Jersey

Published by Clanrye International,
55 Van Reypen Street,
Jersey City, NJ 07306, USA
www.clanryeinternational.com

Digital Image Processing Handbook
Edited by Niceto Salazar

© 2015 Clanrye International

International Standard Book Number: 978-1-63240-145-8 (Hardback)

Contents

Preface

This book was inspired by the evolution of our times; to answer the curiosity of inquisitive minds. Many developments have occurred across the globe in the recent past which has transformed the progress in the field.

The book discusses the recent advances related to 'digital image processing', acknowledging the possibilities offered by digital image processing algorithms in various fields. The book presents graphical representations and illustrative examples in addition to mathematical algorithms for the reader's help. The book is structured for the better understanding of even those readers who have only a basic knowledge and experience in the field of digital image processing. Moreover, the scientists and researchers will be able to use the information given in this book for the advancement of the presented subjects.

This book was developed from a mere concept to drafts to chapters and finally compiled together as a complete text to benefit the readers across all nations. To ensure the quality of the content we instilled two significant steps in our procedure. The first was to appoint an editorial team that would verify the data and statistics provided in the book and also select the most appropriate and valuable contributions from the plentiful contributions we received from authors worldwide. The next step was to appoint an expert of the topic as the Editor-in-Chief, who would head the project and finally make the necessary amendments and modifications to make the text reader-friendly. I was then commissioned to examine all the material to present the topics in the most comprehensible and productive format.

I would like to take this opportunity to thank all the contributing authors who were supportive enough to contribute their time and knowledge to this project. I also wish to convey my regards to my family who have been extremely supportive during the entire project.

Editor

Low Bit Rate SAR Image Compression Based on Sparse Representation

Alessandra Budillon and Gilda Schirinzi

Dipartimento per le Tecnologie - Università degli Studi di Napoli "Parthenope"
Italy

1. Introduction

Synthetic aperture radar (SAR) is an active remote sensing tool operating in the microwave range of the electromagnetic spectrum. It uses the motion of the radar transmitter to synthesize an antenna aperture much larger than the actual antenna aperture in order to yield high spatial resolution radar images (Curlander & McDonough, 1991). It has been applied to military survey, terrain mapping, and other fields for its characteristics of working in all weather during day and night.

In the last few years, high quality images of the Earth produced by SAR systems, carried on a variety of airborne and space borne platforms, have become increasingly available. With the increasing resolution of SAR images, it is of great interest to find efficient ways to store the high volume of SAR image data at real time or to compress SAR images with higher compression performances for limited bandwidth of communication channel.

There are some special characteristics of SAR images so different from incoherent, optical images, to which compression algorithms are commonly applied, that sensitively affect the design of an image compression algorithm: First of all the speckle phenomena, which results from the coherent radiation and processing and severely degrades the quality of SAR images. When illuminated by the SAR, each target contributes backscatter energy which, along with phase and power changes, is then coherently summed for all scatterers. This summation can be either high or low, depending on constructive or destructive interference. Second the very high dynamic range of SAR images also attributable to the coherent nature of the imaging process. Within a resolution cell of an image, the transduced image domain value is related to the radar cross section per unit area of the corresponding patch of illuminated terrain (Eichel & Ives, 1999) This specific cross section can vary over a considerable range. Most natural terrain, being rough relative to the wavelengths employed, exhibit relatively low values of this parameter, in the vicinity of -15 dBsm/m^2; while flat, smooth surfaces such as lake exhibit even lower values. On the other hand, manmade objects, especially of conducting materials with large flat surfaces and right angles, can have specific cross sections of +60 dBsm/m^2 and higher.

These differences mean that encoding/decoding algorithms designed for optical data may not be optimized or even appropriate for SAR data.

Many efforts have been taken place in order to develop suitable compression techniques of the bit stream necessary for raw data and/or focused images coding (Kwok & Jhonson, 1989, Pascazio & Schirinzi, 2003, Eichel & Ives, 1999, Dony & Haykin, 1997, Baxter, 1999).

The most widely used compression techniques are based on Block Adaptive Quantization (BAQ), due to its simplicity for coding and decoding. The algorithm is based on the consideration that the SAR (complex) signal has commonly a Gaussian, with real and imaginary parts mutually independent and practically uncorrelated between adjacent pixels. It divides the data in blocks, and for each block computes the standard deviation σ, in order to determine the optimum quantizer, which adapts to the changing levels of the signal (Kwok & Jhonson, 1989). A non-uniform quantizer (or Lloyd-Max quantizer) that minimizes the Mean Squared Error (MSE) for a given number of quantization levels (Goyal et al., 1998) is commonly used. The minimum block size is selected in order to guarantee a Gaussian statistic within a block; the maximum block size is limited by the fact that the signal power should be approximately constant in the block.

Transform coding algorithms have been also applied on SAR intensity images (Dony & Haykin, 1997, Eichel & Ives, 1999, Baxter, 1999) and on SAR raw data (Pascazio & Schirinzi, 2003). They are based on the decomposition of the signal to be encoded in an orthonormal basis. Then, each decomposition coefficient is approximated by a quantized variable. The role of the signal decomposition is to decorrelate the signal and to make the subsequent quantization process easier. The coding performance depends on the choice of the basis. The best basis compacts the image energy into the fewest coefficients. The small number of significant coefficients in the transformed domain results in a sparse representation, that can be coded with fewer bits, due to its low entropy. An entropy coder can be then used as the last step in the compression scheme. In (Dony & Haykin, 1997) a method which combines Karhunen-Loeve transform and Vector Quantisation is proposed, while in (Eichel & Ives, 1999) simply 2-D Fourier transformation is used, in (Baxter, 1999) a compression system based on the Gabor transform is adopted, in (Pascazio & Schirinzi, 2003) a transform coding compression method using wavelet basis is applied to SAR raw data. Wavelets have also been applied on SAR images by (Zeng & Cumming, 2001, Xingsong et al. 2004), in the first case it has been proposed a tree-structured wavelet transform, while in the second case a compression scheme which combines the wavelet packet transform, the quadtree classification and universal trellis-coded quantization has been adopted.

With the aim of reducing the number of significant representation coefficients, and obtaining a sparse representation, overcomplete dictionaries, or frames, have been recently proposed (Goyal et al., 1998). A frame is a set of column vectors, just as a transform, but with a larger number of vectors than the number of elements in each vector. The representation of the observed data in terms of overcomplete basis in not unique, then a constraint have to be enforced to recover uniqueness. To achieve a sparse representation the introduced constraint can be the minimization of the significant coefficients by using an ℓ_1 norm based penalty. It can be shown that in this case the problem to be solved is a linear programming problem, that can be viewed as a Maximum a Posteriori (MAP) estimation problem with a Laplacian prior distribution assumption (Hyvarinen et al., 1999).

A possible choice of the basis is the overcomplete Independent Component Analysis (ICA) basis (Hyvarinen et al., 1999, Algra, 2000), allowing to model the data as a mixture of non Gaussian and "almost" statistically independent sources, so that the representation coefficients, due to their scarce correlation, can be efficiently coded using a scalar quantizer.

In this paper the performance of a compression method based on an overcomplete ICA representation, coupled with the use of an entropy constrained scalar quantizer (Pascazio & Schirinzi, 2003), optimized for the Laplacian statistics of the ICA coefficients, and using a proper bit allocation strategy, first proposed in (Budillon et al., 2005) is analyzed in details and proved on different set of real data, obtained with ERS1, COSMO SkyMed and TerraSAR-X sensors.

2. Overcomplete ICA

Independent Component Analysis (ICA) (Hyvarinen et al., 1999) has been proposed as a statistical generative model that allows to represent the observed data as a linear transformation of variables that are non Gaussian and mutually independent.
The model is the following:

$$x = As \tag{1}$$

where $x = [x_1, x_2, \ldots x_m]^T$ is the random vector representing the observed data, $s = [s_1, s_2, \ldots s_n]^T$ is the random vector of the independent components, A is an unknown constant matrix, called the mixing matrix or basis matrix.

The overcomplete ICA paradigm (Hyvarinen et al., 1999) assumes $n > m$. This means we have a larger number of independent components and we can more easily adapt to signal statistics. Since the matrix A is not invertible, even if it is known, the estimation of the independent components is an undetermined problem that does not admit a unique solution. Then a constraint on the statistical distribution of the ICA coefficients is introduced to solve the problem.

It can be shown (Hyvarinen et al., 1999) that assuming a Laplacian distribution, the optimal estimation of the coefficients $\hat{s}_i$ leads to the minimization of their ℓ_1-norm with the constraint $x = As$

$$\hat{s} = \underset{x=As}{\arg\min} \sum_i |s_i| \tag{2}$$

The choice of the Laplacian distribution is convenient with respect to the compression application since permits to have a sparse representation with a small number of non zero coefficient $\hat{s}_i$.

For the estimation of the basis matrix we adopted a modification of FastICA proposed in (Hyvarinen et al., 1999), that searches for "quasi-orthogonal" basis.

3. Entropy constrained scalar quantizer and bit allocation

In this section we analyze the performance of a scalar quantizer, optimized for Laplacian-distributed coefficients. In particular, we consider an entropy constrained scalar quantizer, defined as the quantizer minimizing the quadratic distortion for a given value of the entropy of the quantized coefficients (Jayant & Noll, 1984).

It is already known that under the high-resolution quantization hypothesis, i. e. if the number of quantization levels is sufficiently large a uniform quantizer is optimal for a large class of probability distributions [9]. However, at low bit rates, a uniform quantizer is not optimal. Among the non-uniform quantizers, we consider the threshold quantizer (or quasi-uniform quantizer), which assigns zero to the coefficients whose amplitude lies inside a proper interval $[-T, T]$, and uniformly quantizes the others with a quantization step Δ. All the samples whose absolute value exceeds a certain saturation amplitude $K\Delta$ are quantized to the highest or lowest quantization level (see Fig. 1) depending on their sign. The saturation factor K can thus be defined as the ratio between the quantizer saturation value and the standard deviation σ of the coefficient. Note that this quantizer is symmetric and works with an even number of quantization levels.

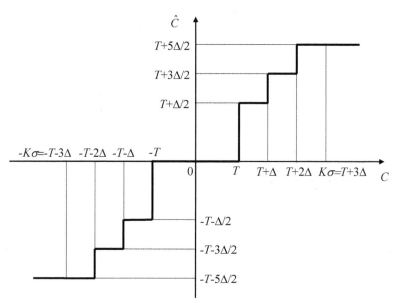

Fig. 1. Six levels threshold quantizer.

If the decomposition basis is chosen so that many coefficients are close to zero and few of them have a large amplitude, the threshold quantizer tends to an optimal entropy constrained quantizer (Mallat & Falzon, 1998). The larger the number of coefficients close to zero, the closer the threshold quantizer is to the optimal one.

At low bit rates, the decomposition coefficients are coarsely quantized, and many are set to zero. Thus it is convenient to scan the coefficients frame in a predefined order and store the position of zero versus non-zero quantized coefficients in a binary significance map. In the same scanning order, the amplitudes of the non-zero quantized coefficients are also entropy encoded with a Huffman or an arithmetic coding and transmitted together with the coded map.

The total number of bits necessary to encode a data frame is given by the number of bits necessary to encode the significance map, plus the number of bits necessary to encode the significant coefficients. Of course, the total bit rates decreases as the coefficients probability density function (pdf) becomes more peaked, so that the number of significant coefficients decreases and the significance map becomes more correlated (Mallat & Falzon, 1998).

The performance of the quantizer considered depends on three parameters: the threshold value T, the number of the quantization levels L, and the saturation factor K. These parameters must be set in such a way as to minimize distortion for an assigned rate value. The optimization of the threshold quantizer performance with respect to parameters T, L and K can be performed once for a unit variance Laplacian variable. Its performance for Laplacian signals with variance σ^2 can be simply inferred by that found for an unit variance Laplacian signal, by simply multiplying the threshold value by σ, and the obtained distortion by the variance σ^2.

A desired bit rate can be achieved for different values of the coder parameters. The optimal coder parameters $\hat{T}, \hat{L}, \hat{K}$ for an assigned bit rate can be found by minimizing the distortion, that for Laplacian distribution can be expressed in an analytical form, following the method presented in (Pascazio & Schirinzi, 2003), for the Gaussian case.

The minimum distortion-rate curve $\hat{D}(R) = D(R, \hat{T}, \hat{L}, \hat{K})$ for a unit variance Laplacian distribution obtained using the threshold entropy constrained quantizer, is shown in Fig. 2 (solid line), where it is compared with the curves obtained with an entropy constrained uniform quantizer (dotted line) (Algra, 2000).

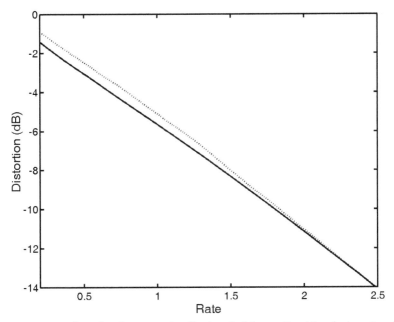

Fig. 2. Distortion-rate function for an optimally threshold quantized Laplacian signal of unit variance (solid line), compared with that obtained with an optimal uniform quantizer (dots).

We can note that the optimal threshold quantizer performs better than a uniform one at very low bit rates (lower than 1.8), and reduces to a uniform one for higher bit rates. This behavior can be conveniently exploited when a proper bit allocation is adopted, since in this case it can happen very often that very low rates must be assigned to certain blocks, even if the total bit budget is not very small. If we apply the same threshold quantizer to the entire frame of the coefficients, we obtain the performance shown in Fig.2. Different results can be obtained by using different quantizer for the different blocks in which the coefficient frame is decomposed. In particular, we can use different quantizers and associated coders optimized for the statistic of each block. A bit allocation algorithm can then be used to distribute bits among the blocks.

A procedure that can be used for optimally distributing the assigned number of bits among the different blocks is described in (Pascazio & Schirinzi, 2003). It imposes an equal average distortion per block and assigns more bits to the blocks with a larger variance respect to those assigned to the blocks with a lower variance. The optimal number of bits for each block is determined by exploiting the minimum distortion curve of Fig. 2 (Pascazio & Schirinzi, 2003).

4. Numerical results

To test the performance of the proposed method we considered different SAR images obtained with different SAR sensors, using ERS1, COSMO SkyMed and TerraSAR-X data. We wanted to test the performance also on different kinds of areas that due to different backscatter characteristics may have different local statistical characteristics: we used three kinds of images that cover agricultural, suburban, and countryside areas.

Each single-look intensity image has been subdivided in data frames in the azimuth and range directions, respectively. Note that the SAR image pixels are floating point valued with a dynamic range of about 50 dB. Moreover, the SAR images are affected by the presence of speckle, typical of images generated by coherent systems, that has to be preserved to keep the information contained in the image.

Each frame has been subdivided in blocks of 8x8 pixels. The overcomplete ICA basis have been computed using the algorithms presented in [6], and starting from a set of 8x8 training vectors. The set size has to be larger than m. The used value for the ratio m/n is about 0.7.

Then, the ICA coefficients of each frame have been computed using Eq. (2). The ICA coefficients have, then, been quantized using the optimal threshold quantizer of Fig. 2, that, besides exhibiting a better performance, has the advantage of allowing any fractional bit rate value. For the bit budget distribution among the different coefficients vectors, the bit allocation procedure referred in Section III has been adopted. To sum up we followed for each image the scheme reported in Fig. 3

Different quality parameters can be considered to evaluate the performance of the compression method. In particular, one of the most meaningful parameters is the signal-to-noise ratio (SNR), or its reciprocal, the normalized average distortion D computed on the SAR images obtained after the processing of the compressed data. We have chosen to evaluate the normalized distortion in order to compare the obtained results with the distortion-rate curve reported in Fig. 2.

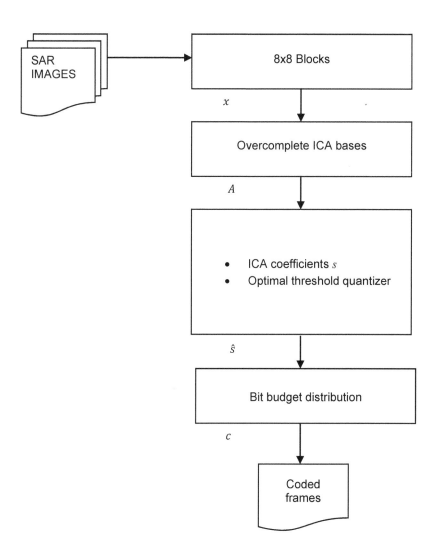

Fig. 3. Scheme of the proposed compression method.

$$D = \frac{\text{quantization noise power}}{\text{SAR data power}} = \frac{\|x - \hat{x}\|^2}{\|x\|^2}.$$

We reported also the distortion evaluated on the ICA coefficients.

$$D_s = \frac{\text{quantization ICA coefficients noise power}}{\text{ICA coefficients power}} = \frac{\|s - \hat{s}\|^2}{\|s\|^2}.$$

First a single look ERS-1 intensity image, relative to Fleevoland, in The Netherlands, was considered. The original image is shown in Fig. 4.

The (equalized) intensity of a frame is shown in Fig. 5. The obtained statistical distribution of each ICA coefficient, as expected, has a Laplacian behaviour as shown in Fig. 6. The ICA basis are reported in Fig. 7.

The average distortion obtained for different bit rates are presented in Table 1. Note that the bit rate values represent the average number of bits per pixel of the image frame. Being the dimension of the ICA basis larger than that of the observation domain, the average number of bits per coefficient is smaller (it is scaled by the factor m/n).

Quantized coefficients have then been used to reconstruct the corresponding image using Eq. (1). The image frame obtained with an average rate per sample $R=2$, is shown in Fig. 8.

Secondly we considered a single look COSMO SkyMed of Naples surroundings, in Italy, shown in Fig. 9.

The (equalized) intensity of a frame is shown in Fig. 10. The obtained statistical distribution of each coefficient, as expected, has a Laplacian behaviour as shown in Fig. 11. The ICA basis are reported in Fig. 12.

The average distortion obtained for different bit rates are presented in Table 2.

The image frame obtained with an average rate per sample $R=2$, is shown in Fig. 13.

Thirdly we considered a single look TerraSAR-X of Frankfurt surrounding, in Germany, shown in Fig. 14.

The (equalized) intensity of a frame is shown in Fig. 15. The obtained statistical distribution of each coefficient, as expected, has a Laplacian behaviour as shown in Fig. 16. The ICA basis are reported in Fig. 17.

The average distortion obtained for different bit rates are presented in Table 3.

The image frame obtained with an average rate per sample $R=2$, is shown in Fig. 18.

It can be noted that in all cases the average image distortions reported in Table 1,2 and 3 are below the value of -11 dB obtained for rate 2 in the curve reported in Fig. 2 for an optimally threshold quantized Laplacian signal of unit variance.

Moreover in all the cases there is no visual appreciable degradation in the reconstructed images using the quantized coefficients of the overcomplete ICA basis.

Fig. 4. SAR single look ERS-1 intensity image, relative to Fleevoland, in The Netherlands.

Fig. 5. SAR ERS-1 frame.

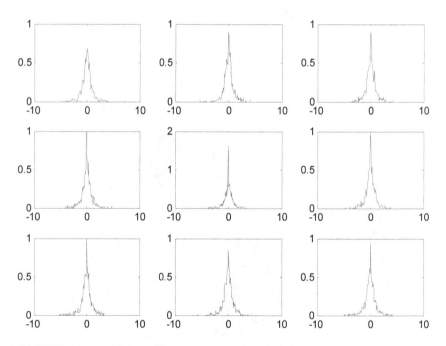

Fig. 6. SAR ERS-1 image ICA coefficients empirical probability distribution functions.

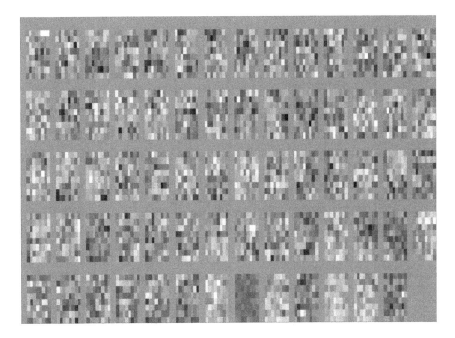

Fig. 7. SAR ERS-1 image overcomplete ICA basis.

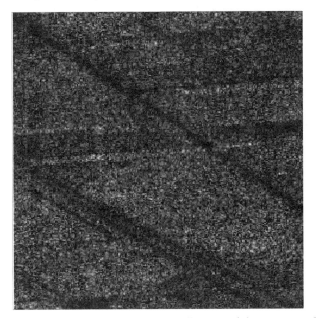

Fig. 8. SAR ERS-1 frame obtained by quantized coefficients of the overcomplete ICA basis with $R=2$.

Average rate	Overcomplete ICA	
	Coefficients average distortion (dB)	Image average distortion (dB)
1	-5.4	-11.1
1.5	-8.3	-13.2
2.	-11.6	-15.3

Table 1. Rate-Distortion values for the SAR ERS-1 image.

Fig. 9. SAR COSMO-SkyMed intensity image of Naples surroundings, Italy.

Fig. 10. SAR COSMO-SkyMed frame.

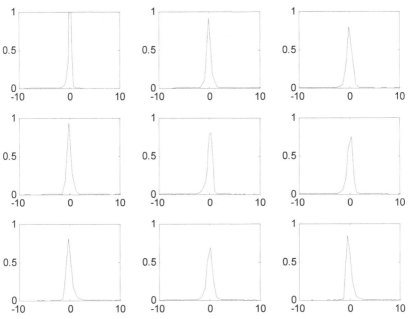

Fig. 11. SAR COSMO-SkyMed image ICA coefficients empirical probability distribution functions.

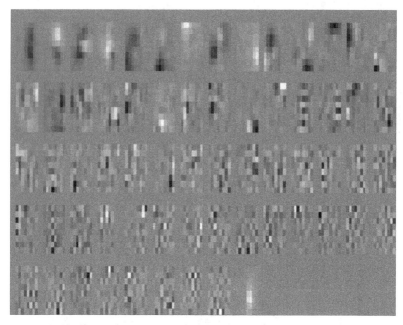

Fig. 12. SAR COSMO-SkyMed image overcomplete ICA basis.

Fig. 13. SAR COSMO-SkyMed frame obtained by quantized coefficients of the overcomplete ICA basis with R=2.

Average rate	Overcomplete ICA	
	Coefficients average distortion (dB)	Image average distortion (dB)
1	-4.4	-8
1.5	-6.9	-10.3
2.	-10.8	-13.2

Table 2. Rate-Distortion values for the SAR COSMO-SkyMed image.

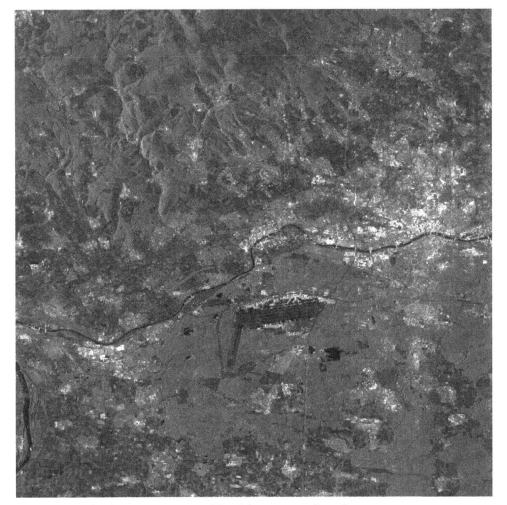

Fig. 14. TerraSAR-X intensity image of Frankfurt surrounding, Germany.

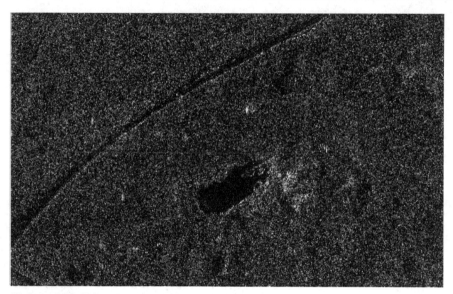

Fig. 15. TerraSAR-X frame.

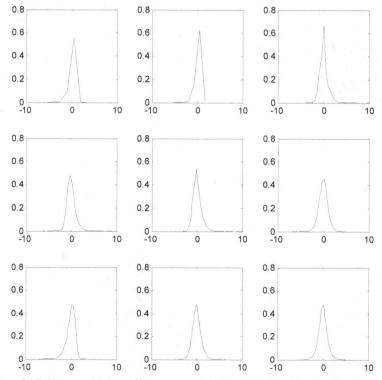

Fig. 16. TerraSAR-X image ICA coefficients empirical probability distribution functions.

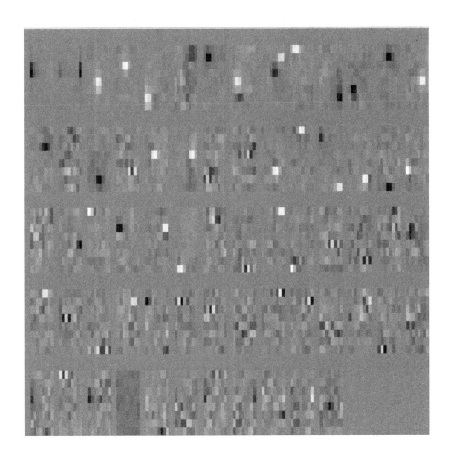

Fig. 17. TerraSAR-X image overcomplete ICA basis.

Fig. 18. TerraSAR-X frame obtained by quantized coefficients of the overcomplete ICA basis with $R=2$.

Average rate	Overcomplete ICA	
	Coefficients average distortion (dB)	Image average distortion (dB)
1	-5.7	-10.6
1.5	-8.5	-13.4
2.	-11.4	-16.4

Table 3. Rate-Distortion values for the TerraSAR-X image.

5. Conclusion

In this paper the performance of a compression method based on an overcomplete ICA representation, coupled with the use of an entropy constrained scalar quantizer, optimized for the Laplacian statistics of the ICA coefficients, and using a proper bit allocation strategy, has been analyzed in details and proved on different set of real data, obtained with ERS1, COSMO SkyMed and TerraSAR-X sensors. The best performances in terms of rate-distortions are obtained on the TerraSAR-X data frame, since it is relative to an enough uniform reflectivity area, while the worse on the COSMO SkyMed image frame, where more details were present. In any cases the image average distortions are below the one obtained with an optimally threshold quantized Laplacian signal of unit variance. The ICA coefficients exhibits the statistical behaviour forced by the fast ICA algorithm, in fact the probability empirical distributions are in all cases a good approximation of a Laplacian distribution. This behaviour allows to use a threshold quantizer optimized for this particular statistical distribution, allowing to discard many coefficients and to use a high bit rate only for few significant coefficients in order to keep low bit rates.

6. Acknowledgment

We thank for providing the real data the Italian Space Agency (ASI) under the contract "Imaging and Monitoring with Multitemporal/Multiview COSMO/SkyMed SAR Data" (ID: 2246) and the German Aerospace Center (Deutsches Zentrum für Luft- und Raumfahrt; DLR) for the TerraSAR-X data (proposal MTH0941).

7. References

Algra, T. (2000). Compression of raw SAR data using entropy-constrained quantization, *Proc. of IEEE Int. Geosci. and Remote Sens. Symp., IGARSS 2000*, pp. 2660-2662, Honolulu, USA, July,2000.

Baxter, R.A., (1999). SAR image compression with the Gabor transform, *IEEE Trans. Geosci. Remote Sensing*, GRS-77, pp. 574-588, 1999.

Budillon, A., Cuozzo, G., D'Elia, C., Schirinzi, G., (2005). Application of overcomplete ICA to SAR image compression, *Proc. of IEEE Int. Geosci. and Remote Sens. Symp., IGARSS 2005*, Seul, South Corea, July, 2005.

Comon, P. (1994). Independent component analysis-a new concept?, *Signal Processing*, vol. 36, pp. 287-314, 1994.

Curlander, J.C., McDonough, R. N. (1991). *Synthetic Aperture Radar, Systems and Signal Processing*, New York: Wiley, 1991.

Dony, R.D., Haykin, S., (1997). Compression of SAR images using KLT, VQ and mixture of principal components, *IEE Proceedings on Radar, Sonar and Navigation*, vol. 144, pp 113-120,1997.

Eichel, P., Ives,R.W. (1999). Compression of Complex-Valued SAR Images, *IEEE Trans. On Image Proc.*, IP-8, pp. 1483-1487, 1999.

Goyal, V. K., Vetterli, M. ,Thao, N. T. (1998). Quantized overcomplete expansions in RN: Analysis, synthesis, and algorithms, *IEEE Trans. Inform. Theory.*, 44, pp. 16-31, 1998.

Hyvarinen, A., Cristescu, R., Oja, E. (1999). A Fast algorithm for estimating overcomplete ICA bases for image windows, *Proc. Int. Joint Conf. on Neural Networks*, pp. 894-899, Washington, D.C., 1999.

Jayant, N. J., Noll, P. (1984), *Digital Coding of Waveforms*, Englewood Cliffs, NJ: Prentice Hall Inc. 1984.

Kwok, R., Jhonson, W. T. K. (1989). Block Adaptive Quantization of Magellan SAR Data, *IEEE Trans. Geosci. Remote Sensing*, GRS-27, pp. 375-383, 1989.

Mallat, S., Falzon, F. (1998). Analysis of Low Bit Rate Image Transform Coding, *IEEE Trans. Signal Processing*, SP-46, pp.1027-1042, 1998.

Pascazio, V., Schirinzi, G. (2003). SAR Raw Data Compression by Sub-Band Coding, *IEEE Trans. Geosci. Rem. Sensing*, GRS-41, pp. 964-976, 2003.

Xingsong, H., Guizhong, L., Yiyang, Z., (2004). SAR image data compression using wavelet packet transform and universal-trellis coded quantization, *IEEE Trans. Geosci. Remote Sensing*, GRS-42, pp. 2632-2641, 2004.

Zhaohui Zeng; Cumming, I.G., (2001). SAR image data compression using a tree-structured wavelet transform, *IEEE Trans. Geosci. Remote Sensing*, GRS-39, pp. 546-552, 2001.

2

Laser Probe 3D Cameras Based on Digital Optical Phase Conjugation

Zhiyang Li

College of Physical Science and Technology, Central China Normal University
Hubei, Wuhan,
P. R. China

1. Introduction

A camera makes a picture by projecting objects onto the image plane of an optical lens, where the image is recorded with a film or a CCD or CMOS image sensor. The pictures thus generated are two-dimensional and the depth information is lost. However in many fields depth information is getting more and more important. In industry the shape of a component or a die, needs to be measured accurately for quality control, automated manufacturing, solid modelling, etc. In auto-navigation, three dimensional coordinates of changing environment need to be acquired in real-time to aid auto path planning for vehicles or intelligent robots. In driving assistant systems any obstacle in front a car should be detected within 0.01 second. Even in making 3D movies for true 3D display in the near future, three dimensional coordinates need to be recorded with a fame rate of at least 25f/s, etc. For the past few decades intensive researches have been carried out and various optical methods have been investigated[Chen, et al., 2000], yet they still could not fulfil every requirement of present-day applications on either measuring speed, or accuracy, or measuring range/area, or convenience, etc. For example, although interferometric methods provide very high measuring precision [Yamaguchi, et al., 2006; Barbosa, & Lino, 2007], they are sensitive to speckle noise and vibration and perform measurement over small areas. The structured light projection methods provide good precision and full field measurements [Srinivasan, et al., 1984; Guan, et al., 2003], yet the measuring width is still limited to several meters. Besides they often encounter shading problems. Stereovision is a convenient means for large field measurements without active illumination, but stereo matching often turns very complicated and results in high reconstruction noise [Asim, 2008].To overcome the drawbacks improvements and new methods appear constantly. For example, time-of-flight (TOF) used to be a point-to-point method [Moring, 1989]. Nowadays commercial 3D-TOF cameras are available [Stephan, et al., 2008]. Silicon retina sensors have also been developed which supports event-based stereo matching [Jürgen & Christoph, 2011]. Among all the efforts those employing cameras appear more desirable because they are non-contact, relatively cheap, easy to carry out, and provide full field measurements, etc.

The chapter introduces a new camera—a so-called laser probe 3D camera, a camera enforced with hundreds and thousands of laser probes projected onto objects, whose pre-known positions help to determine the three dimensional coordinates of objects under investigation. The most challenging task in constructing such a 3D camera is the generation of those huge number of laser probes, with the position of each laser probe independently adaptable according to the shape of an object. In section 2 we will explain how the laser probes could be created by means of digital optical phase conjugation, an accurate method for optical wavefront reconstruction we put forward a little time earlier[Zhiyang, 2010a,2010b]. In section 3 we will demonstrate how the laser probes could be used to construct 3D cameras dedicated for various applications, such as micro 3D measurement, fast obstacle detection, 360-deg shape measurement, etc. In section 4 we will discuss more characteristics like measuring speed, energy consumption, resistance to external interferences, etc., of laser probe 3D cameras. Finally a short summery is given in section 5.

2. Generation of laser probes via digital optical phase conjugation

To build a laser-probe 3D camera, one needs first to find a way to project simultaneously hundreds and thousands of laser probes into preset positions. Looking the optical field formed by all the laser probes as a whole it might be regarded as a problem of optical wavefront reconstruction. Although various methods for optical wavefront reconstruction have been reported, few of them could fulfil above task. For example, an optical lens system can focus a light beam and move it around with a mechanical gear. But it can hardly adjust its focal length so quickly to produce so many laser probes far and near within the time of a snapshot of a camera. Traditional optical phase conjugate reflection is an efficient way for optical wavefront reconstruction [Yariv, & Peper, 1977; Feinberg, 1982]. However it reproduces, or reflects only existing optical wavefronts based on some nonlinear optical effects. That is to say, to generate above mentioned laser probes one should first find another way to create beforehand the same laser probes with high energy to trig nonlinear optical effect. While holography can reconstruct only static optical wavefronts since high resolution holographic plates have to be used.

To perform real-time digital optical wavefront reconstruction it is promising to employ spatial light modulators (SLM) [Amako, et al. 1993; Matoba, et al. 2002; Kohler, et al. 2006]. A SLM could modulate the amplitude or phase of an optical field pixel by pixel in space. For liquid crystal SLMs several millions of pixels are available. And the width of each pixel might be fabricated as small as 10 micrometers in case of a projection type liquid crystal panel. However the pixel size appears still much larger than the wavelength to be employed in a laser probe 3D camera. According to the sensitive wavelength range of a CCD or CMOS image sensor it is preferable to produce laser probes with a wavelength in the range of 0.35~1.2 micrometers, or 0.7~1.2 micrometers to avoid interference with human eyes if necessary. So the wavelength is about ten times smaller than the pixel pitch of a SLM. Therefore with bare SLMs only slowly varying optical fields could be reconstructed with acceptable precision. Unfortunately the resulting optical field formed by hundreds and thousands of laser probes may appear extremely complex.

Recently we introduced an adiabatic waveguide taper to decompose an optical field, however dramatically it changes over space, into simpler form that is easier to rebuild [Zhiyang, 2010a]. As illustrated in Fig.1, such an adiabatic taper consists of a plurality of single-mode waveguides. At the narrow end of the taper the single-mode waveguides couple to each other. While at the wide end the single-mode waveguides become optically isolated from each other. When an optical field incidents on the left narrow end of the taper, it would travel to the right wide end and gets decomposed into fundamental mode field of each isolated single-mode waveguide. Since these fundamental mode fields are separated from each other in space, they could be reconstructed using a pair of low resolution SLMs and a micro lens array (MLA) as illustrated in Fig.2.

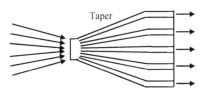

Fig. 1. Structure of an adiabatic waveguide taper.

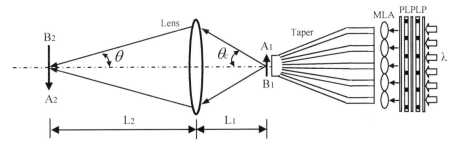

Fig. 2. Device to perform digital optical phase conjugation.

For the device in Fig.2 we may adjust the gray scale of each pixel of SLMs so that it modulates the amplitude and the phase of illuminating laser beam properly [Neto, et al. 1996; Tudela, et al. 2004] and reconstruct a conjugate field proportional to above decomposed fundamental mode field within each isolated single-mode waveguide at the right wide end. Due to reciprocity of an optical path the digitally reconstructed conjugate light field within each isolated single-mode waveguide would travel inversely to the left narrow end of the taper, combine and create an optical field proportional to the original incident optical field. Since the device in Fig.2 rebuilds optical fields via digital optical phase conjugation, it gets ride off all the aberrations inherent in conventional optical lens systems automatically. For example, suppose an object A_2B_2 is placed in front of the optical lens. It forms an image A_1B_1 with poor quality. The reconstructed conjugate image in front of the narrow end of the taper bears all the aberrations of A_1B_1. However, due to reciprocity, the light exited from the reconstructed conjugate image of A_1B_1 would follow the same path and return to the original starting place, restoring A_2B_2 with exactly the same shape. So the resolution of a digital optical phase conjugation device is merely limited by diffraction, which can be described by,

$$dx = \frac{\lambda}{2\sin\theta} \tag{1}$$

where θ is the half cone angle of the light beam arriving at a point at image plane as indicated in Fig.2. The half cone angle θ could be estimated from the critical angle θ_c of incidence of the taper through the relation $\tan(\theta)/\tan(\theta_c)=L_1/L_2=|A_1B_1|/|A_2B_2| = 1/\beta_x$, where β_x being the vertical amplification ratio of the whole optical lens system. When SLMs with 1920×1080 pixels are employed, the width of the narrow end of an adiabatic waveguide taper with a refraction index of 1.5 reaches 0.458mm for λ=0.532 μm, or 0.860mm for λ=1 μm respectively to support Ns=1920 guided eigenmodes. When a 3×3 array of SLMs with same pixels are employed, the width of the narrow end of the taper increases to 1.376mm for λ=0.532 μm, or 2.588mm for λ=1 μm respectively to support a total of Ns=3×1920=5760 guided eigenmodes. The height of reconstructed conjugate image A_1B_1 right in front of the narrow end of the tap may have the same size as the taper. Fig.3 plotted the lateral resolutions at different distances Z from the taper (left), or for different sizes of reconstructed image A_2B_2(middle and right) with θ_c =80°, where the resolution for λ=0.532 μm is plotted in green colour and that for λ=1 μm in red colour. It could be seen that within a distance of Z=0~1000 μm, the resolution is jointly determined by wavelength and the pixel number Ns of the SLMs. The optical lens is taken away temporarily since there is no room for it when Z is less than 1mm. However when $|A_2B_2|$ is larger than 40mm, the resolution becomes irrelevant to wavelength, but decreases linearly with the pixel number Ns of the SLMs and increase linearly with the size of $|A_2B_2|$. When $|A_2B_2|$=100m, the resolution is about 10.25mm for Ns=1920 and 3.41mm for Ns=5760 respectively.

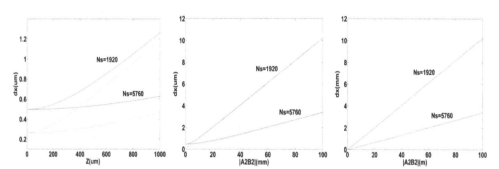

Fig. 3. Lateral resolution of a laser probe at a distance Z in the range of 0~1000μm (left); or with $|A_2B_2|$ in the range of 1~100mm(middle); and 0.1~100m(right) for λ=0.532 μm(green line) and λ=1 μm (red line).

To see more clearly how the device works, Fig.4 simulated the reconstruction of a single light spot via digital optical phase conjugation. The simulation used the same software and followed the same procedure as described in Ref.[Zhiyang, 2010a]. In the calculation λ=1.032μm, the number of eigenmodes equals 200 and the perfectly matched layer has a thickness of - 0.15i. The adiabatic waveguide taper has a refraction index of 1.5. To save time only the first stack of the taper, which has a height of 20 micrometers and a length of 5 micrometers, was taken into consideration. A small point light source was placed 25 micrometers away from the taper in the air. As could be seen from Fig.4a, the light emitted from the point light source propagates from left to right, enters the first stack of the taper and stimulates various eigenmodes within the taper. The amplitudes and phases of all the guided eigenmodes on the right side end of the first stack of the taper were transferred to their conjugate forms and used as input on the right side. As could be seen from Fig.4b the light returned to the left side and rebuilt a point light source with expanded size.

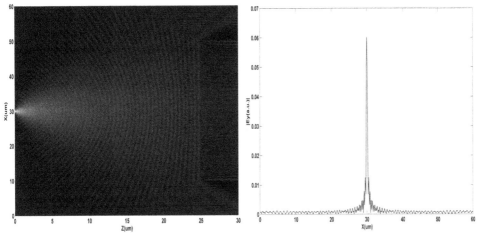

(a). Distribution for incident light, left: 2-D field; right:1-D Electrical component at Z=0

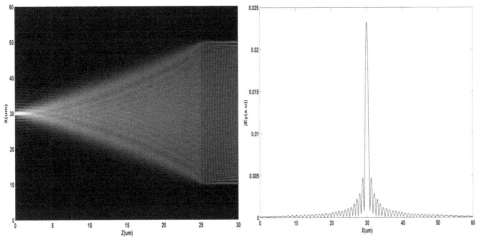

(b). Distribution for rebuilt light, left: 2-D field; right:1-D Electrical component at Z=0

Fig. 4. Reconstruction of a single light spot via digital optical phase conjugation.

From the X-directional field distribution one can see that the rebuilt light spot has a half-maximum-width of about 1μm, which is very close to the predicated resolution of 0.83μm by Eq.1, if the initial width of the point light source is discounted.

Fig.5 demonstrated how multiple light spots could be reconstructed simultaneously via digital optical phase conjugation. The simulation parameters were the same as in Fig.4. Three small point light sources were placed 25 micrometers away from the taper and separated 15 micrometers from each other along vertical direction. As could be seen from Fig.5a, the lights emitted from the three point light sources propagate from left to right, enter the first stack of the taper and stimulate various eigenmodes within the taper.

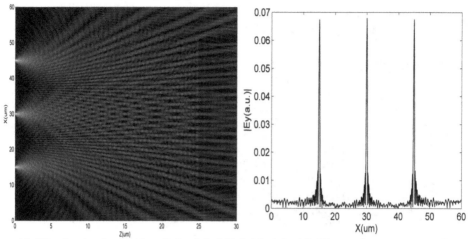

(a). Distribution for incident light, left: 2-D field; right:1-D Electrical component at Z=0

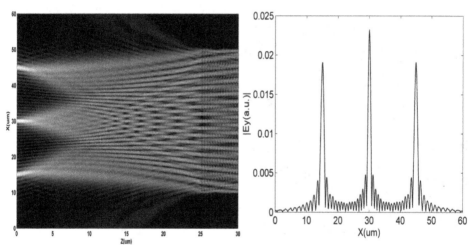

(b). Distribution for rebuilt light, left: 2-D field; right:1-D Electrical component at Z=0

Fig. 5. Reconstruction of three light spots via digital optical phase conjugation.

The amplitudes and phases of all the guided eigenmodes on the right side end of the first stack of the taper were recorded. This can also be done in a cumulative way. That is, at one time place one point light source at one place and record the amplitudes and phases of stimulated guided eigenmodes on the right side. Then for each stimulated guided eigenmode sum up the amplitudes and phases recorded in successive steps. Due to the linearity of the system the resulting amplitudes and phases for each stimulated guided eigenmode appear the same as that obtained by placing all the three point light sources at their paces at a time. Next the conjugate forms of above recorded guided eigenmodes were used as input on the right side. As could be seen from Fig.5b the light returned to the left side and rebuilt three point light sources at the same position but with expanded size. As explained in Ref. [Zhiyang, 2010a] more than 10000 light spots could be generated simultaneously using 8-bit SLMs. Each light spot produces a light cone, or a so called laser probe.

3. Configurations of laser-probe 3D cameras

Once large number of laser probes could be produced we may employ them to construct 3D cameras for various applications. Four typical configurations, each dedicated to a particular application, have been presented in following four subsections. Subsection 3.1 provided a simple configuration for micro 3D measurement, while Subsection 3.2 focused on fast obstacle detection in a large volume for auto-navigation and safe driving. The methods and theory set up in section 3.2 also apply in rest subsections. Subsection 3.3 discussed the combination of a laser probe 3D camera with stereovision for full field real-time 3D measurements. Subsection 3.4 discussed briefly strategies for accurate static 3D measurements, including large size and 360-deg shape measurements for industry inspection. The resolution for each configuration was also analyzed.

3.1 Micro 3D measurement

To measure three dimensional coordinates of a micro object, we may put it under a digital microscope and search the surface with laser probes as illustrated in Fig.6. When the tip of a laser probe touches the surface it produces a light spot with minimum size and the preset position Z_0 of the tip stands for the vertical coordinate of the object. When the tip lays at a height of ΔZ below or above the surface, the diameter of the light spot scattered by the surface expand to Δd. From the geometric relation illustrated in Fig.6 it is easy to see that,

$$\Delta Z = \frac{Z_0}{d} \Delta d \qquad (2)$$

where d is the width of the narrow end of an adiabatic waveguide taper. From Eq.2 it is clear that the depth resolution depends on the minimum detectable size of Δd. The minimum detectable size on the image plane of the objective lens is limited by the pixel size of CCD or CMOS image sensor as W_0/N_0, where W_0 is the width of an image sensor that contains N_0 pixels. When mapped back onto object plane, the minimum detectable size of Δd is $W_0/\beta N_0$,

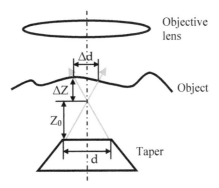

Fig. 6. Set-up for micro 3D measurement with laser probes incident from below the object.

where β is the amplification ratio of the objective lens. However if $W_0/\beta N_0$ is less than the optic aberration, which is approximately $\lambda/2NA$ for a well designed objective lens with a numerical aperture NA, the minimum detectable size of Δd is limited instead by $\lambda/2NA$.

Using Eq.2 we can estimate the resolution of ΔZ. As discussed in previous section, when SLMs with 1920×1080 pixels are employed, the width of the narrow end of an adiabatic waveguide taper with a refraction index of 1.5 reaches d=0.458mm for λ=0.532 μm. When a 3×3 array of SLMs with same pixels are employed, d increases to 1.376mm. Assuming that a 1/2 inch wide CMOS image sensor with 1920×1080 pixels is placed on the image plane of the objective lens, we have $W_0/N_0 \approx 12.7mm/1920 = 6.6μm$. For typical $\times 4$(NA=0.1), $\times 10$(NA=0.25), $\times 40$(NA=0.65) and $\times 100$(NA=1.25) objective lenses, the optic aberrations are about 2.66, 1.06, 0.41, and 0.21μm respectively. At a distance of Z_0=1mm, according to Eq.2, the depth resolutions of ΔZ for above $\times 4, \times 10, \times 40, \times 100$ objective lenses are 5.81, 2.32, 0.89, and 0.46μm for d=0.458mm, or 1.93, 0.77, 0.30, and 0.15μm for d=1.376mm respectively.

In above discussion we have not taken into consideration the influence of the refraction index of the transparent object. Although it is possible to make a proper compensation for the influence once the refraction index is known, there is another way to avoid it by inserting the narrow end of an adiabatic waveguide taper above the objective lens. This could be done with the help of a small half–transparent–half–reflective beam splitter M as illustrated in Fig.7. It is of better depth resolution due to increased cone angle of laser probes at the cost of trouble some calibration for each objective lens. When searching for the surface of an object, the tips of laser probes push down slowly toward object. From monitored successive digital images it is easy to tell when a particular laser probe touches a particular place on the object. Since the laser probes propagate in the air, the influence of the internal refraction index of the object is eliminated.

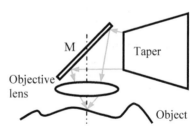

Fig. 7. Set-up for micro 3D measurement with laser probes incident from above the objective lens.

By the way, besides discrete laser probes, a laser probe generating unit could also project structured light beams. That means a laser probe 3D camera could also work in structured light projection mode. It has been demonstrated that by means of structured light projection a lateral resolution of 1μm and a height resolution of 0.1μm could be achieved [Leonhardt, et at. 1994].

3.2 Real-time large volume 3D detection

When investigating a large field, we need to project laser probes into far away distance. As a result the cone angles of the laser probes would become extremely small. A laser probe might look like a strait laser stick, which makes it difficult to tell where the tip is. In such a case we may use two laser probe generating units and let the laser probes coming from different units meet at preset positions. Since the two laser probe generating units could be separated with a relatively large distance, the angle between two laser probes pointing to the same preset position may increase greatly. Therefore the coordinates of objects could be determined with much better accuracy even if they are located at far distances.

Fig.8 illustrated the basic configuration of a laser probe 3D camera constructed with two laser probe generating units $U_{1,2}$ and a conventional CMOS digital camera C. The camera C lies in the middle of $U_{1,2}$. In Fig.8 the laser probe generating unit U_1 emits a single laser probe as plotted in red line while U_2 emits a single laser probe as plotted in green line. The two laser probes meet at preset point A. An auxiliary blue dashed ray is drawn, which originates at the optic centre of the optical lens of the camera C and passes though point A. It is understandable that all the object points lying along the blue dashed line will come onto the same pixel A' of the CMOS image sensor. If an object lies on a plane P_1 in front of point A, the camera captures two light spots, with the light spot produced by red laser probe lying at a pixel distance of $-\Delta j_1$ on the right side of A' and the light spot produced by green laser probe lying at a pixel distance of $-\Delta j_2$ on the left side of A' as illustrated in Fig.9a. When an object lies on a plane P_2 behind point A, the light spots produced by the red and green laser probes exchange their position as illustrated in Fig.9c. When an object sits right at point A the camera captures a single light spot at A' as illustrated in Fig.9b. Suppose the digital camera C in Fig.8 has a total of N pixels along horizontal direction, which cover a scene with a width of W at distance Z, the X-directional distance Δd_1 (or Δd_2) between a red (or green) laser probe and a blue dashed line in real space could be estimated from the pixel distance Δj_1 (or Δj_2) on the captured image by,

$$\Delta d_{1,2} = \frac{W}{N}\Delta j_{1,2} = \frac{2Ztg\alpha}{N}\Delta j_{1,2} \qquad (3)$$

where α is the half view angle. As illustrated in Fig.8 and Fig.9a-c, $\Delta d_{1,2}$ is positive when the light spot caused by red (or green) laser probe laying at the left (or right) side of A'. For illustrative purpose the laser probes emitted from different units are plotted in different

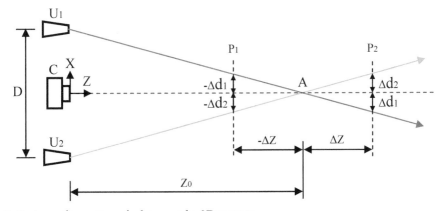

Fig. 8. Basic configuration of a laser probe 3D camera.

colours. In a real laser probe 3D camera all the laser probes may have the same wavelength. To distinguish them we may set the laser probes emitted from one unit slightly higher in vertical direction than the laser probes emitted from another unit as illustrated in Fig.9d-f.

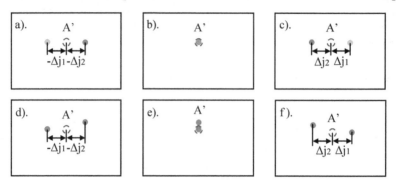

Fig. 9. Images of laser probes reflected by an object located at different distances. Left: in front of A; Middle: right at A; Right: behind A.

From X-directional distance $\Delta d_{1,2}$ it is easy to derive the Z-directional distance ΔZ of the object from the preset position A using the geometric relation,

$$\frac{\Delta d_{1,2}}{\Delta Z} = \frac{D}{2Z_0} \tag{4}$$

where D is the space between two laser probe generating units $U_{1,2}$, Z_0 being the preset distance of point A. From Eq.3-4 it is not difficult to find,

$$Z = Z_0 + \Delta Z = \frac{DNZ_0}{DN - 4Z_0 tg\alpha \Delta j_{1,2}} \tag{5}$$

After differentiation and some rearrangement, Eq.5 yields,

$$dZ = \frac{4Z^2 tg\alpha}{DN} dj_{1,2} \tag{6}$$

where dZ and $dj_{1,2}$ are small deviations, or measuring precisions of ΔZ and $\Delta j_{1,2}$ respectively. In Eq.6 it is noticeable that the preset distance Z_0 of a laser probe exerts little influence on the measuring precisions of ΔZ. Usually $\Delta j_{1,2}$ could be measured with half pixel precision. Assuming D=1000mm, $tg\alpha$=0.5 and $dj_{1,2}$=0.5, Fig.10 plotted the calculated precision dZ based on Eq.6 when a commercial video camera with 1920×1080 pixels, N= 1920 (in blue line), or a dedicated camera with $10k \times 10k$ pixels, N= 10k(in red line) is employed. As could be seen from Fig.10 the depth resolution changes with the square of object distance Z. At a distance of 100,10, 5, and 1m, the depth resolutions are 5263, 53, 13, and 0.5mm for N=1920, which reduce to 1000, 10, 2.5, and 0.1mm respectively for N=10k. The depth resolutions are acceptable in many applications considering the field is as wide as 100 m at a distance of 100 mm. From Eq.6 it is clear that to improve the depth resolution one can increase D or N, or both. But the most convenient way is to decrease α, that is, to make a close-up of the object. For example, when $tg\alpha$ decreases from 0.5 to 0.05, the measuring precision of Z would improve by 10 times. That is to say, a 0.5m wide object lying at a distance of 5m from the camera could be measured with a depth precision of 1.3mm (N= 1920), or 0.25mm(N=10k), if its image covers the whole area of the CCD or CMOS image sensor.

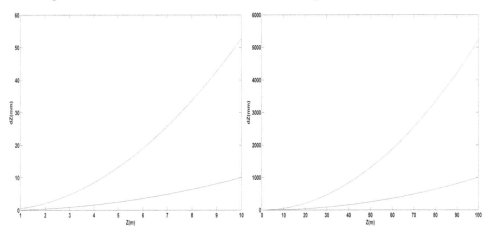

Fig. 10. Depth resolution of a laser probe 3D camera in the range of 0~10m(left) and 0~100m(right) with D=1000mm, $tg\alpha$=0.5, $dj_{1,2}$=0.5, and N=1920(blue) or 10k(red).

To acquire the three dimensional coordinates of a large scene the laser probe generating units should emit hundreds and thousands of laser probes. For convenience, in Fig.8 only one laser probe is shown for each unit. In Fig.11 six laser probes are plotted for each unit. It

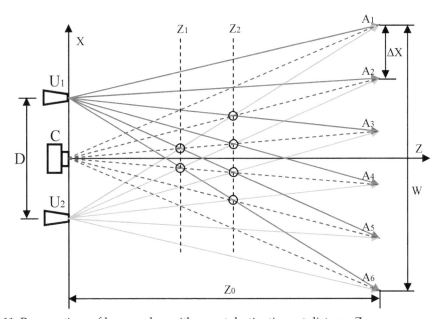

Fig. 11. Propagations of laser probes with preset destinations at distance Z_0.

is easy to see that as the number of laser probes increases the situation becomes quite complicated. It is true that each laser probe from one unit meets with one particular laser probe from another unit at six preset points A_{1-6} respectively. However the same laser probe would also come across other five laser probes from another unit at points other than A_{1-6}. Actually, if each laser probe generating unit produces N_p laser probes, a total of $N_p \times N_p$ cross points will be made by them, and only N_p points among them are at preset positions. The other $(N_p - 1) \times N_p$ undesired cross points might probably cause false measurements. See the two cross points on plane Z_1 and four cross points on plane Z_2 that are marked with small black circles, we could not distinguish them from preset points A_{2-5}, since they all sit on the blue dashed lines, sharing the same preset pixel positions on captured images. As a result it will be impossible to tell whether the object is located around the preset points A_{1-6} or near the plane Z_1 or Z_2. To avoid this ambiguity we should first find where the plane Z_1 or Z_2 is located.

As illustrated in Fig.11, since the optic centre of the optical lens of digital camera C is placed at the original point (0,0), the X-Z coordinates of the optic centres of the two laser probe emitting units $U_{1,2}$ becomes (D/2,0) and (-D/2,0) respectively. Denoting the X-Z coordinates of N_p preset points A_i as (X_i, Z_0), i=1,2,...,N_p, the equations for red, blue and green lines could be written respectively as,

$$X = \frac{D}{2} + (X_i - \frac{D}{2})\frac{Z}{Z_0} \qquad i = 1,2,...,N_p \tag{7}$$

$$X = X_j\frac{Z}{Z_0} \qquad j = 1,2,...,N_p \tag{8}$$

$$X = -\frac{D}{2} + (X_k + \frac{D}{2})\frac{Z}{Z_0} \qquad k = 1,2,...,N_p \tag{9}$$

where i, j and k are independent indexes for preset points A_i, A_j and A_k. The cross points where a red line, a blue line and a green line meet could be find by solving the linear equations Eq.7-9, which yields,

$$Z = \frac{D}{D + X_k - X_i}Z_0 \tag{10a}$$

$$X = X_j\frac{Z}{Z_0} \tag{10b}$$

$$X_j = \frac{X_k + X_i}{2} \tag{10c}$$

When $X=X_i=X_j=X_k$, according to Eq.10a, $Z=Z_0$. They stand for the coordinates of N_p preset points. When $X_k \neq X_i$, we have $Z \neq Z_0$, which gives the coordinates of cross points that cause ambiguity, like the cross points marked with black circles on plane Z_1 or Z_2 in Fig.11.

One way to eliminate above false measurements is to arrange more laser probes with preset destinations at different Z_0 that helps to verify whether the object is located near the preset points. To avoid further confusion it is important that laser probes for different Z_0 should be arranged on different planes as indicated in Fig.12. For laser probes arranged on the same plane perpendicular to Y-Z plane they share the same cut line on Y-Z plane. Since the optic centres of the two laser probe emitting units $U_{1,2}$ and the optical lens of digital camera C all sit at (0, 0) on Y-Z plane, if we arrange the laser probes for a particular distance Z_0 on the same plane perpendicular to Y-Z plane, they will come across with each other on that plane with no chance to come across with other laser probes arranged on other planes perpendicular to Y-Z plane.

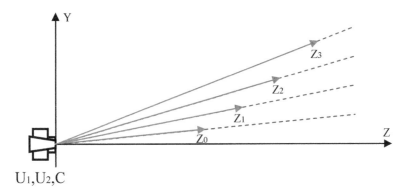

Fig. 12. Laser probes arranged on different planes perpendicular to Y-Z plane.

In what follows, we will design a laser probe 3D camera for auto-navigation and driving assistant systems, demonstrating in detail how the laser probes could be arranged to provide accurate and definite depth measurement. In view of safety a 3D camera for auto-navigation or driving assistant systems should detector obstacles in very short time and acquiring three dimensional coordinates within a range from 1 to 100m and a relatively large view angle 2α. In following design we let $\alpha \approx 26.6°$, so that $tg\alpha=0.5$. Since the device is to be mounted within a car, we may chose a large separation for two laser probe generating units as D=1m, which provides a depth resolution as plotted in Fig.10. To avoid above false measurements we project laser probes with preset destinations at seven different planes at Z_0=2,4,8,14,26,50, and 100m. In addition the X-directional spaces between adjacent preset destinations are all set as $\Delta X=X_i-X_{i+1}=2m$, where the preset destination with lower index number assumes larger X coordinate. The propagations of these laser probes in the air are illustrated in Fig.13-14. In Fig.13 the propagations of the laser probes over a short range between zero to the preset destinations are drawn on the left side, while the propagations of the same laser probes over the entire range between 0~100m are drawn on the right side. In Fig.14 only the propagations of the laser probes over the entire range between 0~100m are shown. The optic centres of the first and second laser probe generating units $U_{1,2}$ are located at (0.5,1) and (-0.5,0) respectively, while the camera C sits at the original point (0,0). The red and green lines stand for the laser probes emitted from U_1 and U_2 respectively. The solid blue lines connect the optic centre of the optical lens with the preset destinations of the laser probes on a given plane at Z_0, which plays the same auxiliary function as the dashed blue lines in Fig.8.

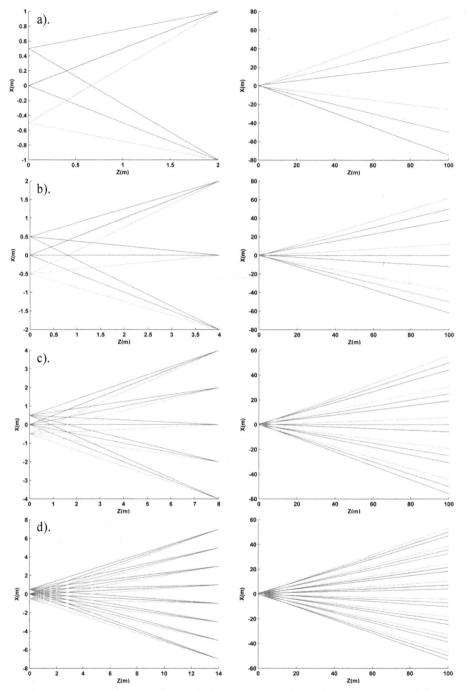

Fig. 13. Propagations of laser probes with destinations at a). 2m; b). 4m; c). 8m; and d). 14m.

First lets check Fig.13a for $Z_0=2m$. Since $\Delta X=X_i-X_{i+1}=2m$, Eq.10a becomes,

$$Z = \frac{1}{1+(k-i)\Delta X}Z_0 = \frac{1}{1+2n}Z_0 \tag{11}$$

where $n=k-i$ is an even integer. For an odd integer of n Eq.10c does not hold true. Therefore $Z \leq Z_0/5$, if $n \neq 0$, which implies that all the possible undesired cross points are located much closer to the camera C. In addition since the field width at Z_0 is $W=2Z_0 tg\alpha=Z_0$, the total number of laser probes that could be arranged within a width of W is

$$N_P = \frac{W}{\Delta X}+1 = \frac{Z_0}{2}+1 \tag{12}$$

According to Eq.12, $N_P=2$ at $Z_0=2m$. As the maximum value for n in Eq.11 is $N_P-1=1$ and n should be even integer, we have n=0. It means that beside 2 preset points there are no other cross points. In Fig.13a, from the left figure we see only two cross points at preset destinations at 2m. We find no extra cross points in the right figure which plotted the propagations of the same laser probes over a large range of 0~100m. In addition we see by close observation that at large distances the X-directional distance between a red (or green) line and an adjacent blue line approaches one forth of the X-directional distance between two adjacent blue lines. This phenomenon could be explained as follows.

From $Z=Z_0$ to $Z=Z_0+\Delta Z$, the X-directional distance between a red (or green) line and an adjacent blue line increases from zero to $\Delta d_{1,2}$ as described by Eq.4, meanwhile the X-directional distance between adjacent blue lines changes from ΔX to $\Delta X'$. It is easy to find that,

$$\frac{\Delta X}{Z_0} = \frac{\Delta X'}{Z_0+\Delta Z} \tag{13}$$

Rearrange Eq.13 as,

$$\Delta X' = \frac{\Delta X}{Z_0}(Z_0+\Delta Z) \tag{14}$$

Dived Eq.4 by Eq.14, we get,

$$\frac{\Delta d_{1,2}}{\Delta X'} = \frac{D}{2\Delta X}\frac{\Delta Z}{Z_0+\Delta Z} \tag{15}$$

From Eq.15 we can see that $\Delta d_{1,2}/\Delta X'$ approaches 1/4 when $\Delta Z \gg Z_0$. It could also be seen that $\Delta d_{1,2}/\Delta X'$ becomes -1/4 when $\Delta Z = -Z_0/2$. In combination, start from $Z_0/2$ to infinity, both red and green lines are centred round blue lines with X-directional deviations no larger than one fourth of the X-directional distances between adjacent blue lines at the same distance, obtaining no chance to intersect with each other. It implies that no ambiguity would occur if the laser probes with preset destinations at Z_0 are used to measure the depth of an object located within the range from $Z_0/2$ to infinity. As shown in Fig.13a using laser probes with preset destinations at $Z_0=2m$, from monitored pictures we can definitely tell whether there is an object and where it is within the range of 1~100m if we search round the

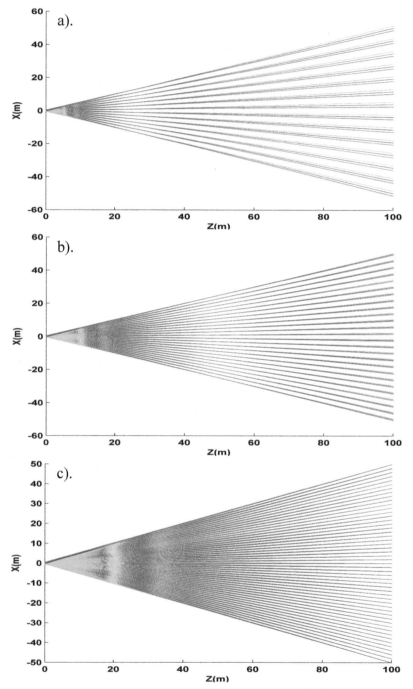

Fig. 14. Propagations of laser probes with destinations at a). 26m; b). 50m; and c). 100m.

preset image position A' and confine the searching pixel range Δj less than one fourth of the pixel number between two adjacent preset image positions. Since N_p preset points distribute evenly over a width of W, which cover a total of N pixels, $\Delta j \leq N/4N_p$. If N=1000, $\Delta j \leq 125$.

Next lets check Fig.13b for Z_0=4m. Using Eq.12, we have N_p=3. Since the maximum value for n in Eq.11 is N_p-1=2 and n should be even integer, we have n=0, 2. It means that beside 3 preset points there is N_p-n=3-2=1 extra cross point at $Z=Z_0/5$=0.8m, which are clearly seen in the left figure in Fig.13b. The number of extra cross points decreases by n because j=(k+i)/2=k-n/2 as required by Eq.10c is unable to adopt every number from 1 to N_p. As discussed above using laser probes with preset destinations at Z_0=4m, from captured pictures we can definitely tell whether there is an object and where it is within the range of 2~100m if we confine the searching pixel range to $\Delta j \leq N/4N_p$. If N=1000, $\Delta j \leq 83$.

Similarly both the preset points and the extra cross points are observed exactly as predicated by Eq.12 for Z_0=8,14,26,50, and 100m as illustrated in Fig.13c-d and Fig.14. With above arrangement a wide object at a certain distance Z might be hit by laser probes with preset destinations on different planes, while a narrow object might still be missed by all above laser probes since the X-directional spaces between adjacent laser probes are now more than ΔX=2m if $Z>Z_0$, although they decrease to $\Delta X/2$=1m at $Z_0/2$. To detect narrow objects we may add another 100 gropes of laser probes with same preset destinations at Z_0 but on different planes perpendicular to Y-Z plane, each grope shifting $\Delta X/100$=20mm along X-directional as illustrated in Fig.15. With all these laser probes a slender object as narrow as 20mm, see the object O_1 in Fig.15a, would be caught without exception at a single measurement. But if an object is not tall enough to cover several rows of laser probes, see the object O_2 in Fig.15a, it may also escape from detection. To increase the possibility of detecting objects with small height we may re-arrange the positions of the laser probes by inserting each row of laser probes from the lower half part into every row of laser probes at upper half part. As a result the maximum X-directional shift between adjacent rows of laser probes reduces from 2-0.02=1.98m to 1m as illustrated in Fig.15b. As could be seen the same object O_2 now gets caught by a laser probe in the fourth row.

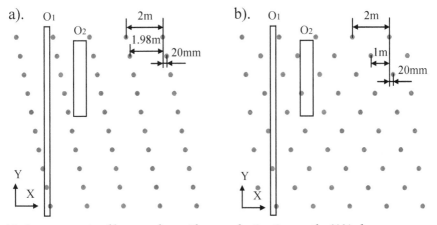

Fig. 15. Arrangements of laser probes with same destination on the X-Y plane.

In above design we arranged 100 group of laser probes with destinations at Z_0=2,4,8,14, 26,50, and 100m respectively. That is to say a total of $100\times(1+3+5+8+14+26+51)+1=10801$ laser probes have been employed. With so many laser probes an object as narrow as 20mm might be detected within a single measurement, or a single frame, without ambiguity. If the object is located between 50 and 100m, it could be detected correctly by any laser probe hitting on it. If it comes closer to the camera, although it might be incorrectly reported by laser probes with destinations at Z_0=100m, or 50m, etc, it will be correctly reported by laser probes with destinations at smaller Z_0. Considering the facts that the measuring range of the laser probes overlap greatly, the X-directional space between adjacent laser probes reduces by a half at $Z_0/2$ than that at Z_0, and the car bearing the camera, or the object itself, is moving, an object as narrow as 10mm or much less has great chance to be detected, or hit by at least one laser probe, within one or several frames.

3.3 Real-time large volume full field 3D measurement

Usually a laser probe 3D camera discussed in previous subsection could acquire at maximum about 10^4 three dimensional coordinates every frame using 8-bit SLMs. If dense three dimensional coordinates need to be acquired in real time a laser probe 3D camera could be incorporated with a pair of stereovision cameras. The accurate three dimensional coordinates come directly from the laser probe 3D camera plus those derived from stereovision make a complete description of the full field. More importantly, the laser probe 3D camera helps greatly in matching, noise depression and calibration for stereovision. As illustrated in Fig.16, a pair of digital cameras $C_{1,2}$ for stereovision have been added to the device in Fig.8, which are separated by a distance of D_1. D_1 might adopt a value larger or

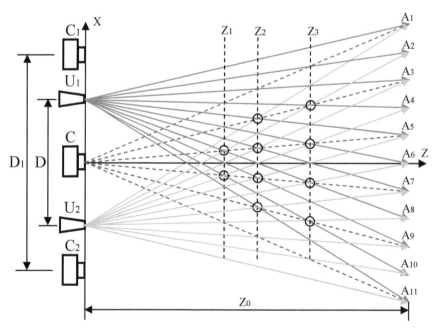

Fig. 16. A laser probe 3D camera combined with a stereo vision camera.

smaller than D. Each laser probe puts a mark on the object. From the image captured by camera C the absolute location of the object could be calculated using Eq.5 and the positions of the same mark on the pictures captured by camera C_1 and C_2 could then be predicated. In other word, one mark on the pictures captured by camera C_1 could easily be matched with the same mark on the pictures captured by camera C_2. Without these marks the matching between the pictures captured by cameras C_1 and C_2 might be very difficult or impossible over many pixels, creating serious noises in 3D reconstruction. The matching of the rest pixels around the marks could be performed quickly with reduced searching range. The marks also serve as an accurate and efficient means for the calibration of cameras C_1 and C_2. In stereovision it is very important to align one camera accurately with another camera, which brings great trouble when changing the focal length of one camera to zoom in or out, since the same amount of changes must be made instantly to the focal length of another camera. With the help of the laser marks, one camera needs only to follow roughly the changes of another camera. This is because all the pictures captured by cameras are projections of objects on the image plane, which is determined by the location, orientation and the focal length of the camera. Usually camera C is fixed at the origin of coordinates as illustrated in Fig.16. The only unknown parameter $tg\alpha$ in Eq.5, which is related to the focal length, is pre-calibrated. It could also be determined on the spot for every picture captured by camera C based on the fact that the same object detected by neighbouring laser probes with different preset destination Z_0 should have nearly the same depth Z as predicated by Eq.5. Even for very rough objects $tg\alpha$ could be properly determined after a least squares fit over the depths of many pairs of neighbouring laser probes. Next the unknown locations, orientations and the focal lengths of the camera $C_{1,2}$ could be derived from the image positions of hundreds of laser probes whose absolute coordinates are pre-calculated using Eq.5. Then by stretching, or rotation, or a combination of them, the pictures come from camera C_1 could easily be transformed to match with the pictures from camera C_2. After above pre-processing, stereo matching might be performed on the overlapped region of the image pairs from camera $C_{1,2}$.

When laser probes are arranged as discussed in previous subsection, we say that the laser probe 3D camera is working in detection mode. For continuous measurements, once the location of all the objects are found in a frame, laser probes could be rearranged much more densely near the surfaces of known objects so that more three dimensional coordinates could be acquire within successive frames. In this case we say that the laser probe 3D camera is working in tracing mode. After some frames in tracing mode, a laser probe 3D camera should return to detection mode for one frame to check whether there are new objects appearing in the field. In Fig.16 the number of laser probes increased to 11 for tracing mode. It could be seen that as the number of laser probes increases the number of extra crossing points also increases as compared with that in Fig.11. Nevertheless these extra cross points are harmless since we already known the object lies around Z_0, away from Z_1 to Z_3.

The stereovision pictures recorded by cameras $C_{1,2}$ bear the images of lots of laser probes. They are harmful for later 3D display. Although these marks could be cleaned away via post imaging processing, a more preferable approach is to separate the visible light from infrared laser probes with a beam splitter. As illustrated in Fig.17, the beam splitter BS reflects the infrared laser probes onto image transducer CCD_1, while passing the visible light onto image transducer CCD_2. The advantage to employ two image transducers within one camera is that the electronic amplifier for each image transducer may adopt a different gain value so that the dark one does not get lost in the bright one. This is beneficial especially when working in strong day light. If both cameras C_1 and C adopted the same structure as illustrated in Fig.17, camera C_2 could be taken away because images for visible light from cameras C_1 and C are enough to make up a stereovision.

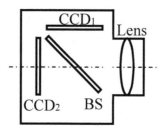

Fig. 17. A digital camera capable of recording infrared and visible light images separately.

3.4 Static large size or 360-deg shape measurement

In shape measurement for industry inspection the measuring accuracy is more crucial than measuring speed. Usually the component under investigation stays at a fixed position or moves slowly on a line during measurement. To improve measuring precision we can first divide the entire area under investigation into lot of subdivisions, say 10×10 subdivisions. Then measure each subdivision with much improved depth resolution due to reduced view angle as discussed in section 2. Dense and accurate three dimensional coordinates of the entire area could be obtained by patching all the measurements together [Gruen, 1988; Heipke, 1992]. The patching or aligning between adjacent subdivisions becomes easy and accurate with the help of laser probes. We can arrange adjacent subdivisions in a way so that they overlap slightly. As illustrated in Fig.18, when shifting from one subdivision S_1 to an adjacent subdivision S_2 we move the camera C and laser probe generating units $U_{1,2}$ separately. First we move the camera C to the new subdivision S_2 and keep $U_{1,2}$ unchanged, see Fig.18b. From the images of laser probes on the overlap region on the pictures taken before and after the movement of camera C, we can find exactly how much the camera C have moved. This could be accomplished using the fact that the laser probes on the overlap region stay at fixed positions. Next we move $U_{1,2}$ to the new subdivision S_2 with the camera

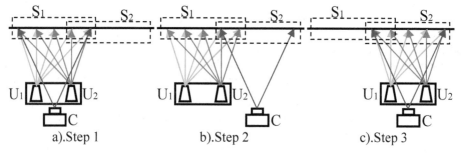

Fig. 18. Steps to move laser probe generating unit $U_{1,2}$ and camera C separately to adjacent subdivision.

C unchanged, see Fig.18c. From captured picture before and after the movement of $U_{1,2}$ the exact displacement could be calculated from the displacements of the same laser probes. Then measurement on the new subdivision S_2 could be carried out.

For 360-deg shape measurement, we can mount the two laser probe generating units $U_{1,2}$ and the camera C on two separate circular tracks, with the object under investigation placed at the centre. When the measurement at a certain angle is done, the camera C and laser probe generating units $U_{1,2}$ could be move to a new view angle separately following the same strategies as discussed above. With the help of laser probes on the overlapped region we can determine over how much angle have $U_{1,2}$ and camera C each moved, which makes it easy to transfer the local coordinates at a certain view angle accurately to the global coordinates. Otherwise additional measure has to be taken to monitor the positions of $U_{1,2}$ and camera C.

In shape measurement we can chose CCD or CMOS image sensors with large pixel number to achieve high vertical and lateral resolution at the cost of reduced frame rate. Usually shape measurements are carried out at small fixed distances, if we let D = 2Z, Eq.6 simplifies to,

$$dZ = \frac{W}{N} dj_{1,2} \qquad (16)$$

Eq.16 implies that the vertical resolution is the same as the lateral resolution determined by the image sensor. When an image sensor with a total of $10k \times 10k$ pixels is used, we have N=10000. Then for a subdivision with an area of $100 \times 100mm^2$, i.e., W=100mm, both vertical and lateral resolutions reach 5μm for $dj_{1,2}$=0.5. By a least squares fit method sub-pixel resolution for the image position of laser probes are possible [Maalen-Johansen, 1993; Clarke, et al., 1993]. When 1/20 sub-pixel resolution is obtained after least squares fit, $dj_{1,2}$=0.05, above said resolution improves to 0.5 μm and the relative error reaches 5×10^{-6}.

As discussed in subsection 3.2 within a single frame about 10801 points could be acquired using a laser probe 3D camera, each providing a three dimensional coordinate for the detected object. Usually this number of three dimensional coordinates is enough for industry inspection. The feature sizes, such as width, height, diameter, thickness, etc., could all be derived from measured data. If dense coordinates are needed for very complex shapes, they could be acquired from successive frames. For example, within 100 successive frames, which last 10 seconds at a frame rate of 10f/s, a total of about $100 \times 10801 \approx 10^6$ three dimensional coordinates could be acquired. Between each frame the laser probes shift a little their preset positions along horizontal or vertical direction. When combined together these 10^6 three dimensional coordinates provide a well description of the entire component. In addition, to detect possible vibrations of the object during successive frames we can fix the positions of a small fraction of laser probes throughout the measurements. The movements of the images of these fixed laser probes help to reveal and eliminate the movements of the objects relative to the camera.

4. Characteristics of laser-probe 3D cameras

In previous section we discussed four typical configurations of laser probe 3D cameras and their measuring precision. In this section we will provide more analysis concerning such characteristics as processing speed, power consumption, and resistance to external interferences and compare them with that of other measuring methods.

4.1 Image processing speed

The processing, or the derivation of depth information from pictures captured by a laser probe 3D camera is simple compared with many other methods like structured light projection, stereovision, etc. One need only to search on the left and right side of pre-known image positions of preset laser probes to see whether there is a pair of light spots reflected by objects. In other words one need only to check whether there are local intensity maximums, or whether the image intensities exceed a certain value on the left and right sides of N_p pre-known pixels with a searching range of $\pm N/4N_p$ pixels. The searching stops once the pair of light spots is found. Therefore on one image row, a total of $N_p \times 2N/4N_p$ $=N/2$ pixels need to be checked at maximum. Considering pairs of light spots reflected by objects lie symmetrically around pre-known image positions, when one light spot is detected another light spot could be found easily on other side after one or two steps of searching. It implies that the maximum searching steps could be reduced to about $N/4$. Usually the pre-known pixels are arranged on every other row, so only about one eighth of the total pixels of an image need to be checked. Once a pair of light spots is detected the depth of the object could be calculated easily using Eq.5 with less than 10 operations. For the laser probe 3D camera given in the last section, at most 10801 points need to be calculated. Since the working frequencies of many ARM, FPGA chips have reached 500MHz~1 GHz, one operation could be perform within 100ns on many embedded systems. Then the total time to calculate 10801 points is less than $10801 \times 10 \times 100ns \approx 0.01s$. It means that an obstacle in front of a car could be reported within a single frame.

4.2 Laser power

Since the laser power is focused into each laser probe rather than projected over the entire field, a laser probe 3D camera may be equipped with a relatively low power laser source. For micro 3D measurement a laser power less than 20mW might be enough, because almost all the laser energy might be gathered by objective lens and shed onto the image transducer except the adsorption by SLMs and optical lenses. However if optical manipulation of micro- or nano-particles is to be carried out higher energy might be necessary [MacDonald, 2002; Grier, 2003]. For industry inspection a laser power less than 2W might be enough since the measurements are usually carried out within about 1m. For obstacle detection within a range of 1~100m, if on average 1~5mW should be assigned to each laser probe for a total of 10801 laser probes, considering an adsorption of 90% by SLMs and optical lenses, a laser power of 100~500W might be necessary. To reduce energy adsorption dedicated gray scale SLMs should be employed. In a gray scale SLM the colour filters could be omitted, which results in triple decrease of energy adsorption as well as triple increase of available pixel number. In addition, among said 10801 laser probes, those with preset destinations at near distances might be assigned with much lower energy. Therefore the total energy for a laser probe 3D camera to measure an area of 100m $\times$ 100m at a distance of 100m might be reduced to within 20~100W, much less than the lamp power in a LCD projector. The laser power could be further reduced by several times if sensitive CCD or CMOS image sensors are employed. Other optical methods could hardly work with such low light power over so large area. For example, in structured light projection method, if an output light energy of 20~100W is projected over the same area, the illuminating intensity is only 2~10mW per square meter. In contrast, at a distance of 100m, the diameter of a laser probe could be as small as ~10mm as discussed in section 2. It means that even with an average energy of 1~5mW, the illuminating intensity provide by each laser probe could reach $1{\sim}5mW/25\pi$ per square millimetre, which is about 15708 times higher than that available in structured light projection method at the same distance.

4.3 Resistance to interferences

There are various interferences that may decrease measuring accuracy, to name a few, environmental light, vibration, colour, reflectivity and orientation of the object under investigation, etc. In subsection 3.3 we discussed how to eliminate the influence of environment light with a beam splitter. In subsection 3.4 we introduced a method to detect and eliminate the vibration of an object during successive measuring frames. Since a laser probe 3D camera determines the absolute location of an object by the positions rather than the exact intensities of reflected images of laser probes that are focused with diffraction limited precision, the colour, reflectivity or orientation of the object exerts limited influence on the measuring results, especially in fast obstacle detection.

There is another interference source that usually receives little attention but is of vital importance in practice, i.e., mutual interferences between same active devices. When several users turn on their laser probe 3D cameras at the same time, will every camera produce good results like it usually does when it works alone? It is true that one camera would now capture the laser probes projected by other cameras. Fortunately few of the images of laser probes projected by other cameras would lie symmetrically round the pre-known image positions of the laser probes projected by itself, since the laser probes from different devices are projected from different places with different angles. In image processing, to depress this mutual interference, we can discard all the single light spots or pairs of light spots lying asymmetrically round the pre-known image positions. In addition, referring Fig.15, we may store in each camera many sets of laser probe arrangements that differ in their vertical pattern, or rotated with a different angle within the vertical plane. When it observed the existence of laser probes from other cameras by turning off its own laser probes, it may chose one arrangement of laser probes that coincides least with existing laser probes. Considering the number of laser probes projected by one camera is about 100 times less than the camera's total pixel number, about ten cameras might work side by side at the same time without much interference to each other. In addition a laser probe 3D camera could also distinguish its own laser probes from that emitted by other cameras from at least 4 successive frames with its own laser probes turning on and off repeatedly. Those light spots that appear and disappear properly are very likely the images produced by its own laser probes. Further more, for a professional laser probe 3D camera, several laser sources with different wavelengths may be incorporated. Accordingly narrow band changeable beam splitters should be used in Fig.17. When other cameras exist, it may shift to a least occupied wavelength. With all above strategies several tens of laser probe 3D cameras may work well side by side at the same time.

5. Conclusion

In summery, the chapter puts forth a laser probe 3D camera that offers depth information lost in conventional 2D cameras. Via digital optical phase conjugation, it projects hundreds and thousands of laser probes precisely onto preset destinations to realize accurate and quick three dimensional coordinate measurement. A laser probe 3D camera could be designed with vertical and lateral resolutions from sub-micrometer to several micrometers for micro object or medium sized component measurement. It could also be configured for real-time 3D measurement over a large volume — for example, over a distance of 1~100m with a view angle larger than 50° — and detect any obstacle as narrow as 20mm or much less within a single frame or 0.01 second, which is of great use for auto-navigation, safe-driving, intelligent robot, etc.

The laser probes in a 3D camera not only make a 3D measurement simple and quick, but also help a lot in accurate patching for large size or 360-deg shape measurement, monitoring and elimination of vibration, depression of mutual influence when many laser probe 3D cameras work side by side, etc. When incorporated with stereovision they make the stereo matching easy and accurate. More than that, they offer an efficient means for camera calibration so that when one camera zooms in or out, another camera may follow only roughly rather than exactly, alleviating the stringent equipment requirements in stereo movie industry.

With its diffraction limited resolution to digitally reconstruct any optical wavefront, however complex it is, digital optical phase conjugation opened a way for many new techniques. The laser probe 3D camera discussed in the chapter is only one of the many possible applications. Since huge number of laser probes with varying intensity could be created precisely at lots of preset points, pointing more laser probes into each preset point using a large array of laser probe generating units and taking one such preset point as a 3D pixel, real-time true 3D display over a very large space with fine quality could become a reality. High power laser beams could also be formed, accurately focused and steered via digital optical phase conjugation, which may find wide applications in such fields as nuclear fusion, space laser communication, and so on. In micro world arrays of laser probes with sub-micrometer resolution could be employed for fast micro- or nano-partical assembling, operations on DNA, stereo information storage, etc.

6. Acknowledgment

The work is financially supported by self-determined research funds of CCNU from the colleges' basic research and operation of MOE. It is also partly supported by a key project No.104120 from Ministry of Education of P.R.China.

7. References

Amako, J.; Miura, H. & Sonehara, T. (1993). Wavefront control using liquid-crystal devices, *Appl.Opt.*, Vol.32, No.23, pp.4323-4329.

Asim, B. (2008). *Stereo Vision*, InTech, ISBN: 978-953-7619-22-0, Vienna, Austria.

Barbosa, E. A. & Lino, A. (2007). Multiwavelength electronic speckle pattern interferometry for surface shape measurement, *Appl. Opt.*, Vol.46, pp.2624–2631.

Chen, F.; Brown, G. M. & Song, M. (2000). Overview of three-dimensional shape measurement using optical methods, *Opt. Eng.* Vol.39, No.1, pp.10–22.

Clarke, T.A.; Cooper, M.A.R. & Fryer, J.G.(1993). An estimation for the random error in sub-pixel target location and its use in the bundle adjustment, *Proc.SPIE*, Vol.2252, pp.161-168.

Feinberg, J. (1982). Self-pumped continuous-wave phase-conjugation using internal reflection, *Opt.Lett.*, Vol.7, pp.486.

Grier, D.G. (2003). A revolution in optical manipulation, *Nature*, Vol.424, pp.810-816.

Gruen, A.W. (1988). Geometrically constrained multiphoto matching, Photogramm. *Eng. Remote Sens.*, Vol.54, No.5, pp.633-641.

Guan, C.; Hassebrook, L.G. & Lau D.L. (2003). Composite structured light pattern for three-dimensional video. *Opt Express*, Vol.11, pp.406–417.

Heipke, C. (1992). A global approach for least squares image matching and surface recognition in object space, *Photogramm. Eng. Remote Sens.*, Vol.58, No.3, pp.317-323.

Leonhardt, K; Droste, U. & Tiziani, H.J. (1994). Microshape and rough surface analysis by fringe projection, *Appl. Opt.*, Vol.33, pp.7477-7488.

Jürgen, K. & Christoph S. (2011), Address-event based stereo vision with bio-inspired silicon retina imagers, In: *Advances in theory and applications of stereo vision*, Asim Bhatti, pp.165-188, InTech, ISBN:978-953-307-516-7, Vienna, Austria

Kohler, C.; Schwab, X. & Osten, W. (2006). Optimally tuned spatial light modulators for digital holography, *Appl.Opt.*, Vol.45, No.5, pp.960-967.

Maalen-Johansen, I.(1993). On the precision of sub-pixel measurements in videometry, *Proc.SPIE*, Vol.2252, pp.169-178.

MacDonald, M.P., et al. (2002). Creation and manipulation of three-dimensional optically trapped structures, *Since*, Vol.296, pp.1101-1103.

Matoba, O., et al. (2002). Real-time three-dimensional object reconstruction by use of a phase-encoded digital hologram, *Appl.Opt.*, Vol.41, No.29, pp.6187-6192.

Moring, I. (1989). Active 3-D vision system for automatic model-based shape inspection, *Opt. Lasers Eng.*, Vol.10, pp.3-4.

Neto, L.G.; Roberge, D.; & Sheng, Y. (1996). Full-range, continuous, complex modulation by the use of two coupled liquid-crystal televisions, *Appl.Opt.*, Vol.23, No.23, pp.4567-4576.

Srinivasan, V.; Liu, H.C. & Halioua M. (1984). Automated phase-measuring profilometry of 3-D diffuse objects. *Appl Opt.*, Vol.23, pp.3105–3108.

Stephan, H.; Thorsten, R & Bianca, H. (2008). A Performance Review of 3D TOF Vision Systems in Comparison to Stereo Vision Systems, In: *Stereo Vision*, Asim Bhatti, pp.103-120, InTech, ISBN: 978-953-7619-22-0, Vienna, Austria.

Tudela, R., et al. (2004). Wavefront reconstruction by adding modulation capabilities of two liquid crystal devices, *Opt.Eng.*, Vol.43, No.11, pp.2650-2657.

Yamaguchi, I. et al. (2006). Surface shape measurement by phase-shifting digital holography with a wavelength shift, *Appl. Opt.*, Vol.45, pp.7610–7616.

Yariv, A. & Peper, D.M. (1977). Amplified reflection, phase conjugation, and oscillation in general four wave mixing, *Opt.Lett.*,Vol.1,No.1, p.16.

Zhiyang, L. (2010a). Accurate optical wavefront reconstruction based on reciprocity of an optical path using low resolution spatial light modulators, *Optics Communications,* Vol. 283, pp.3646-3657. (2010b). *SciTopics.* Retrieved December 30, 2010, from http://www.scitopics.com/Real_time_accurate_optical_wave_front_reconstruction_based_on_digital_ optical_phase_conjugation.html

3

ISAR Signal Formation and Image Reconstruction as Complex Spatial Transforms

Andon Lazarov
Burgas Free University
Bulgaria

1. Introduction

Inverse aperture synthesis in the radar theory is a recording of the complex reflective pattern (complex microwave hologram) of a moving target as a complex signal. The trajectory of moving target limited by the radar's antenna pattern or time of observation is referred to as synthetic aperture, and radar using the principle of inverse aperture synthesis is inverse synthetic aperture radar (ISAR). The spatial distribution of the reflectivity function of the target referred to as a target image can be retrieved from the received complex signals by applying image reconstruction techniques.

Conventional ISAR systems are coherent radars. In case the radars utilize a range-Doppler principle to obtain the desired image the range resolution of the radar image is directly related to the bandwidth of the transmitted radar signal, and the cross-range resolution is obtained from the Doppler frequency gradient generated by the radial displacement of the object relative to the radar.

A common approach in ISAR technique is division of the arbitrary movement of the target into radial displacement of its mass centre and rational motion over the mass centre. Radial displacement is compensated considered as not informative and only rotational motion is used for signal processing and image reconstruction. In this case the feature extraction is decomposed into motion compensation and image reconstruction (Li et al., 2001). Multiple ISAR image reconstruction techniques have been created, which can be divided into parametric and nonparametric methods in accordance with the signal model description and the methods of a target features extraction. (Berizzi et al., 2002; Mrtorella et al., 2003; Berizzi et al., 2004). The range-Doppler is the simplest non parametric technique implemented by two-dimensional inverse Fourier transform (2-D IFT). Due to significant change of the effective rotation vector or large aspect angle variation during integration time the image becomes blurred, then motion compensation is applied, which consist in coarse range alignment and fine phase correction, called autofocus algorithm. It is performed via tracking and polynomial approximation of signal history from a dominant or well isolated point scatterer on the target (Chen & Andrews, 1980), referred to as dominant scatterer algorithm or prominent point processing, a synthesized scatterer such as the centroid of multiple scatterers (Wu et al., 1995), referred to as multiple scatterer algorithm. Autofocus technique for random translational motion compensation based on definition of an entropy image cost function is developed in (Xi et al., 1999). Time window technique for suitable selection of the signals to be coherently processed and to provide a focused image is suggested in (Martorella& Berizzi, 2005). A robust autofocus algorithm based on a flexible parametric signal model for motion estimation and feature extraction in ISAR imaging of moving targets via minimizing a nonlinear least squares cost function is proposed in (Li et al., 2001). Joint time-frequency transform for radar range-Doppler imaging and ISAR motion compensation via adaptive joint time-frequency technique is presented in (Chen & Qian, 1998; Qian &, Chen 1998).

In the present chapter assuming the target to be imaged is an assembly of generic point scatterers an ISAR concept, comprising three-dimensional (3-D) geometry and kinematics, short monochromatic, linear frequency modulated (LFM) and phase code modulated (PCM) signals, and target imaging algorithms is thoroughly considered. Based on the functional analysis an original interpretation of the mathematical descriptions of ISAR signal formation and image reconstruction, as a direct and inverse spatial transform, respectively is suggested. It is proven that the Doppler frequency of a particular generic point is congruent with its space coordinate at the moment of imaging. In this sense the ISAR image reconstruction in its essence is a technique of total radial motion compensation of a moving target. Without resort to the signal history of a dominant point scatterer a motion compensation of higher algorithm based on image entropy minimization is created.

2. ISAR complex signal of a point target (scatterer)

2.1 Kinematic equation of a moving point target

The Doppler frequency induced by the radial displacement of the target with respect to the point of observation is a major characteristic in ISAR imaging. It requires analysis of the kinematics and signal reflected by moving target. Consider an ISAR placed in the origin of the coordinate system (Oxy) and the point **A** as an initial position with vector **R**(0) at the moment $t = 0$, and the point **B** as a current or final position with vector **R**(t) at the moment t (Fig. 1).

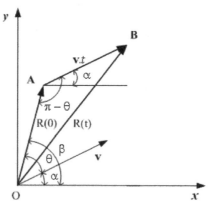

Fig. 1. Kinematics of a point target.

Assume a point target is moving at a vector velocity **v**, and then the kinematic vector equation can be expressed as

$$R(t) = R(0) + \mathbf{v}.t \tag{1}$$

which in matrix form can be rewritten as

$$\begin{bmatrix} x(t) \\ y(t) \end{bmatrix} = \begin{bmatrix} x(0) \\ y(0) \end{bmatrix} + \begin{bmatrix} v_x \\ v_y \end{bmatrix}.t \tag{2}$$

where $x(0) = R(0).\cos\beta$, $y(0) = R(0).\sin\beta$ are the coordinates of the initial position of the target (point **A**); $R(0) = \sqrt{x^2(0) + y^2(0)}$ is the module of the initial vector; β is the initial aspect angle; $v_x = v.\cos\alpha$, $v_y = v.\sin\alpha$ are the coordinates of the vector velocity; v is the module of the vector velocity and α is the angle between vector velocity and Ox axis.

The time dependent distance ISAR – point target can be expressed as

$$R(t) = \sqrt{R^2(0) + (v.t)^2 + 2(\mathbf{R}(0).\mathbf{v}).t} \ , \tag{3}$$

where $\mathbf{R}(0).\mathbf{v}$ is the inner product, defined by $\mathbf{R}(0).\mathbf{v} = x(0)v_x + y(0)v_y$ or $\mathbf{R}(0).\mathbf{v} = R(0).v.\cos\theta$; $\theta = \beta - \alpha$ is the angle between position vector $\mathbf{R}(0)$ and vector velocity $\mathbf{v}$, defined by the equation

$$\theta = \arccos\frac{x(0).v_x + y(t).v_y}{R(0).v} . \tag{4}$$

Then Eq. (3) can be rewritten as

$$R(t) = \sqrt{R^2(0) + (v.t)^2 + 2R(0)(v.t)\cos\theta} \ , \tag{5}$$

where $R(0)$ is the distance to the target at the moment $t = 0$, measured on OA, the initial line of sight (LOS).

The radial velocity of the target at the moment t is defined by differentiation of Eq. (5), i.e.

$$v_r(t) = \frac{dR(t)}{dt} = \frac{v^2 t + R(0).v.\cos\theta}{\sqrt{R^2(0) + (v.t)^2 + 2R(0).v.t.\cos\theta}} . \tag{6}$$

If $t = 0$, the radial velocity $v_r(0) = v\cos\theta$. In case the angle $\theta = 0$, then $v_r(0) = v$. At the moment $t = T$ when $v.T = -R(0)\cos\theta$ the target is on the traverse, then $v_r(T) = 0$, and $T = \dfrac{-R(0)\cos\theta}{v}$, which for the kinematics in Fig. 1 requires an angle θ to have a value $\theta \geq \pi/2$. The time variation of the radial velocity of the target causes a time dependent Doppler shift in the frequency of the signal reflected from the target.

2.2 Doppler frequency of a moving point target

Assume that the ISAR emits to the target a continuous sinusoidal waveform, i.e.

$$s(t) = A_0 \exp(j\omega t),$$ (7)

where A_0 is the amplitude of the emitted waveform, $\omega = 2\pi f = \dfrac{2\pi.c}{\lambda}$ is the angular frequency, f is the carrier frequency, λ is the wavelength of the emitted waveform, $c = 3.10^8$ m/s is the speed of the light in vacuum.

The signal reflected from the target can be defined as a time delayed replica of the emitted waveform, i.e.

$$s(t) = A_i \exp(j\omega(t - t_i))$$ (8)

where A_i is the amplitude of the reflected signal, $t_i = \dfrac{2R_i(t)}{c}$ is the time delay of the replica of the emitted waveform, $R_i(t)$ is the radial slant range distance to the target, calculated by Eq. (5). Define the general phase of the reflected signal as

$$\Phi(t) = \omega\left(t - \frac{2R_i(t)}{c}\right).$$ (9)

Then the current angular frequency of the reflected signal can be determined as

$$\hat{\omega}(t) = \frac{d\Phi(t)}{dt} = \omega - 2\frac{\omega}{c}.\frac{dR_i(t)}{dt},$$ (10)

$$\hat{\omega}(t) = \frac{d\Phi(t)}{dt} = \omega - \frac{4\pi}{\lambda}.\frac{dR_i(t)}{dt},$$ (11)

where $\omega_D(t) = \dfrac{4\pi}{\lambda}.\dfrac{dR_i(t)}{dt}$ is the angular time dependent Doppler frequency.

For the closing target $\dfrac{dR_i(t)}{dt} < 0$, then the angular Doppler frequency is a negative, $\omega_D(t) < 0$, and current angular frequency of the signal reflected from the target, $\hat{\omega}(t)$, increases, i.e. $\hat{\omega}(t) = \omega + \omega_D(t)$. For a receding target $\dfrac{dR_i(t)}{dt} > 0$, then the angular Doppler frequency is a positive, $\omega_D(t) > 0$, and current frequency of the signal reflected from the target, $\hat{\omega}(t)$, decreases, i.e. $\hat{\omega}(t) = \omega - \omega_D(t)$.

Based on Eq. (6) the angular Doppler frequency can be expressed as

$$\omega_D(t) = \frac{4\pi}{\lambda}\frac{v^2.t + R(0).v.\cos\theta}{\sqrt{R^2(0) + (v.t)^2 + 2R(0).v.t\cos\theta}}.$$ (12)

Accordingly the absolute Doppler frequency can be defined as

$$F_D(t) = \frac{2}{\lambda}.\frac{v^2.t + R(0).v.\cos\theta}{\sqrt{R^2(0) + (v.t)^2 + 2R(0).v.t.\cos\theta}}.$$ (13)

If $t = 0$, then $F_D(0) = \frac{2}{\lambda}.v.\cos\theta$. If $\theta = 0$, then $F_D(0) = \frac{2}{\lambda}.v$. At the moment $t = T$, i.e

$v.T = -R(0)\cos\theta$ the target is on the traverse, then $F_D(T) = 0$. At the particular moment t

and $\theta = 0$, $F_D(t) = \frac{2}{\lambda}.v$ is constant, and for $\theta = \pi/2$, $F_D(t) = \frac{2}{\lambda}.\frac{v^2.t}{\sqrt{R^2(0) + (v.t)^2}}$. Hence in

case $\theta \neq 0$ the Doppler frequency is time dependent during the aperture syntheses, coherent processing interval (CPI), but only one value has a meaning for ISAR imaging, the value defined at the moment of imaging, which will be proven in subsection 3.3.

2.3 Numerical experiments

2.3.1 Example 1

Assume that the point target is moving at the velocity v =29 m/s and illuminated by a continuous waveform with wavelength λ = 3.10^{-2} m (frequency $f = 10^{10}$ Hz). CPI time t = 712 -722 s s, initial distance $R(0) = 10^5$ m, guiding angle α = 0.9.π, position angle β = $\pi/3$. The calculation results of the current signal frequency and Doppler frequency are illustrated in Figs 2, (a), and (b).

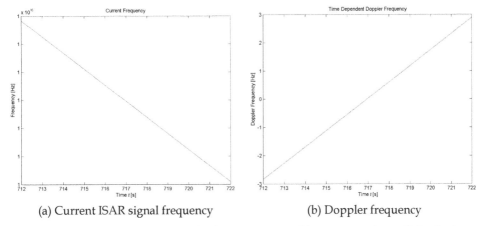

(a) Current ISAR signal frequency   (b) Doppler frequency

Fig. 2. Current ISAR signal and Doppler frequency caused by time varying radial velocity.

It is worth noting that the current signal frequency decreases during CPI due to the alteration of the value and sign of the Doppler frequency varying from -3 to 3 Hz. At the moment t = 717 s the Doppler frequency is zero. The time instance where Doppler changes its sign (zero Doppler differential) can be regarded as a moment of target imaging.

Computational results of the imaginary and real part of ISAR signal reflected by a point target with time varying radial velocity are presented in Figs. 3, (a), and (b). It can be clearly seen the variation of the current frequency of the signal due to the time dependent Doppler frequency of the point target. The existence of wide bandwidth of Doppler variation in the signal allows multiple point scatterers to be potentially resolved at the moment of imaging.

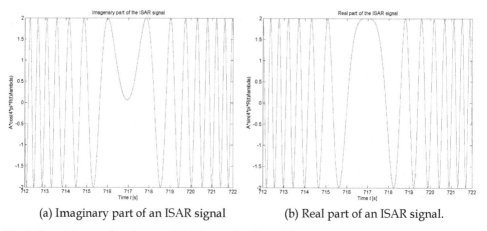

(a) Imaginary part of an ISAR signal   (b) Real part of an ISAR signal.

Fig. 3. Imaginary and real part of ISAR signal reflected by a point target.

2.3.2 Example 2

It is assumed that the point target moves at the velocity v =29 m/s and is illuminated with continuous waveform with wavelength λ = 10^{-2} m (frequency $f = 3.10^{10}$ Hz). CPI time $t = 0$ - 2 s, initial distance $R(0)$ = 30 m, guiding angle $\alpha = \pi$ and position angle, $\beta = 0$. The calculation results of the current signal frequency and Doppler frequency are illustrated in Figs 4, (a), and (b).

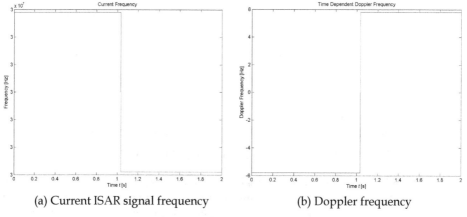

(a) Current ISAR signal frequency   (b) Doppler frequency

Fig. 4. Current ISAR signal frequency and Doppler frequency with a constant radial velocity.

It can be seen that the current signal frequency has two constant values during CPI due to the constant Doppler frequency with two signs, -5.8 Hz and +5.8 Hz. At the moment $t = 1.04$ s the Doppler frequency alters its sign. The time instance where Doppler changes its sign (zero Doppler differential) can be regarded as a moment of point target imaging that means one point target can be resolved.

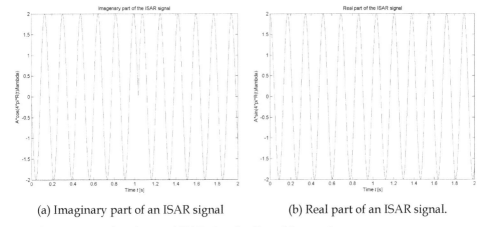

(a) Imaginary part of an ISAR signal   (b) Real part of an ISAR signal.

Fig. 5. Imaginary and real part of ISAR signal reflected by a point target.

Computational results of the imaginary and real part of ISAR signal reflected by a point target with constant radial velocity are presented in Figs. 5, (a), and b. It can be clearly seen the change of the phase in the imaginary part of the ISAR signal.

3. ISAR signal formation and imaging with a sequence of monochromatic short pulses

3.1 3-D ISAR geometry and kinematics

The basic characteristic in ISAR imaging is the time dependent distance between a particular generic point from the target and ISAR. Consider 3-D geometry of ISAR scenario with radar and moving target in the coordinate system $Oxyz$ (Fig. 6). The target is located in a regular grid, defined in the coordinate system $O'XYZ$. The generic point scatterer $\mathbf{g}$ from the target area is specified by the index vector (i,j,k), i.e. $\mathbf{g} = (i,j,k)$. The position vector $\mathbf{R}_{ijk}(p)$ of the ijk th generic point scatterer in the coordinate system $Oxyz$ at the moment p is described by the following vector equation

$$\mathbf{R}_{ijk}(p) = \mathbf{R}_{00}(0) + \mathbf{V}T_p\left(\frac{N}{2} - p\right) + \mathbf{AR}_{ijk}, \tag{14}$$

where $\mathbf{R}_{ijk}(p) = \left[x_{ijk}(p), y_{ijk}^{\,2}(p), z_{ijk}^{\,2}(p)\right]^T$, $x_{ijk}(p), y_{ijk}(p)$, and $z_{ijk}(p)$ are the current coordinates of the generic point, T_p denotes the pulse repetition period; $p = \overline{1,N}$ denotes the index of the emitted pulse, N denotes the full number of the emitted pulses during CPI; $\mathbf{R}_{00'}(0) = \left[x_{00'}(0), y_{00'}(0), z_{00'}(0),\right]^T$ is the position vector of the target geometric center, that locates a point O' at the moment $p = \dfrac{N}{2}$, $\mathbf{V} = [V_x, V_y, V_z]^T$ denotes the vector velocity with coordinates $V_x = V\cos\alpha$, $V_y = V\cos\beta$ and $V_z = V\cos\delta$; $\mathbf{R}_{ijk} = [X_{ijk}, Y_{ijk}, Z_{ijk}]^T$ denotes the position vector of the ijk th generic point; $X_{ijk} = i(\Delta X)$, $Y_{ijk} = j(\Delta Y)$ and $Z_{ijk} = k(\Delta Z)$ denote the discrete coordinates of the ijk th generic point in the coordinate system $O'XYZ$; ΔX, ΔY and ΔZ denote the dimensions of the grid cell; $\cos\alpha$, $\cos\beta$ and $\cos\delta = \sqrt{1 - \cos^2\alpha - \cos^2\beta}$ are the guiding cosines; V is the module of the vector velocity.

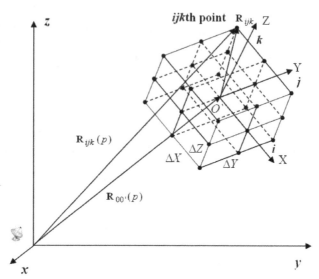

Fig. 6. Geometry of 3-D ISAR scenario.

The elements of the transformation matrix $\mathbf{A}$ in Eq. (14) are determined by the Euler expressions

$$
\begin{aligned}
a_{11} &= \cos\psi\cos\varphi - \sin\psi\cos\theta\sin\varphi; \\
a_{12} &= -\cos\psi\sin\varphi - \sin\psi\cos\theta\cos\varphi; \\
a_{13} &= \sin\psi\sin\theta; \\
a_{21} &= \sin\psi\cos\varphi + \cos\psi\cos\theta\sin\varphi; \quad a_{31} = \sin\theta\sin\varphi; \\
a_{22} &= -\sin\psi\sin\varphi + \cos\psi\cos\theta\cos\varphi; \quad a_{32} = \sin\theta\cos\varphi; \\
a_{23} &= -\cos\psi\sin\theta; \quad a_{33} = \cos\theta.
\end{aligned}
\tag{15}
$$

The projection angles ψ, θ and φ, defining the space orientation of the 3-D grid are calculated by components A, B, C of the normal vector to the plane that specifies the position of the target, and coordinates of the vector velocity, i.e.

$$
\psi = \arctan\left(-\frac{A}{B}\right); \theta = \arccos\frac{C}{[(A)^2 + (B)^2 + (C)^2]^{\frac{1}{2}}}
\tag{16}
$$

$$
\varphi = \arccos\frac{V_x B - V_y A}{\{[(A)^2 + (B)^2][(V_x)^2 + (V_y)^2 + (V_z)^2]\}^{\frac{1}{2}}}.
\tag{17}
$$

The components A, B, C of the normal vector are determined by the components of the position vector $\mathbf{R}_{00'}(0) = [x_{00'}(0), y_{00'}(0), z_{00'}(0),]^T$, vector velocity of the target and vector position of an arbitrary reference point $\mathbf{R}_0 = [x_0(0), y_0(0), z_0(0)]^T$ in the coordinate system $Oxyz$ by expressions

$$
\begin{aligned}
A &= V_z[y_{00'}(0) - y_0(0)] - V_y[z_{00'}(0) - z_0(0)]; \\
B &= V_x[z_{00'}(0) - z_0(0)] - V_z[x_{00'}(0) - x_0(0)]; \\
C &= V_y[x_{00'}(0) - x_0(0)] - V_x[y_{00'}(0) - y_0(0)].
\end{aligned}
\tag{18}
$$

The projection of the vector equation (14) on Cartesian coordinates yields

$$
\begin{bmatrix} x_{ijk}(p) \\ y_{ijk}(p) \\ z_{ijk}(p) \end{bmatrix} =
\begin{bmatrix} x_{00'}(0) + V_x\left(\dfrac{N}{2} - p\right)\cdot T_p \\ y_{00'}(0) + V_y\cdot\left(\dfrac{N}{2} - p\right)\cdot T_p \\ z_{00'}(0) + V_z\cdot\left(\dfrac{N}{2} - p\right)\cdot T_p \end{bmatrix} +
\begin{bmatrix} a_{11} & a_{12} & a_{13} \\ a_{21} & a_{22} & a_{23} \\ a_{31} & a_{32} & a_{33} \end{bmatrix} \cdot
\begin{bmatrix} X_{ijk} \\ Y_{ijk} \\ Z_{ijk} \end{bmatrix},
\tag{19}
$$

then the distance between the generic point and ISAR can be expressed as

$$
R_{ijk}(p) = \left[x_{ijk}{}^2(p) + y_{ijk}{}^2(p) + z_{ijk}{}^2(p) \right]^{\frac{1}{2}}
\tag{20}
$$

Eq. (20) is used in calculation of the time delay of the signal reflected by a particular generic point scatterer from the target area while signal modeling.

3.2 Short pulse ISAR signal formation

Consider 3-D ISAR scenario (Fig. 6) and a generic point $\mathbf{g}$ from the target illuminated by sequence of short monochromatic pulses, each of which is described by

$$
s(t) = A.\mathrm{rect}\left(\frac{t}{T}\right)\exp(j.\omega t),
\tag{21}
$$

$$
\mathrm{rect}\frac{t}{T} = \begin{cases} 1, \ 0 \le \dfrac{t}{T} < 1, \\ 0, \ \text{otherwise.} \end{cases}
$$

where A is the amplitude of the emitted signal, $\omega = 2\pi\dfrac{c}{\lambda}$ is the angular frequency; $c = 3.10^8$ m/s is the speed of the light in vacuum; λ is the wavelength of the signal; T is the timewith of the emitted pulse.

The signal reflected by the generic point scatter can be written as

$$
s_\mathbf{g}(p,t) = a_\mathbf{g}\, \mathrm{rect}\frac{t - t_\mathbf{g}(p)}{T}\exp\{j\omega[t - t_\mathbf{g}(p)]\},
\tag{22}
$$

$$\text{rect}\frac{t-t_g(p)}{T} = \begin{cases} 1, 0 \le \dfrac{t-t_g(p)}{T} < 1, \\ 0, \text{ otherwise.} \end{cases}$$

where $t_g(p) = \dfrac{2R_g(p)}{c}$ is the time delay of the signal, $\mathbf{g}$ stands for the discrete vector coordinate that locates the generic point scatterer in the target area $\mathbf{G}$, a_g stands for the magnitude of the 3-D discrete image function, $\tilde{t} = t \bmod T_p$ is the slow time, p denotes the number of the emitted pulse, T_p is the pulse repetition period, $t = \tilde{t} - pT_p$ is the fast time, presented as $t = k.T$, where k is the number of range bin, where the ISAR signal is placed. The demodulated ISAR signal from the target area is

$$s(p,k) = \sum_{g \in G} a_g \text{ rect}\frac{k.T - t_g(p)}{T}.\exp\{-j\omega t_g(p)]\} \cdot \tag{23}$$

The expression (23) is a weighted complex series of finite complex exponential base functions. It can be regarded as an asymmetric complex transform of the 3-D image function a_g, $\mathbf{g} \in \mathbf{G}$, defined for a whole discrete target area $\mathbf{G}$ into 2-D signal plane $s(p,k)$.

3.3 Image reconstruction from a short pulse ISAR signal

Eq. (23) can be rewritten as

$$s(p,k) = \sum_{g \in G} a_g.\text{rect}\frac{k.T - \dfrac{2R_g(p)}{c}}{T}.\exp\left[-j\frac{4\pi}{\lambda}R_g(p)\right] \tag{24}$$

Formally for each kth range cell the image function can be extracted by the inverse transform

$$\hat{a}_g = \sum_{p=1}^{N} s(p,k)\exp\left[j\frac{4\pi}{\lambda}R_g(p)\right] \tag{25}$$

where p is the number of emitted pulse, N is the full number of emitted pulses during CPI.

Because $s(p,k)$ is a 2-D signal, only a 2-D image function $\hat{a}_g$ can be extracted. Eq. (25) is a symmetric complex inverse spatial transform or inverse projective operation of the 2-D signal plane $s(p,k)$ into 2-D image function $\hat{a}_g$, and can be regarded as a spatial correlation between $s(p,k)$ and $\exp\left[j\dfrac{4\pi}{\lambda}R_g(p)\right]$. Moreover, Eq. (25) can be interpreted as a total compensation of phases, induced by radial displacement $R_g(p)$ of the target. Taylor expansion of the distance to the generic point, $R_g(p)$ at the moment of imaging is

$$R_g(p) = r_g + v_g(pT_p) + \frac{a_g}{2!}(pT_p)^2 + \frac{h_g}{3!}(pT_p)^3 + \dots, \tag{26}$$

where r_g, v_g, a_g and h_g is the distance, radial velocity, acceleration and jerk of the generic point, respectively at the moment of imaging.

Due to range uncertainty of generic points placed in the kth range resolution cell, r_g can be assumed constant, and (25) can be written as

$$\hat{a}_g = \exp\left(j\frac{4\pi}{\lambda}r_g \right) \sum_{p=1}^{N} s(p,k) \exp\left(j\frac{4\pi}{\lambda}[v_g(pT_p) + \frac{a_g}{2!}(pT_p)^2 + \frac{h_g}{3!}(pT_p)^3 + ...] \right). \qquad (27)$$

Eq. (27) stands for a procedure of total motion compensation of every generic point from kth range resolution cell. The range distance r_g does not influence on the image reconstruction and can be removed from the equation (27), i.e.

$$\hat{a}_g = \sum_{p=1}^{N} s(p,k) \exp\left(j2\pi[\frac{2}{\lambda}v_g(pT_p) + \frac{1}{\lambda}a_g(pT_p)^2 + \frac{1}{3}h_g(pT_p)^3 + ...] \right). \qquad (28)$$

For each kth range cell the term $\frac{2}{\lambda}v_g$ stands for the Doppler frequency whereas terms as $\frac{2}{\lambda}a_g$, $\frac{2}{\lambda}h_g$ ...., denote the higher order derivations of the time dependent Doppler frequency, defined at the moment of imaging.

If the Doppler frequency of generic points in the kth range cell is equal or tends to constant during CPI the equation (28) reduces to the following equation of radial motion compensation

$$\hat{a}_g = \sum_{p=1}^{N} s(p,k) \exp\left(j2\pi.\left(\frac{2}{\lambda}v_g\right)(pT_p) \right). \qquad (29)$$

Denote $\frac{2}{\lambda}v_g = \hat{p}.\Delta F_D$, where $\Delta F_D = \frac{1}{NT_p}$ is the Doppler frequency step; $\hat{p}$ is the unknown Doppler index at the moment of imaging; then the complex image function $\hat{a}_g = \hat{a}_g(\hat{p},k)$ in discrete space coordinates can be written as

$$\hat{a}_g(\hat{p},k) = \sum_{p=1}^{N} s(p,k) \exp\left(j2\pi\frac{p\hat{p}}{N} \right). \qquad (30)$$

The equation (30) stands for an IFT of $s(p,k)$ for each kth range resolution cell and can be considered as phase and/or motion compensation of first order.

Denote $a_1 = \frac{2}{\lambda}v_g$, $a_2 = \frac{2\pi}{\lambda}a_g$, $a_3 = \frac{2\pi}{3\lambda}h_g$, then (28) can be rewritten as

$$\hat{a}_g = \sum_{p=1}^{N} s(p,k) \exp\left(j[a_2(pT_p)^2 + a_3(pT_p)^3 + ...] \right) \exp\left(j2\pi a_1(pT_p) \right) \qquad (31)$$

Denote $\Phi(p) = a_2(pT_p)^2 + ... + a_m(pT_p)^m$ as a phase correction and/or motion compensation function of higher order, then

$$\hat{a}_g(\hat{p},k) = \sum_{p=1}^{N} \left[s(p,k) \exp(j\Phi(p)) \right].\exp\left(j2\pi\frac{p\hat{p}}{N} \right). \qquad (32)$$

where $\hat{a}_g(\hat{p},k)$ denotes the complex azimuth image of the target, $\hat{p}$ denotes the unknown index of the azimuth space coordinate equal to the unknown Doppler index of the generic point scatterer from the target at the moment of imaging. The polynomial coefficients a_m, m = 2, 3, are calculated iteratively via applying image quality criterion, which will be discussed in subsections 4.4.

Eq. (32) can be interpreted as an ISAR image reconstruction procedure implemented through inverse Fourier transform (IFT) of a phase corrected ISAR signal into a complex azimuth image $\hat{a}_g(\hat{p},k)$ for each kth range cell. In this sense the ISAR signal $s(p,k)$ can be referred to as a spatial frequency spectrum whereas $\hat{a}_g(\hat{p},k)$ can be referred to as a spatial image function defined at the moment of imaging. Based on Eq. (32) two steps of image reconstruction algorithm can be outlined.

Step 1 Compensate the phases, induced by higher order radial movement, by multiplication of $s(p,k)$ with the exponential term $\exp[j\Phi(p)]$, i.e.

$$\hat{s}(p,k) = s(p,k)\exp[j\Phi(p)] \tag{33}$$

Step 2 Compensate the phases induced by first order radial displacement of generic points in the kth range cell by applying IFT (extract complex image), i.e.

$$\hat{a}_g(\hat{p},k) = \sum_{p=1}^{N} \hat{s}(p,k).\exp\left(j2\pi\frac{p\hat{p}}{N}\right) \tag{34}$$

Complex image extraction can be implemented by inverse fast Fourier transform (IFFT). The algorithm can be implemented if the phase correction function $\Phi(p)$ is preliminary known.

Otherwise only IFT can be applied. Then non compensated radial acceleration and jerk of the target still remain and the image becomes blurred (unfocused). In order to obtain a focused image motion compensation of second, third and/or higher order has to be applied, that means coefficients of higher order terms in $\Phi(p)$ have to be determined. The definition and application of these terms in image reconstruction is named an autofocus procedure accomplished by an optimization step search algorithm (SSA) which will be discussed in subsection 4.4.

4. ISAR signal formation and imaging with a sequence of LFM waveforms

4.1 LFM waveform

Consider 3-D ISAR scenario (Fig. 6) and a target illuminated by sequence of LFM waveforms, each of which is described by

$$s(t) = A.\mathrm{rect}\left(\frac{t}{T}\right)\exp\left[-j\left(\omega t + bt^2\right)\right], \tag{35}$$

where $t = \tilde{t} - pT_p$ is the fast time and $\tilde{t} = t\,\mathrm{mod}\,T_p$ is the slow time; p is the index of emitted pulse; T_p is the pulse repetition period; $\omega = 2\pi\frac{c}{\lambda}$ is the carrier angular frequency; $c = 3.10^8$ m/s is the speed of the light; λ is the wavelength of the signal; T is the timewidth of a LFM waveform; $b = \dfrac{2\pi\Delta F}{T}$ is the LFM rate. The bandwidth $2\Delta F$ of the transmitted waveform provides the dimension of the range resolution cell, i.e. $\Delta R = c / 2\Delta F$.

4.2 LFM ISAR signal model

The deterministic component of the ISAR signal, reflected by the **g**th generic point scatterer has the form

$$s_g(p,t) = a_g \operatorname{rect}\frac{t - t_g(p)}{T} \exp\left\{ -j\left[\omega\big(t - t_g(p)\big) + b\big(t - t_g(p)\big)^2 \right] \right\} \tag{36}$$

$$\operatorname{rect}\frac{t - t_g(p)}{T} = \begin{cases} 1, 0 \le \dfrac{t - t_g(p)}{T} < 1 \\ 0, \text{otherwise} \end{cases},$$

where a_g is the reflection coefficient of the **g**th generic point scatterer, a 3-D image function; $t_g(p) = \dfrac{R_g(p)}{c}$ is the round trip time delay of the signal from **g**th generic point scatterer; $R_g(p) = \operatorname{mod}[\mathbf{R}_g(p)]$, $t = [k_{g\min}(p) + k - 1]\Delta T$ is the fast time, $k = \overline{1, K(p) + K}$ is the sample number of a LFM pulse; $K = T / \Delta T$ is the full number of samples of the LFM pulse, ΔT is the time duration of a LFM sample, $k_{g\min}(p) = \left\lceil \dfrac{t_{g\min}(p)}{\Delta T} \right\rceil$ is the number of the radar range cell where the signal, reflected by the nearest point scatterer of the target is detected, $t_{g\min}(p) = \dfrac{2R_{g\min}(p)}{c}$ is the minimal time delay of the SAR signal reflected from the nearest point scatterer of the target, $K(p) = k_{g\max}(p) - k_{g\min}(p)$ is the relative time dimension of the target; $k_{g\max}(p) = \left\lceil \dfrac{t_{g\max}(p)}{\Delta T} \right\rceil$ is the number of the radar range bin where the signal, reflected by farthest point scatterer of the target is detected; $t_{g\max}(p) = \dfrac{2R_{g\max}(p)}{c}$ is the maximum time delay of the SAR signal reflected from the farthest point scatterer of the target.

The ISAR signal in discrete form can be written as

$$s(p,k) = \sum_{g \in G} s_g(p,k) = \sum_{g \in G} a_g \operatorname{rect}\left[\frac{\hat{t}(p,k)}{T}\right] \exp\left\{ -j\left[\omega \hat{t}(p,k) + b\big(\hat{t}(p,k)\big)^2 \right] \right\} \tag{37}$$

$$\operatorname{rect}\left[\frac{\hat{t}_g(p,k)}{T}\right] = \begin{cases} 1 \text{ if } 0 \le \dfrac{\hat{t}_g(p,k)}{T} < 1, \\ 0 \text{ otherwise.} \end{cases}$$

where $\hat{t}_g(p,k) = [k_{g\min}(p) + k - 1]\Delta T - t_g(p)$.

Demodulation of the ISAR signal return is performed by its multiplication by the complex conjugated emitted waveform, i.e.

$$\hat{s}(p,t) = \sum_{g \in G} a_g \operatorname{rect} \frac{t - t_g(p)}{T} \exp\left\{ j\left[\omega\left(t - t_g(p)\right) + b\left(t - t_g(p)\right)^2 \right] \right\} \cdot \exp\left[-j\left(\omega t + bt^2 \right) \right] \tag{38}$$

which yields

$$\hat{s}(p,t) = \sum_{g \in G} a_g \operatorname{rect} \frac{t - t_g(p)}{T} \exp\left\{ -j\left[(\omega + 2bt) t_g(p) - bt_g^2(p) \right] \right\} . \tag{39}$$

Denote the current angular frequency of emitted LFM pulse as $\omega(t) = \omega + 2bt$, which in discrete form can be expressed as $\omega_k = \omega + 2b(k-1)\Delta T$, where ω is the carrier angular frequency, and b is the chirp rate, k is the LFM sample number, ΔT is the time length of the sample, then Eq. (39) can be rewritten as

$$\hat{s}(p,t) = \sum_{g \in G} a_g \operatorname{rect} \frac{t - \dfrac{R_g(p)}{c}}{T} \exp\left[-j\left(2\omega(t) \frac{R_g(p)}{c} - b\left(\frac{2R_g(p)}{c} \right)^2 \right) \right], \tag{40}$$

which in discrete form can be expressed as

$$\hat{s}(p,k) = \sum_{g \in G} a_g \operatorname{rect} \frac{\hat{t}_g(p,k)}{T} \exp\left[-j\left(2\omega_k \frac{R_g(p)}{c} - b\left(\frac{2R_g(p)}{c} \right)^2 \right) \right]. \tag{41}$$

Eq. (41) can be interpreted as a spatial transform of the 3-D image function a_g into 2-D ISAR signal plane $\hat{s}(p,k)$ by the finite transformation operator, the exponential term

$$\exp\left[-j\left(2\omega_k \frac{R_g(p)}{c} - b\left(\frac{2R_g(p)}{c} \right)^2 \right) \right]. \tag{42}$$

Formally the 3-D image function a_g should be extracted from 2-D ISAR signal plane by the inverse spatial transform but due to theoretical limitation based on the number of measurement parameters only a 2-D image function may be extracted, i.e.

$$\hat{a}_{g \in G} = \sum_{p=1}^{N} \sum_{k=1}^{K(p)+K} \hat{s}(p,k) \cdot \exp\left[j\left(2\omega_k \frac{R_g(p)}{c} - b\left(\frac{2R_g(p)}{c} \right)^2 \right) \right]. \tag{43}$$

Extraction of the image function is a procedure of complete phase compensation of the signals reflected by all point scatterers from the object that means total compensation of target movement during CPI. The argument of the exponential term (43),

$\left(2\omega_k \dfrac{R_g(p)}{c} - b\left(\dfrac{2R_g(p)}{c} \right)^2 \right)$ is a complex function infinitely differentiable in a neighborhood of the moment of imaging that allows 2-D Taylor expansion on range and azimuth direction to be applied, i.e. the following polynomial of higher order to be defined

$$\left(2\omega_k \frac{R_g(p)}{c} - b\left(\frac{2R_g(p)}{c}\right)^2\right) = a_0 + a_1.(pT_p) + a_2.(pT_p)^2 + \dots + a_m(pT_p)^m$$

$$+b_1.(k\Delta T) + b_2.(k\Delta T)^2 + \dots + b_m(k\Delta T)^m + c_2(pT_p)(k\Delta T) + \dots$$

(44)

The constant terms a_0 has noting to do with phase correction and can be neglected. The linear terms $a_1.(pT_p)$ and $b_1.(k\Delta T)$ are redefined as $a_1(pT_p) = 2\pi\frac{p\hat{p}}{N}$ and $b_1(k\Delta T) = 2\pi\frac{k\hat{k}}{\hat{K}}$, where $\hat{k} = \hat{k}(g), \hat{p} = \hat{p}(g)$ denote the new unknown range and cross-range space coordinates of the gth generic point at the instant of imaging, $\hat{K} = K + K(p)$ denotes the number of range cells for each emitted pulse. The sum of higher order terms is signified as

$$\Phi(p,k) = a_2.(pT_p)^2 + \dots + a_m(pT_p)^m + b_2.(k\Delta T)^2 + \dots + b_m(k\Delta T)^m + c_2(pT_p)(k\Delta T) + \dots$$

(45)

then

$$\left(2\omega_k \frac{R_g(p)}{c} - b\left(\frac{2R_g(p)}{c}\right)^2\right) = 2\pi\frac{p\hat{p}}{N} + 2\pi\frac{k\hat{k}}{K} + \Phi(p,k).$$

(46)

Substitute (46) in (43), then

$$\hat{a}_g(\hat{p},\hat{k}) = \sum_{p=1}^{N}\sum_{k=1}^{\hat{K}}\hat{s}(p,k)\exp\left[j\left(\Phi(k,p) + 2\pi\frac{p\hat{p}}{N} + 2\pi\frac{k\hat{k}}{K}\right)\right],$$

(47)

where $\hat{p} = \overline{1,N}$, $\hat{k} = \overline{1,K(p) + K}$.

Eq. (47) can be rewritten as

$$\hat{a}_g(\hat{p},\hat{k}) = \sum_{p=1}^{N}\left[\sum_{k=1}^{\hat{K}}\hat{s}(p,k).\exp[j\Phi(k,p)].\exp\left(j2\pi\frac{k\hat{k}}{K}\right)\right]\exp\left(j2\pi\frac{p\hat{p}}{N}\right).$$

(48)

Eq. (48) can be considered as an image reconstruction computational procedure, which does reveal the 2-D discrete complex image function $\hat{a}_g(\hat{p},\hat{k})$.

4.3 LFM ISAR image reconstruction algorithm

Based on the previous analysis the following image reconstruction steps can be defined.

Step 1 Compensate phase terms of higher order by multiplication of complex matrix $\hat{s}(p,k)$ by a complex exponential function $\exp[j\Phi(p,k)]$, i.e.

$$\tilde{s}(p,k) = \hat{s}(p,k).\exp[j\Phi(p,k)]$$

(49)

Step 2 Range compress $\tilde{s}(p,k)$ by discrete IFT, i.e.

$$\tilde{s}(p,\hat{k}) = \frac{1}{K}\sum_{k=1}^{\hat{k}}\tilde{s}(p,k).\exp\left(j2\pi\frac{k\hat{k}}{K}\right). \tag{50}$$

Step 3 Azimuth compress $\tilde{s}(p,\hat{k})$, i.e. extract a complex image by IFT

$$a_g(\hat{p},\hat{k}) = \frac{1}{N}\sum_{p=1}^{N}\tilde{s}(p,\hat{k}).\exp\left(j2\pi\frac{p\hat{p}}{N}\right). \tag{51}$$

Step 4 Compute the module of the complex image by

$$\left|a_g(\hat{p},\hat{k})\right| = \left|\frac{1}{N}\sum_{p=1}^{N}\tilde{s}(p,\hat{k}).\exp\left(j2\pi\frac{p\hat{p}}{N}\right)\right|. \tag{52}$$

The aforementioned algorithm is feasible if the phase correction function $\Phi(p,k)$ is a priory known. Otherwise, a focused image is impossible to extract. In this case taking into account the linear property of computational operations in (48) the image extraction algorithm may start with 2-D IFT (range and cross range compression) of the demodulated ISAR signal, the complex matrix $\hat{s}(p,k)$, i.e.

$$a_g(\hat{p},\hat{k}) = \sum_{p=1}^{N}\left[\sum_{k=1}^{\hat{k}}\hat{s}(p,k).\exp\left(j2\pi\frac{k\hat{k}}{\hat{K}}\right)\right]\exp\left(j2\pi\frac{p\hat{p}}{N}\right). \tag{53}$$

It is worth noting that 2-D IFT are interpreted as a spatial correlation of the complex frequency spectrum, $\hat{s}(p,k)$ with the exponential terms $\exp\left(j2\pi\frac{k\hat{k}}{\hat{K}}\right)$ and $\exp\left(j2\pi\frac{p\hat{p}}{N}\right)$ that reveal unknown range, $\hat{k}$ and cross range, $\hat{p}$ space coordinates of a 2-D image function $a_g(\hat{p},\hat{k})$ in the area of all possible values $\hat{p} = \overline{1,N}$ and $\hat{k} = \overline{1,K(p)+K}$.

4.4 Autofocusing phase correction by image entropy minimization

If the image obtained by only range (50) and azimuth (51) compression is blurred a higher order phase correction has to be applied, i.e. to perform $\tilde{s}(k,p) = \hat{s}(k,p).\exp\left[j\Phi(p)\right]$. The phase correction or motion compensation of higher order is an autofocus procedure. It requires determination of coefficients $a_2 \dots a_m$, $b_2 \dots b_m$ and c_2 of the polynomial (45). The computational load is reduced if $\Phi(p,k) = \Phi(p)$ for each k, i.e. (45) is limited to

$$\Phi(p) = a_2.(pT_p)^2 + \dots + a_m(pT_p)^m \tag{54}$$

An iterative SSA is applied to find out optimal values of the coefficients using entropy as a cost function to evaluate the quality of the image. At first step a_2 is calculated, at second - a_3, etc. The exact value of each coefficient a_m, $m = 2,3,\dots$ is computed iteratively, starting from

$a_m = 0$ and increasing by $\Delta a_m = 0.01$ in case the image quality gets better. If the image quality does not improve or gets worse go to computation of the next coefficient a_{m+1} or stop the procedure. In practice the quadratic term has a major impact on the phase correction process.

Let $\Phi_s(p)$ be a phase correction function, defined at the sth iteration, and then the phase correction is accomplished by

$$\tilde{s}_s(p,k) = \hat{s}(p,k)\exp(-j\Phi_s(p)). \tag{55}$$

After current phase correction and image extraction by range and cross-range (azimuth) compression, calculate a power normalized image as

$$I_s(\hat{p},\hat{k}) = \frac{\left|a_{g,s}(\hat{p},\hat{k})\right|^2}{\sum\limits_{p=1}^{N}\sum\limits_{k=1}^{\hat{K}}\left|a_{g,s}(\hat{p},\hat{k})\right|^2}. \tag{56}$$

Calculate entropy of the normalized ISAR image

$$H_s = -\sum\limits_{p=1}^{N}\sum\limits_{k=1}^{\hat{K}}I_s(\hat{p},\hat{k})\ln[I_s(\hat{p},\hat{k})]. \tag{57}$$

The estimate of the optimal values of coefficients corresponds to the minimum of the entropy image cost function, i.e.

$$\hat{a}_m = \arg\min_{a_m}\left\{H_s[I_s(\hat{p},\hat{k})]\right\}. \tag{58}$$

The procedure is repeated until the global minimum value of the entropy H_s is acquired.

4.5 Numerical experiment

To verify the properties of the LFM ISAR signal model and to prove the correctness of the image reconstruction algorithm a numerical experiment is carried out. Assume the target, Mig-35, detected in 3-D coordinate system $O'XYZ$ is moving rectilinearly in a coordinate system $Oxyz$. Kinematical parameters: velocity $V = 400$ m/s; guiding angles $\alpha = 0.92\pi$; $\beta = -0.5\pi$; $\gamma = 0.42\pi$, coordinates of the mass-center at the moment ($p = N/2$): $x_{00'}(0) = 36,3.10^3$ m; $y_{00'}(0) = 71,3.10^3$ m; $z_{00'}(0) = 5.10^3$ m; reference coordinates: $x_0(0) = 10$ m; $y_0(0) = 5.10^4$ m; $z_0(0) = 2.10^3$ m. LFM emitted pulse: wavelength $\lambda = 3.10^{-2}$ m; pulse repetition period $T_p = 1.32.10^{-2}$ s, LFM pulse timewidth $T = 10^{-6}$ s; number of LFM samples $K = 300$; timewidth of LFM sample $\Delta T = 0.33.10^{-8}$ s; bandwidth $\Delta F = 1.5.10^8$ Hz, LFM rate $b = 3.10^{14}$ s^{-2}; number of emitted pulses during CPI $N = 500$. Dimensions of the grid cell: $\Delta X = \Delta Y = \Delta Z = 0.5$ m; reference points on grid axes X,Y,Z, $i = \overline{1,64}$, $j = \overline{1,64}$ $k = \overline{1,10}$. Target intensities $a_{ijk} = 0.01$, out of target intensities $a_{ijk} = 0.001$.

The complex spatial frequency spectrum and 2-D space image function are presented in Figs. 7 and 8, respectively. The entropy and final focused image of Mig-35 are illustrated in Figs. 9 and 10, respectively.

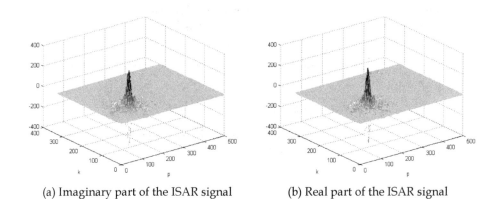

(a) Imaginary part of the ISAR signal   (b) Real part of the ISAR signal

Fig. 7. Complex ISAR signal - complex spatial frequency spectrum.

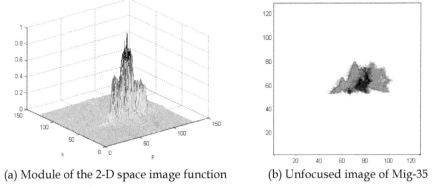

(a) Module of the 2-D space image function   (b) Unfocused image of Mig-35

Fig. 8. 2-D isometric space image function and 2-D unfocused image of Mig-35 after azimuth compression by second IFT.

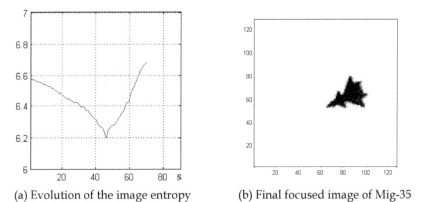

(a) Evolution of the image entropy   (b) Final focused image of Mig-35

Fig. 9. Image entropy and final focused image of Mig-35 by step 47 and minimal entropy 6.2.

5. ISAR signal formation and imaging with a sequence of PCM waveforms

5.1 PCM waveform

Consider 3-D ISAR scenario (Fig. 6) and a target a sequence of phase-code modulated (PCM) pulse trains (bursts). Each PCM pulse train is described by

$$s(t) = A \mathbf{rect} \frac{t}{T} \exp\{-j[\omega t + \pi b(t) + \varphi_0]\}, \tag{59}$$

where $t = \tilde{t} - pT_p$ is the fast time and $\tilde{t} = t \bmod T_p$ is the slow time; p is the index of the emitted pulse train; T_p is the burst repetition period; φ_0 is the initial phase of a PCM pulse, $k = \overline{1,K}$ is the index of the PCM segment, $K = T / \Delta T$ is the full number of PCM segments; T is the time duration of the phase-code modulated pulse train, ΔT is the timewidth the phase segment, $b(t) \in \{0,1\}$ is the binary parameter of the PCM train.

5.2 PCM ISAR signal model

Deterministic component of the ISAR signal return reflected by the gth generic point scatterer if $\varphi_0 = 0$ is defined by

$$s_g(p,t) = a_g \mathbf{rect} \frac{t - t_g(p)}{T} \exp\{-j[\omega(t - t_g(p)) + \pi b(t)]\}, \tag{60}$$

$$\mathbf{rect} \frac{t - t_g(p)}{T} = \begin{cases} 1, & \text{if } 0 \le \dfrac{t - t_g(p)}{T} < 1; \\ 0, & \text{otherwise.} \end{cases}$$

The deterministic component of the ISAR signal return reflected from the target for every p th pulse train is described by

$$s(p,t) = \sum_{g \in G} a_g \mathbf{rect} \frac{t - t_g(p)}{T} \exp\{-j[\omega(t - t_g(p)) + \pi b(t)]\}. \tag{61}$$

Eq. (61) is a weighted complex series of finite base functions, ISAR signals from all generic points. It can be regarded as an asymmetric complex transform of the 3-D image function $a_{g \in G}$, into a 2-D signal plane $\hat{s}(k,p)$. Computing $\mathbf{rect}[t - t_g(p)/T]$ time delays $t_g(p)$ are arranged in ascending order. An index $\hat{k}$ different from this order is introduced i.e. $t_g^{\hat{k}}(p)$. Denote $\hat{t}_g^{\hat{k}}(p) = (k_{g\min}(p) + k - 1)\Delta T - t_g^{\hat{k}}(p)$, then Eq. (60) in discrete form can be written as

$$s(p,k) = \sum_{g \in G} a_g \mathbf{rect} \frac{\hat{t}_g^{\hat{k}}(p)}{T} . \exp\{-j[\omega \hat{t}_g^{\hat{k}}(p) + \pi b(k - \hat{k} + 1)\Delta T]\}, \tag{62}$$

$$\mathbf{rect} \frac{\hat{t}_g^{\hat{k}}(p)}{T} = \begin{cases} 1, & \text{if } 0 \le \dfrac{\hat{t}_g^{\hat{k}}(p)}{T} < 1 . \\ 0, & \text{otherwise} \end{cases}$$

where $\hat{k}$ stands for a current range number k for which $\text{rect}[\hat{t}_g^k(p)/T]$ yields 1 first time. It is possible for many time delays, $t_g(p)$ the index $\hat{k}$ to have one and the same value. The index $\hat{k}$ is considered as a space discrete range coordinate of a gth generic point at the moment of imaging.

5.3 PCM ISAR image reconstruction procedure

Based on the phase demodulated ISAR signal

$$\hat{s}(p,k) = \sum_{g\in G} a_g \, \text{rect} \frac{\hat{t}_g^{\hat{k}}(p)}{T} \exp\left\{-j\left[\omega(k_{g\min}(p)\Delta T - t_g^{\hat{k}}(p)) + \pi b((k-\hat{k}+1)\Delta T)\right]\right\}. \quad (63)$$

formally the 3-D image function a_g should be extracted from 2-D ISAR signal plane by the inverse spatial transform but due to theoretical limitation based on the number of measurement parameters only a 2-D image function may by determined, i.e.

$$\hat{a}_g = \sum_{p=1}^{N} \sum_{k=\hat{k}}^{\hat{k}+K} s(p,k)\exp\left\{j\left[\omega(k_{g\min}(p)\Delta T - t_g^{\hat{k}}(p)) + \pi b((k-\hat{k}+1)\Delta T)\right]\right\}, \quad (64)$$

Eq. (64) can be rewritten as

$$\hat{a}_g = \sum_{p=1}^{N} \sum_{k=\hat{k}}^{\hat{k}+K} \left[\hat{s}(p,k)\exp[j\pi b(k-\hat{k}+1)\Delta T]\right].\exp\left\{j\omega\left[k_{g\min}(p)\Delta T - t_g^{\hat{k}}(p)\right]\right\}. \quad (65)$$

Taylor expansion of the phase term $\left[t_{ijk\min}(p)-t_{ijk}^{\hat{k}}(p)\right]$ can be presented as a polynomial function of higher order, i.e.

$$\left[k_{g\min}(p) - t_{ijk}^{\hat{k}}(p)\right] = a_0 + a_1(pT_p) + a_2(pT_p)^2 + ... + a_m(pT_p)^m. \quad (66)$$

The linear term $a_1(pT_p)$ is reduced to $\dfrac{2\pi}{N}\hat{p}.p$ and considered as a Fourier operator, $\hat{p}$ is the discrete unknown coordinate of the gth generic point scatterer placed in the kth range cell, N is the number of emitted PCM trains during CPI. The constant term has nothing to do with the image reconstruction and is removed. The rest sum of the terms in (66) are denoted as

$$\Phi(p) = a_2(pT_p)^2 + ... + a_m(pT_p)^m, \quad (67)$$

then (65) can expressed as

$$\hat{a}_g(\hat{p},\hat{k}) = \sum_{p=1}^{N} \sum_{k=\hat{k}}^{\hat{k}+K} \left\{\hat{s}(p,k)\exp\left[j\pi b(k-\hat{k}+1)\Delta T\right]\right\}\exp\left\{j\left[\frac{2\pi}{N}p\hat{p} + \Phi(p)\right]\right\}, \quad (68)$$

Based on the linearity of the operations (68) can be rewritten as

$$\hat{a}_g(\hat{p},\hat{k}) = \sum_{p=1}^{N} \left\{\sum_{k=\hat{k}}^{\hat{k}+K} [\hat{s}(p,k).\exp(j\Phi(p)).\exp[j\pi b(k-\hat{k}+1)\Delta T)]\right\}\exp\left\{j\left[\frac{2\pi}{N}\hat{p}p\right]\right\}. \quad (69)$$

Accordingly, the image extraction algorithm can be outlined as follows.

Step 1 Phase correction by multiplication of the phase demodulated ISAR signal with an exponential phase correction function, i.e.

$$\tilde{s}(p,k) = \hat{s}(p,k).\exp[j\Phi(p)]. \tag{70}$$

Step 2 Range compression is by correlating of the phase corrected ISAR signal $\tilde{s}(p,k)$ with reference function, complex conjugated of the transmitted PCM signal $\exp[j\pi b(k - \hat{k} + 1)\Delta T]$, i.e.

$$\tilde{s}(\hat{p},\hat{k}) = \sum_{k=\hat{k}}^{\hat{k}+K} \tilde{s}(p,k)\exp[j\pi b(k - \hat{k} + 1)\Delta T], \tag{71}$$

where $p = \overline{1,N}$, $\hat{k} = \overline{1,K(p)}$.

Step 3 Azimuth compression and complex image extraction by Fourier transform of the range compressed ISAR data, i.e.

$$\hat{a}_g(\hat{p},\hat{k}) = \sum_{p=1}^{N} \tilde{s}(p,\hat{k})\exp\left\{ j\left[\frac{2\pi}{N}\hat{p}p \right]\right\}. \tag{72}$$

Then the module of the target image can be calculated by

$$\left|\hat{a}_g(\hat{p},\hat{k})\right| = \left| \sum_{p=1,N} \tilde{s}(p,\hat{k})\exp\left\{ j\left[\frac{2\pi}{N}\hat{p}p \right]\right\}\right|. \tag{73}$$

The aforementioned algorithm is feasible if the phase correction function $\Phi(p,k)$ is a priory known. Otherwise, a focused image is impossible to extract. In this case taking into account the linear property of computational operations in (68) the image extraction algorithm may start with correlation along range coordinate (range compression) and Fourier transform along cross range coordinate (range compression) of the demodulated ISAR signal, the complex matrix $\hat{s}(p,k)$, i.e.

$$\hat{a}_g(\hat{p},\hat{k}) = \sum_{p=1}^{N} \left\{ \sum_{k=\hat{k}}^{\hat{k}+K} \hat{s}(p,k).\exp[j\pi b((k - \hat{k} + 1)\Delta T)]\right\}\exp\left\{ j\left[\frac{2\pi}{N}\hat{p}p \right]\right\}. \tag{74}$$

If the image obtained by only range (71) and azimuth (72) compression is blurred a higher order phase correction algorithm has to be applied. It requires determination of coefficients $a_2 \dots a_m$ in polynomial (67) using a phase correction SSA described in 4.4.

5.4 Numerical experiment

A numerical experiment is carried out to verify the properties of the PCM ISAR signal model and to prove the correctness of the image reconstruction algorithm. It is assumed that the target, helicopter is detected in a coordinate system $O'XYZ$ and illuminated by Barker's

PCM burst and moving rectilinearly in a coordinate system $Oxyz$. Kinematic parameters: velocity module $V = 25$ m/s; velocity guiding angles $\alpha = 0$, $\beta = 0.5\pi$, $\gamma = 0.5\pi$; coordinates of the mass-centre: $x_{00'}(0) = 0$ m, $y_{00'}(0) = 5.10^4$ m, $z_{00'} = 3.10^3$ m. Barker's PCM binary function $b(t)$: $b(t) = 0$ if $t = (\overline{1,5,8,9},11,13)\Delta T$, and $b(t) = 1$ if $t = (\overline{6,7},10,12)\Delta T$; wavelength $\lambda = 3.10^{-2}$ m; burst repetition period $T_p = 5.10^{-3}$ s; PCM sample timewidth $\Delta T = 3.3.10^{-9}$ s; number of burst samples $K = 13$; sample index $k = \overline{1,13}$; PCM burst timewidth $T = 42.9.10^{-9}$ s; number of bursts emitted during CPI $N = 500$. Grid's cell dimensions $\Delta X = \Delta Y = \Delta Z = 0.5$ m. Reference points on axes X,Y,Z $i = j = \overline{1,100}$ and $k = \overline{1,40}$, respectively. Isotropic point scatterers are placed at each node of the regular grid. Target's intensities $a_{ijk} = 0.01$, out of target's intensities $a_{ijk} = 0.001$.

The real and imaginary part of the complex Barker's PCM ISAR signal is presented in Fig. 10, the final image – 2-D space image function - in Fig. 11, and entropy evolution in Fig. 12.

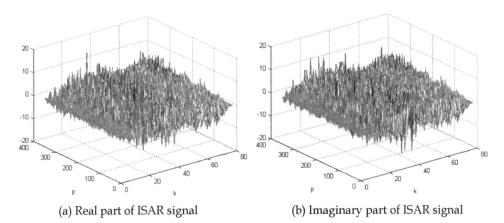

(a) Real part of ISAR signal   (b) Imaginary part of ISAR signal

Fig. 10. Complex Barker's PCM ISAR signal as a complex spatial frequency spectrum.

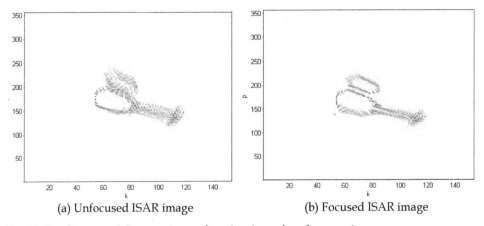

(a) Unfocused ISAR image   (b) Focused ISAR image

Fig. 11. Final image – 2-D space image function (pseudo color maps).

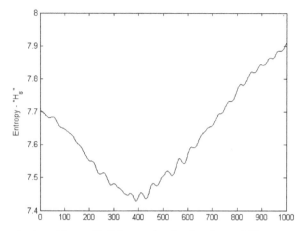

Fig. 12. Entropy evolution: $H_{min} = 7{,}43$ by optimal vale of $a_2 = 390$.

6. Conclusion

In the present chapter a mathematical description and original interpretation of ISAR signal formation and imaging has been suggested. It has been illustrated that both of these operations can be interpreted as direct and inverse spatial complex transforms, respectively. It has been proven that the image extraction is a threefold procedure; including phase correction, range compression performed by IFT in case LFM waveforms and by cross-correlation in case PCM waveforms, and azimuth compression performed by IFT in both cases. It has been underlined that the image reconstruction is a procedure of total motion compensation, i.e. compensation of all phases induced by the target motion. Only phases proportional to the distances from ISAR to all point scatterers on the target at the moment of their imaging still remain. These phases define a complex character of the ISAR image. The drawback of the proposed higher motion compensation algorithm is the existence of multiple local minimums in entropy evolution in case the target is fast maneuvering. In order to find out a global minimum in the entropy and optimal values of the polynomial coefficients the computation process has to be enlarged in wide interval of their variation. The subject of the future research is the exploration of the image reconstruction algorithm with higher order terms and cross-terms of the phase correction polynomial while the target exhibits complicated movement.

7. Acknowledgement

This chapter is supported by NATO Science for Peace and Security (SPS) Programme: NATO: ESP. EAP. CLG 983876.

8. References

Li, J.; Wu, R.; Chen, V. (2001). Robust autofocus algorithm for ISAR imaging of moving targets, *IEEE Transactions on Aerospace and Electronic Systems*, Vol. 37, No 3, (July 2001), pp. 1056-1069, ISSN 0018-9251

Berizzi, F.; Dalle Mese, E. & Martorella, M. (2002). Performance analysis of a contrast-based ISAR autofocusing algorithm. *Proceedings of 2002 IEEE Radar Conference*, pp. 200-205, ISBN 0-7803-7357-X, Long Beach, CA, USA, Apr. 22-25, 2002

Martorella, M.; Haywood, B.; Berizzi, F. & Dalle Mese, E. (2003). Performance analysis of an ISAR contrast-based autofocusing algorithm using real data. *Proceedings of 2003 IEEE Radar Conference*, pp. 30-35, ISBN 0-7803-7870-9, Adelaide, SA, Australia, Sept. 3-5, 2003

Berizzi, F.; Martorella, M.; Haywood, B. M.; Dalle Mese, E. &Bruscoli, S. (2004). A survey on ISAR autofocusing techniques. *Proceedings of IEEE ICIP 2004*, Singapore, Oct. 24-27, 2004

Chen, C. & Andrews, H.C. (1980). Target motion induced radar imaging. *IEEE Transactions on Aerospace and Electronic Systems*, Vol. 16, (January 1980), pp. 2-14, ISSN 0018-9251

Wu, H.; Delisle, G. Y. & Fang, D. G. (1995). Translational motion compensation in ISAR image processing. *IEEE Transactions on Image Processing*, Vol. 4, No 11, (November 1995), pp. 1561-1571, ISSN 0018-9251

Xi, L.; Guosui, L.& Ni, J. (1999). Autofocusing of ISAR images based on entropy minimization, *IEEE Transactions on Aerospace and Electronic Systems*, Vol. 35, No 4, (October 1999), pp. 1240-1252, ISSN 0018-9251

Martorella M. & Berizzi, F. (2005). Time windowing for highly focused ISAR image reconstruction," *IEEE Transactions on Aerospace and Electronic Systems*, Vol 41, No 3, (July 2005), pp. 992-1006, ISSN 1729-8806

Chen, V. & Quint, S. (1998). Joint time-frequency transform for radar range Doppler imaging. *IEEE Transactions on Aerospace and Electronic Systems*, Vol. 34, No 2, (April 1998) pp. 486-499, ISSN 0018-9251

Qian, S. & Chen, V. (1998). ISAR motion compensation via adaptive joint time-frequency technique, *IEEE Transactions on Aerospace and Electronic Systems*, Vol. 34, No 2, pp. 670-677, (April 1999), ISSN 0018-9251

4

Polygonal Representation
of Digital Curves

Dilip K. Prasad[1] and Maylor K. H. Leung[2]
[1]Nanyang Technological University
[2]Universiti Tunku Abdul Rahman (Kampar)
[1]Singapore
[2]Malaysia

1. Introduction

Approximating digital curves using polygonal approximations is required in many image processing applications [Kolesnikov & Fränti, 2003, 2005; Lavallee & Szeliski, 1995; Leung, 1990; Mokhtarian & Mackworth, 1986; Prasad, *et al.*, 2011; Prasad & Leung, 2010a, 2010b; Prasad & Leung, 2010; Prasad & Leung, 2012; Prasad, *et al.*, 2011a]. Such representation is used for representing noisy digital curves in a more robust manner, reducing the computational resources required for processing and storing them, and for computing various geometrical properties of digital curves. Specifically, properties like curvature estimation, tangent estimation, detecting inflexion points, perimeter of the curves, etc., which are very sensitive to the digitization noise. Polygonal approximation is also useful in topological representation, segmentation and contour feature extraction in the applications of object detection, face detection, etc.

Most contemporary methods require some form of control parameter for selecting the most representative points (referred to as the dominant points) in the digital curve to be used as the vertices of the polygonal approximation [Arcelli & Ramella, 1993; Bhowmick & Bhattacharya, 2007; Carmona-Poyato, *et al.*, 2005; Carmona-Poyato, *et al.*, 2010; Carmona-Poyato, *et al.*, 2011; Chung, *et al.*, 2008; Chung, *et al.*, 1994; Davis, 1999; Debled-Rennesson, *et al.*, 2005; Douglas & Peucker, 1973; Gritzali & Papakonstantinou, 1983; Kanungo, *et al.*, 1995; Kolesnikov, 2008; Kolesnikov & Fränti, 2003, 2005, 2007; Latecki, *et al.*, 2009; Lavallee & Szeliski, 1995; Leung, 1990; Lowe, 1987; Marji & Siy, 2004; Mokhtarian & Mackworth, 1986; Pavlidis, 1976; Perez & Vidal, 1994; Phillips & Rosenfeld, 1987; Prasad & Leung, 2010c; Ramer, 1972; Ray & Ray, 1992; Rosin, 1997, 2002; Salotti, 2002; Sankar & Sharma, 1978; Sarkar, 1993; Sato, 1992; Sklansky & Gonzalez, 1980; Tomek, 1975; Wall & Danielsson, 1984; Wang, *et al.*, 2008]. The value of control parameter in all the known algorithms is chosen heuristically. In reality, choosing such control parameter can be very challenging because a suitable value of such control parameters depends upon the nature of the digital curve and one value may not be suitable for all the curves in an image and definitely not suitable for all images in a dataset or an application. In section 2, we first propose a parameter independent method for polygonal approximation of the digital curves.

In addition to the heuristics, another issue is the problem of measuring the quality of the polygon fitted by an algorithm. It was shown in [Carmona-Poyato, et al., 2011; Rosin, 1997] that most contemporary metrics to compare and benchmark such algorithms are ineffective for different types of digital curves. The reason for this is that the polygonal approximation has conflicting requirements in terms of the local and global quality of fit. In section 3, we show explicitly that these requirements are conflicting. Quality metrics for local and global characteristics are presented in section 3.5. The presented metrics can be used to measure the quality of not only one edge of the approximated polygons, but also for the complete polygon for a digital curve and for all curves in an image.

A few contemporary methods are discussed qualitatively in section 4 and numerical comparisons are provided in section 5. The conclusions are presented in section 6.

2. Parameter independent polygonal approximation method

The proposed method uses the framework of the method proposed by Lowe [Lowe, 1987] and Ramer-Douglas-Peucker [Douglas & Peucker, 1973; Ramer, 1972] (referred to as L-RDP method for convenience). The L-RDP method of fitting a series of line segment over a digital curve is described here. For a digital curve $e = \{P_1 \quad P_2 \quad \ldots \quad P_N\}$, where P_i is the i th edge pixel in the digital curve e. The line passing through a pair of pixels $P_a(x_a, y_a)$ and $P_b(x_b, y_b)$ is given by:

$$x(y_a - y_b) + y(x_b - x_a) + y_b x_a - y_a x_b = 0. \tag{1}$$

Then the deviation d_i of a pixel $P_i(x_i, y_i) \in e$ from the line passing through the pair $\{P_1, P_N\}$ is given as:

$$d_i = \left| x_i (y_1 - y_N) + y_i (x_N - x_1) + y_N x_1 - y_1 x_N \right|. \tag{2}$$

Accordingly, the pixel with maximum deviation can be found. Let it be denoted as $P_{\max}$. Then considering the pairs $\{P_1, P_{\max}\}$ and $\{P_{\max}, P_N\}$, we find two new pixels from e using the concept in the equations (1) and (2). It is evident that the maximum deviation goes on decreasing as we choose newer pixels of maximum deviation between a pair. This process can be repeated till a certain condition (depending upon the method) is satisfied by all the line segments. This condition shall be referred to as the optimization goal for the ease of reference.

The condition used by L-RDP [Douglas & Peucker, 1973; Lowe, 1987; Ramer, 1972] is that for each line segment, the maximum deviation of the pixels contained in its corresponding edge segment is less than a certain tolerance value:

$$\max(d_i) < d_{\text{tol}}. \tag{3}$$

where d_{tol} is the chosen threshold.

In general, the value of d_{tol} is chosen heuristically to be a few pixels and d_{tol} functions as the control parameter. Now, we present the method to choose the value of d_{tol} automatically using the characteristics of the line, such that the user does not need to specify the value of d_{tol} [Prasad, *et al.*, 2011a]. First we show that if a continuous line segment is digitized then the maximum distance between that digital line segment and the continuous line segment is bounded and can be computed analytically. Then, this bound can be used to choose the value of d_{tol} adaptively.

We consider the effect of digitization on the slope of a line connecting two points (which may or may not be pixels) [Prasad, *et al.*, 2011a]. Due to digitization in the case of images, a general point $P(x,y)$ is approximated by a pixel $P'(x',y')$ as follows:

$$x' = \text{round}(x); \quad y' = \text{round}(y); \quad \Rightarrow x', y' \in \mathbb{Z} \tag{4}$$

where $\text{round}(x)$ denotes the rounding of the value of real number x to its nearest integer. $P'(x',y')$ satisfy the following:

$$x' = x + \Delta x; \quad y' = y + \Delta y; \quad -0.5 \le \Delta x \le 0.5, \quad -0.5 \le \Delta y \le 0.5 \tag{5}$$

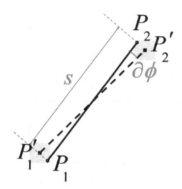

Fig. 1. Representation of the line $P_1 P_2$ and the digitized line $P_1' P_2'$.

Let the slope of the line $P_1 P_2$ (actual line) be denoted as m and the slope of the line $P_1' P_2'$ (digital line) be denoted as m', where P_1' and P_2' are obtained by digitization of P_1 and P_2 using (4). See Fig. 1 for the illustration. Then m and m' are given as:

$$m = \frac{y_2 - y_1}{x_2 - x_1} \tag{6}$$

$$m' = \frac{y_2' - y_1'}{x_2' - x_1'} = \left(m + \frac{\Delta y_2 - \Delta y_1}{x_2 - x_1} \right) \bigg/ \left(1 + \frac{\Delta x_2 - \Delta x_1}{x_2 - x_1} \right) \tag{7}$$

The angular difference between the numeric tangent and the digital tangent is used as the estimate of the error. This angular difference is given as:

$$\partial\phi = \left|\tan^{-1}(m) - \tan^{-1}(m')\right| = \left|\tan^{-1}\left(\frac{m-m'}{1+mm'}\right)\right|$$

$$= \left|\tan^{-1}\left(\frac{m(\Delta x_2 - \Delta x_1) - (\Delta y_2 - \Delta y_1)}{(1+m^2)(x_2-x_1) + (\Delta x_2 - \Delta x_1) + m(\Delta y_2 - \Delta y_1)}\right)\right| \tag{8}$$

$$= \left|\tan^{-1}\left(\left(\frac{x_2-x_1}{s^2}\right)(1+t)^{-1}\left(m(\Delta x_2 - \Delta x_1) - (\Delta y_2 - \Delta y_1)\right)\right)\right|$$

where, $s = \sqrt{(x_2-x_1)^2 + (y_2-y_1)^2}$ and $t = \frac{(\Delta x_2 - \Delta x_1)(x_2-x_1)}{s^2} + \frac{(\Delta y_2 - \Delta y_1)(y_2-y_1)}{s^2}$. Due

to (5), the maximum value of $|\Delta x_2 - \Delta x_1|$ and $|\Delta y_2 - \Delta y_1|$ is 1. Further, $|(x_2-x_1)/s|$ and $|(y_2-y_1)/s|$ are both less than 1. Thus, $|t| < 1$ if $s > \sqrt{2}$, which is true for any line made of more than 2 pixels (i.e. 3 pixels or more). Thus, infinite geometric series expansion can be used in (8) and $\partial\phi$ can be approximated as:

$$\partial\phi \approx \left|\tan^{-1}\left(\left(\frac{x_2-x_1}{s^2}\right)\left(m(\Delta x_2 - \Delta x_1) - (\Delta y_2 - \Delta y_1)\right)\left(1-t+t^2\right)\right)\right|$$

$$\approx \left|\left(\frac{x_2-x_1}{s^2}\right)\left(m(\Delta x_2 - \Delta x_1) - (\Delta y_2 - \Delta y_1)\right)\left(1-t+t^2\right)\right| \tag{9}$$

Further we note that, $\partial\phi$ has a maximum value when $|\Delta x_2 - \Delta x_1| = |\Delta y_2 - \Delta y_1| = 1$:

$$\partial\phi_{max} = max\left(\frac{1}{s^3}(|\sin\phi \pm \cos\phi|)\left(\left|s^2 - s(\pm\cos\phi \pm \sin\phi) + (\pm\cos\phi \pm \sin\phi)^2\right|\right)\right) \tag{10}$$

where, $\phi = \tan^{-1}(m)$. Then, the maximum deviation is given by:

$$d_{max} = s\partial\phi_{max}. \tag{11}$$

Based on the above analysis, in L-RDP, the suggested value of d_{tol} at every iteration is $d_{max} = s\partial\phi_{max}$. At each step in the recursion, if the length of the line segment most fit on the curve (or sub-curve) is s and the slope of the line segment is m, then using (10), we compute $d_{tol} = s\partial\phi_{max}$ and use it in (3).

3. Global vs. local characteristics of line fit

It is expected that while fitting a polygon on a digital curve, which is effectively fitting a series of line segments on the digital curve, either we have to take very small local area in order to achieve high precision or we have to take a larger area in order to have a reliable and practically usable fit. This was formally stated and explained by Strauss in the context of Hough transform [Strauss, 1996; Strauss, 1999], "This duality could be set out as follows: as the shape detection precision increases, the reliability of the detection decreases. This seems to be due to the binary aspect of the vote in the classical Hough transform."

While Strauss is right in pointing out the duality between the precision (quality of local fit) and reliability (quality of global fit), he is incorrect in attributing it to the nature of Hough transform. It can be shown using simple metrics, precision and reliability measures, that there is a perennial conflict in the quality of fit in the local scale (precision at the level of few pixels) and global scale (reliability at the level of complete curve) [Prasad & Leung, 2010c]. It is due to this reason, most absolute measures fail in quantifying the quality of fit properly [Carmona-Poyato, et al., 2011; Rosin, 1997].

Assuming that we are not bound by the limitation that the points used for representing the digital curve should be a subset of the digital curve, we just use least squares method to get the best line(s) fit for a digital curve and show that the precision and reliability measures are at conflict with each other. Suppose, for a digital curve with the sequence of pixels $S = \{P_i(x_i, y_i)\}$, $i = 1$ to N, we intend to fit a line $ax + by = 1$. Then, the coefficients of the line, a and b, can be determined by casting the problem of fitting into the following matrix equation [Acton, 1984]:

$$\mathbf{X}\bar{\mathbf{A}} = \bar{\mathbf{J}},\tag{12}$$

where $\mathbf{X} = \begin{bmatrix} [x_1 & x_2 & \cdots & x_M]^T & [y_1 & y_2 & \cdots & y_M]^T \end{bmatrix}$, $\bar{\mathbf{A}} = [a \quad b]^T$, the superscript T denotes the transpose operation, and $\bar{\mathbf{J}}$ is a column matrix containing M rows, whose every element is 1.

3.1 Precision

The precision of fitting can be modeled using the residue of the least squares method:

$$\varepsilon_p = \left\| \mathbf{X}\bar{\mathbf{A}} - \bar{\mathbf{J}} \right\| = \left\| \mathbf{B}\bar{\mathbf{J}} - \bar{\mathbf{J}} \right\|,\tag{13}$$

where $\|\cdot\|$ represents the Euclidean norm, $\mathbf{B} = \mathbf{X}\left(\mathbf{X}^T\mathbf{X}\right)^{-1}\mathbf{X}^T$ is obtained by substituting $\mathbf{A}$ obtained using (12). The subscript p in ε_p represents precision, and we shall refer to ε_p as the precision parameter for the ease of reference. The lower the value of ε_p, the greater the precision. Noting that $\mathbf{B} = \mathbf{B}^T = \mathbf{B}^T\mathbf{B}$, (13) can simplified as $\varepsilon_p = \sqrt{\left(\mathbf{B}\bar{\mathbf{J}} - \bar{\mathbf{J}}\right)^T \left(\mathbf{B}\bar{\mathbf{J}} - \bar{\mathbf{J}}\right)} = \sqrt{\left(\|\bar{\mathbf{J}}\|\|\bar{\mathbf{J}} - \mathbf{B}\bar{\mathbf{J}}\|\cos\theta\right)} = \sqrt[4]{M}\sqrt{\left(\|\bar{\mathbf{J}} - \mathbf{B}\bar{\mathbf{J}}\|\cos\theta\right)}$, where $\|\bar{\mathbf{J}}\| = \sqrt{N}$ (since $\bar{\mathbf{J}}$ contains N elements, each equals to 1) and θ is the angle between $\bar{\mathbf{J}}$ and $\left(\bar{\mathbf{J}} - \mathbf{B}\bar{\mathbf{J}}\right)$. However, since $\varepsilon_p = \|\bar{\mathbf{J}} - \mathbf{B}\bar{\mathbf{J}}\|$, ε_p can be written as:

$$\varepsilon_p = \sqrt{N}\cos\theta.\tag{14}$$

It is evident that by choosing lesser number of pixels, i.e., reducing N, ε_p can be reduced and hence, the precision can be increased. It should be noted that with the decrease in the number of pixels, $\mathbf{X}$ and consequently $\mathbf{B}$ change, and thus the contribution from $\cos\theta$ may vary. However, if continuous pixels are considered, the overall variance in $\mathbf{X}$ is reduced, and hence the impact of $\cos\theta$ is also reduced. In effect, this means that fitting the line in a smaller local region is more precise than a large region.

3.2 Reliability

In this sub-section, we first present a quantitative measure of reliability that can be understood and compared with respect to the precision measure. Generally, for the reliability of a fit, the fit is expected to satisfy at least two conditions. First, the fit should be valid for a sufficiently large region (or in this case a long edge) and second, it should not be sensitive to occasional spurious large deviations in the edge. A combination of both these properties can be sought by defining a reliability parameter as follows:

$$\varepsilon_r = \sum_i \left| \mathbf{X}_i \overline{\mathbf{A}} - 1 \right| \Big/ s_{\max} \tag{15}$$

where $\mathbf{X}_i = \begin{bmatrix} x_i & y_i \end{bmatrix}$, $|\cdot|$ represents the magnitude and $s_{\max}$ is the maximum Euclidean distance between any two pair of pixels. Subscript r in ε_r denotes reliability. As before, lower the value of ε_r, higher the reliability.

3.3 Duality

As evident from (14) and (15), and the discussion between them, there is always a contradiction between precision and reliability. In order to increase the precision, we need to consider smaller regions for fitting, whereas for increasing the reliability, we need to consider larger regions for fitting (largest region being the region spanned by the connected edge pixels under consideration). Indeed the contradiction does not occur in ideal lines as shown in Fig. 2(a)-(d). It is also not an issue if the lines are in general smooth, so that the precision within a large region is already very high, such that reliability and precision are already sufficiently high and there is no practical need to increase the precision or reliability. Some such examples are presented in Fig. 2(e)-(g). This is illustrated in Fig. 3 and Table 1. However, if indeed an application calls for still higher precision, the reliability will have to be compromised and the duality comes into picture. Examples of more practical cases are shown in Fig. 2(h)-(p). In such cases, the duality comes into picture strongly and a balance has to be achieved in order to obtain a fit that is sufficiently reliable as well as precise.

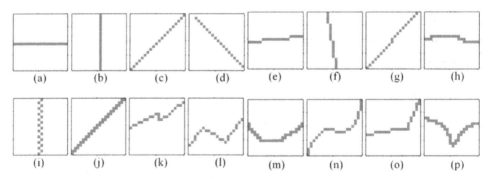

Fig. 2. Example of small images. Each image is of size 20×20 pixels. The grey pixels are the edge pixels, on which line has to be fit.

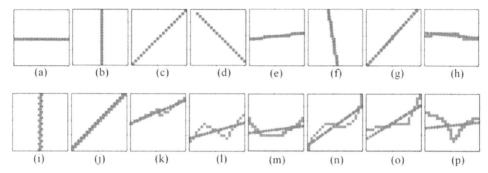

Fig. 3. Lines that have been fit on the images using least squares approach. The lines are shown in red asterisk.

Image	(a)	(b)	(c)	(d)	(e)	(f)	(g)	(h)
ε'_p	0.000	0.000	0.000	0.000	0.024	0.035	0.013	0.071
ε_r	0.000	0.000	0.000	0.000	0.022	0.031	0.008	0.066
Image	(i)	(j)	(k)	(l)	(m)	(n)	(o)	(p)
ε'_p	0.047	0.015	0.072	0.121	0.150	0.111	0.121	0.233
ε_r	0.048	0.007	0.057	0.114	0.135	0.107	0.115	0.248

Table 1. Value of parameters ε'_p and ε_r corresponding to Fig. 3. Values are shown till 3 decimal points.

3.4 Performance measures in the context of precision and reliability

We use various performance measures for comparing various algorithms.

1. Maximum deviation of any pixel on the edge from the fitted polygon (ε_{max}):

In the context of a general line given by (12), the maximum deviation ε_{max} is specified by $\varepsilon_{max} = \left\| \mathbf{X}\bar{\mathbf{A}} - \bar{\mathbf{J}} \right\|_\infty / \left\| \bar{\mathbf{A}} \right\|$, where $\left\| \cdot \right\|_\infty$ denotes the infinity norm (i.e. maximum norm). Since $\left\| \cdot \right\|_\infty \le \left\| \cdot \right\|$, $\varepsilon_{max} \le \varepsilon_p / \left\| \bar{\mathbf{A}} \right\|$. Thus, it can be concluded that ε_{max} is a form of precision measure.

2. Integral square error (ISE):

This is the sum of squares of deviation of each pixel from the approximated polygon. It is given by $\text{ISE} = \left(\varepsilon_p / \left\| \bar{\mathbf{A}} \right\| \right)^2 = \varepsilon_p^2 / \left(\bar{\mathbf{A}}^T \bar{\mathbf{A}} \right)$. Thus, effectively, ISE is also a precision measure.

3. Dimensionality reduction (DR) ratio or compression ratio (CR):

The compression ratio is the ratio of number of pixels in the digital curve (N) to the number of vertices of the polygonal approximation (M), $CR = N/M$. Though this measure is not related to either precision or reliability, it is an important performance metric in practice. In addition to other metrics representing precision and/or reliability, a larger value of this is beneficial for reduction of data and computational resources. Instead of compression ratio, its reciprocal dimensionality reduction ratio $DR = CR^{-1} = M/N$ can be used as a minimization metric (i.e. the lesser, the better).

4.   Figure of merit (FOM)

Figure of merit is given by $FOM = CR/ISE$. This is a maximization metric, i.e., larger value of FOM is preferred over a lower value. However, it is well known that FOM is biased towards ISE [Carmona-Poyato, et al., 2010]. For example, if the break points of a digital curve [Masood, 2008] are considered as the dominant points, the ISE is zero and inconsequent of the CR, FOM is infinity. If we intend to use a minimization metric, we may consider $WE^1 = 1/FOM$ [Marji & Siy, 2004]. It suffers with the same deficiency as FOM.

5.   Fidelity, Efficiency and Merit

Researchers tried relative measures like fidelity, efficiency, merit to quantify the quality of fit [Carmona-Poyato, et al., 2011; Rosin, 1997]. In relative measures, a so-called optimal algorithm is considered as the reference for comparing the performance of the algorithm being tested. The method proposed by Perez and Vidal [Perez & Vidal, 1994] based on dynamic programming is generally used by the researchers as the reference algorithm. This is because it targets $\min-\varepsilon$ and $\min-\#$ such that the fitting error is minimized for a certain number of points ($\min-\varepsilon$) or the number of points for fitting is minimized for a given value of fitting error ($\min-\#$). It is logical that there is no way of determining an optimal value for the fixed number of points ($\min-\varepsilon$) or the fixed value of fitting error ($\min-\#$), because such a value depends upon the nature of the digital curve for which polygonal approximation is sought.

3.5 Proposed performance measures

As seen in section 3.4, none of the existing methods cater for the global nature of the fit. Thus, the reliability measure is very important addition to the performance metrics of the polygonal approximation method. For the line segments (edges of the polygon), the precision and reliability measures are computed:

$$\varepsilon'_p = \frac{\overline{\mathbf{J}} \cdot (\overline{\mathbf{J}} - \mathbf{X}\overline{\mathbf{A}})}{|\overline{\mathbf{A}}|} \tag{16}$$

$$\varepsilon_r = \sum_i |\mathbf{X}_i \overline{\mathbf{A}} - 1| / s_{max} \tag{17}$$

where ε'_p and ε_r are the precision and reliability measures, $\mathbf{X}_i = [x_i \quad y_i]$, and s_{max} is the maximum Euclidean distance between any two pair of pixels [Prasad & Leung, 2010c]. Notation $|\cdot|$ represents the magnitude in the scalar case and the Euclidean norm in the case of vectors.

1.   Precision measure for an edge

Suppose J line segments are fitted upon a digital curve. Then we define the net precision measure for the digital curve as follows:

$$\left(\varepsilon'_p\right)_{\text{Curve}} = \text{mean}\left(\varepsilon'^j_p; j = 1 \text{ to } J\right), \tag{18}$$

where ε'^j_p is the precision measure of the j th line segment, defined using (16).

2. Reliability measure for an edge
The net reliability measure of the digital curve is defined as follows:

$$\left(\varepsilon_r\right)_{\text{Curve}} = \frac{\sum\limits_{j=1}^{J}\sum\limits_{i}\left|\mathbf{X}^j_i\overline{\mathbf{A}}^j - 1\right|}{\sum\limits_{j=1}^{J}s^j_{\max}}, \tag{19}$$

where $\mathbf{X}^j_i$, $\overline{\mathbf{A}}^j$, and $s^j_{\max}$ correspond to $\mathbf{X}_i$, $\overline{\mathbf{A}}$, and $s_{\max}$ defined after (17) for the j th line segment.

3. Precision measure for a dataset of images
Suppose a dataset contains L number of images, the number of edges in the l th image is K_l, then, the precision measure for the dataset is:

$$\begin{aligned}\left(\varepsilon'_p\right)_{\text{Dataset}} &= \text{mean}\left(\left(\varepsilon'_p\right)^l_{\text{Image}}; l = 1 \text{ to } L\right)\\\left(\varepsilon'_p\right)_{\text{Image}} &= \text{max}\left(\left(\varepsilon'_p\right)^k_{\text{Curve}}; k = 1 \text{ to } K\right)\end{aligned}, \tag{20}$$

4. Reliability measure for a dataset of images
In a manner similar to (20), the reliability measure for a dataset is:

$$\begin{aligned}\left(\varepsilon_r\right)_{\text{Dataset}} &= \text{mean}\left(\left(\varepsilon_r\right)^l_{\text{Image}}; l = 1 \text{ to } L\right)\\\left(\varepsilon_r\right)_{\text{Image}} &= \text{max}\left(\left(\varepsilon_r\right)^k_{\text{Curve}}; k = 1 \text{ to } K\right)\end{aligned}, \tag{21}$$

4. Contemporary polygonal approximation method in the perspective of duality and the upper bound

4.1 Optimal polygonal representation of Perez and Vidal [Perez & Vidal, 1994]

The algorithm proposed by Perez and Vidal (PV) [Perez & Vidal, 1994] is by far the most popular algorithm used as a benchmark for comparing the performance of polygonal fitting algorithms. The reason for its popularity is twofold. For a given number of points $N' \leq N$, where N is the number of pixels in the digital curve, it computes the optimal choice of N' points from the digital curve such that some error metric is minimized. Since the error metric can be flexibly defined by a user, it is versatile in its use. Further, for the purpose of benchmarking, the designers of other algorithms can first perform the polygonal fitting using their own algorithms, obtain a value of N' as obtained by their own algorithms, use this value of N' in the algorithm by PV and simply compare the points obtained by their method against the optimal points obtained by PV.

Since PV can use any error metric to be minimized, it is interesting to note that we can either use the precision score or the reliability score as the error to be minimized. If precision score is used as the error function, PV attempts to fit segments such that all the line segments are of approximately the same length. If reliability score is used as the error function, PV attempts to fit segments that are combination of two types: first type are the small segment with small value of d_{max} but with very small (close to zero) value of $\sum_i \left| X_i \bar{A} - 1 \right|$; the second type are long segments with comparatively larger values of $\sum_i \left| X_i \bar{A} - 1 \right|$ but significantly larger value of d_{max} such that the reliability score is also small valued.

On the other hand, PV do not guarantee that the maximum deviation of the pixels in curve is within the upper limit of the error due to digitization. If the value of N' is very large, it is likely that PV will fit the segments such that the maximum deviation is lesser than the upper bound. This means that the polygonal approximation will over fit and be sensitive to the error due to digitization. On the other hand, if the value of N' is small, the maximum deviation of the fitted segments is larger than the upper bound, thus indicating under-fitting. In essence, this means that using a fixed value of N' or solving min-ε problem is not suitable for optimal polygonal approximation of the digital curves.

4.2 Lowe [Lowe, 1987] and Ramer-Douglas-Peucker [Douglas & Peucker, 1973; Ramer, 1972] (L-RDP method)

Lowe [Lowe, 1987] and Ramer-Douglas-Peucker [Douglas & Peucker, 1973; Ramer, 1972] is basically a splitting method in which the point of maximum deviation is found recursively till the maximum deviation of any edge pixel from the nearest line segment is less than a fixed value. Since this is a splitting algorithm, it begins with a very high value of d_{max}, which reduces as the edge is split further. The algorithm stops at a point where the maximum deviation satisfies a minimum criterion. Thus, this algorithm focuses more on reliability and attempts to barely satisfy a precision requirement.

In the sense of the upper bound, this algorithm gives a mixed performance. For a few segments, the chosen threshold may be below the upper bound and the result is an over-fitting for this segment. On the other hand, the chosen threshold may be above the upper bound for certain line segments, thus resulting in under-fitting for such segments.

4.3 Precision and reliability based optimization (PRO)

In this method, though the method of optimization is the same as the L-RDP method, the optimization goal is different than (3). Instead of (3), the optimization goal is:

$$\max\left(\varepsilon'_p, \varepsilon_r\right) < \varepsilon_0, \tag{22}$$

where, ε_0 is the chosen heuristic parameter. Since this method explicitly uses the precision and reliability measures as the optimization functions, this method is expected to perform well for both precision and reliability measures.

However, this method does not take into account the upper bound of the error due to digitization.

4.4 Break point supression method of Masood [Masood, 2008]

Masood begins with the sequence of the break points, i.e., the smallest set of line segments such that each pixel of the curve lies exactly on the line segments, which is considered as the initial set of dominant points. Then, he proceeds with recursively deleting one break point at a time such that removing it has a minimum impact in its immediate neighborhood and optimizing the locations of the dominant points for minimum precision score. Although the aim of optimization is to improve the global fit and thus indirectly improve the reliability, evidently, Masood's method is tailored for optimizing the precision and performs poorly in terms of reliability.

Since Masood begins with largest possible set of dominant points and removes the dominant points till a certain termination criterion is satisfied, if the termination criterion is not very relaxed, the maximum deviation is in general lesser than the upper bound. Thus, in essence, Masood's method is sensitive to the digitization effects and gives an unnecessarily close fit to the digital curve.

4.5 Dominent point detection method of Carmona-Poyato [Carmona-Poyato, *et al.*, 2010]

Like Masood [Masood, 2008], Carmona also begins with the sequence of break points and the initial set of dominant points. However, unlike Masood, Carmona recursively deletes the dominant points with minimum impact on the global fit of the line segments. Thus, inherently Carmona-Poyato focuses more on reliability than on precision. It is evident in the results reported in [Carmona-Poyato, *et al.*, 2010] that this method has a tendency to be lenient in the maximum allowable deviation in the favor of general shape representation for the whole curve.

5. Numerical examples

We consider the following methods for comparison:

1. L-RDP_max (from section 2)
2. L-RDP0.5, L-RDP1.0, L-RDP1.5, and L-RDP2.0 (from sections 2 and 4.2) correspond to the values of d_{tol} as 0.5, 1.0, 1.5, and 2.0 pixels respectively.
3. PRO0.2, PRO0.4, PRO0.6, PRO0.8, and PRO1.0 (from section 4.3) correspond to the values of ε_0 as 0.2, 0.4, 0.6, 0.8, and 1.0, respectively.
4. Masood (section 4.4, [Masood, 2008]) using the termination criterion specified in [Masood, 2008], i.e., $\varepsilon_{max} < 0.9$.
5. Carmona-Poyato (section 4.5, [Carmona-Poyato, *et al.*, 2010]), using the termination condition specified in [Carmona-Poyato, *et al.*, 2010], i.e., $r_i < 0.4$.

5.1 Images of Fig. 2

First, we consider L-RDP_max. The results are in the second row of Fig. 4. We see that L-RDP_max is able to avoid the fluctuations due to digitization and noise (in Fig. 4, see columns (g-p), row 2). In the meanwhile, it is able to retain good fit for snippets with important curvature changes, see columns (h,m,n,p), row 2 of Fig. 4. Conclusively, due to the consideration of the upper bound of digitization error, L-RDP_max considers the general features of the digital curve rather than concentrating on every single small scale feature of the curve.

The first observation is that L-RDP algorithms are very sensitive to the tolerance values. L-RDP0.5 algorithm gives a performance comparable to PRO0.2 and PRO0.4, both qualitatively (specifically note the columns (h,i,m,n) of Fig. 4) and quantitatively (see Table 2). A slight increase in tolerance from 0.5 to 1 changes the quality and performance parameters of the line fitting significantly, as evident in Fig. 4 and Table 2. The performance of L-RDP1 is closer to PRO0.6 and the performance of L-RDP1.5 is closer to L-RDP_max and PRO0.8. As the tolerance is increased further in L-RDP algorithms, the fitted line segments start losing information about the major curvature changes and represent the digital curves only crudely. Thus, though L-RDP2.0 provides significant dimensionality reduction (see DR in Table 2), it performs poorly for all the remaining performance parameters.

Next, we consider the results of PRO algorithms. It can be seen in the row PRO0.2 of Fig. 4 that it follows the digital curves very closely. As a consequence it is very sensitive to digitization and generates numerous small line segments to represent the curve, strongly evident in columns (e-i,k-p) of Fig. 4. Though definitely very reliable and precise, as evident from $\left(\varepsilon_p'\right)_{\text{Dataset}}$ and $\left(\varepsilon_r\right)_{\text{Dataset}}$ in Table 1, due to the tendency to fit the curves very closely, it performs poorly in dimensionality reduction (see DR values in Table 1). In the next set: PRO0.4-0.8, we see that these algorithms tend to follow the curvature of the digital curve, better than PRO0.2. We highlight the results in column (m) of Fig. 4. While PRO0.2 generated many line segment for the right side of the curve, PRO0.4-0.8 are more selective in fitting the line segments and fit the line segments focusing at the location of changes in curvature. Further, as the value of ε_0 increases from 0.4 to 0.8, the tendency to concentrate further on the general characteristics of the curve (rather than following every small scale feature of the curve) increases. This is significantly evident in the results in columns (h), (n), and (p) of Fig. 4. In the last PRO algorithm, PRO1.0, we see that rather than focusing on small features of the digital curve, these algorithms tend to follow the general characteristics of the digital curve on a relatively larger scale. Due to this reason, the results of PRO0.8-1.0 are closer to L-RDP_max. As a consequence of this characteristic, PRO0.8-1.0 and L-RDP_max have significantly better dimensionality reduction as compared to other PRO algorithms (see DR in Table 2).

With lower value of $\left(\varepsilon_p'\right)_{\text{Dataset}}$ than $\left(\varepsilon_r\right)_{\text{Dataset}}$ in Table 2, we see that Masood targets improving the precision (reducing) rather than the reliability. Thus, as noted in columns (k-m) of Fig. 4, Masood fails in representing the nature of the curves effectively. On the other hand, for Carmona-Poyato, the value of $\left(\varepsilon_r\right)_{\text{Dataset}}$ is lower than $\left(\varepsilon_p'\right)_{\text{Dataset}}$ in Table 2. However, due to the small length of the digital curves here and the fact that Carmona fits the polygonal approximation depending upon the length of the curve, in these figures with very small digital curves, it tends to fit the curves very closely (see columns (e,f,i,n,o) of Fig. 4), thus demonstrating better precision as well as reliability as compared to Masood. On the other hand for these images, L-RDP_max gives a performance in between Masood and Carmona-Poyato. This indicates that L-RDP_max avoids both under-fitting and over fitting.

5.2 Example of large closed curve

In this section, we consider an example of digital closed curve which is significantly large and contains 458 pixels. The digital curve is derived by scanning the image of dog from Figure 14 of [Masood, 2008] at 300 dpi, followed with blurring using Adobe Photoshop with a brush size of 2 pixels. Then the polygonal approximation obtained using various methods are presented in Fig. 5. As in section 5.1, the performance of L-RDP_max, L-RDP1.5, and PRO0.8 are similar. For this curve, the performance of Carmano-Poyato is also similar to L-RDP_max. Not only the number of vertices in the polygonal approximation for these cases are similar, the location of the vertices are also similar. L-RDP0.5 and PRO0.2 over fit the curve with numerous points. The quantitative performances are listed in Table 2.

5.3 Large datasets used in real applications

We consider 7 datasets used in object detection algorithms for the purpose of training. These datasets, namely afright [McCarter & Storkey, 2003], Caltech101 [Fei-Fei, *et al.*, 2007], Caltech 256 [Griffin, *et al.*], Pascal 2007 [Everingham, *et al.*, 2007], Pascal, 2008 [Everingham, *et al.*, 2008], Pascal 2009 [Everingham, *et al.*, 2009], and Pascal 2010[Everingham, *et al.*, 2010], contain a total of 97178 images, with the smallest image being only 80 pixels wide and the largest image being 748 pixels wide. The values of $\left(\varepsilon_p'\right)_{\text{Dataset}}$, $\left(\varepsilon_r\right)_{\text{Dataset}}$ and DR for all the datasets and algorithms are plotted in Fig. 6, Fig. 7, and Fig. 8 respectively. Even over such wide range of images, L-RDP and PRO algorithms give consistent performances, as seen in Fig. 6, Fig. 7, and Fig. 8. Further, all L-RDP and PRO algorithms give better performance in terms of precision and reliability, as seen in Fig. 6 and Fig. 7. As a final note, L-RDP_max gives better DR than both Masood and Carmona-Poyato, as seen in Fig. 8.

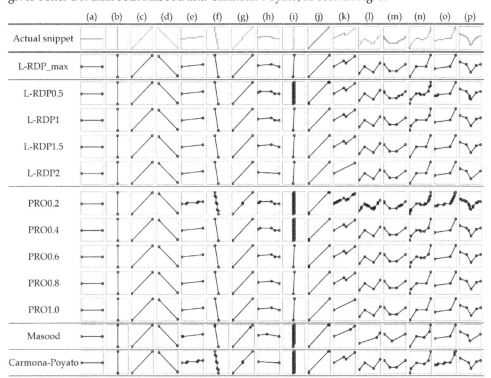

Fig. 4. The polygonal approximations obtained using various methods for images in Fig. 2.

	Dataset of the 16 images in Fig. 2			Digital curve in section 5.2			
	$\left(\varepsilon'_p\right)_{\text{Dataset}}$	$\left(\varepsilon_r\right)_{\text{Dataset}}$	DR	$\left(\varepsilon'_p\right)_{\text{Dataset}}$	$\left(\varepsilon_r\right)_{\text{Dataset}}$	DR	Time (seconds)
L-RDP_max	0.2751	0.2198	0.1286	0.3954	0.3189	0.1114	0.3059
L-RDP0.5	0.1108	0.0931	0.2233	0.0897	0.0964	0.2642	0.8533
L-RDP1	0.2295	0.1884	0.1356	0.2829	0.2397	0.1332	0.3498
L-RDP1.5	0.2751	0.2198	0.1286	0.4133	0.3508	0.1048	0.2571
L-RDP2	0.3650	0.2899	0.1174	0.5298	0.4341	0.0917	0.2225
PRO0.2	0.0032	0.0030	0.3933	0.0055	0.0062	0.4672	1.6157
PRO0.4	0.1486	0.1227	0.2008	0.1629	0.1607	0.1769	0.5004
PRO0.6	0.1974	0.1700	0.1405	0.2748	0.2467	0.1288	0.3330
PRO0.8	0.2563	0.2086	0.1307	0.4066	0.3483	0.1048	0.2613
PRO1.0	0.3185	0.2471	0.1228	0.5626	0.4635	0.0873	0.2100
Masood	0.2970	0.3144	0.1845	0.1203	0.1155	0.2249	26.1754
Carmona-Poyato	0.1306	0.1110	0.2436	0.3349	0.3152	0.1157	0.6324

Table 2. Performance metrics for the dataset of the 16 images in Fig. 2 and the digital curve in section 5.2.

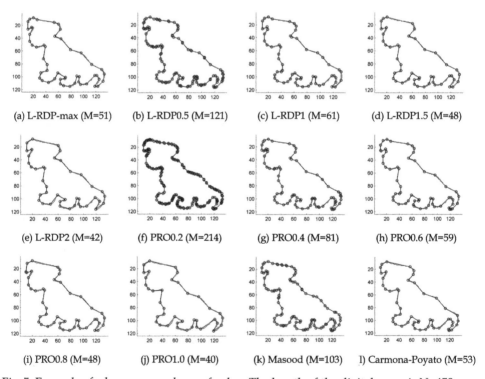

(a) L-RDP-max (M=51)   (b) L-RDP0.5 (M=121)   (c) L-RDP1 (M=61)   (d) L-RDP1.5 (M=48)

(e) L-RDP2 (M=42)   (f) PRO0.2 (M=214)   (g) PRO0.4 (M=81)   (h) PRO0.6 (M=59)

(i) PRO0.8 (M=48)   (j) PRO1.0 (M=40)   (k) Masood (M=103)   l) Carmona-Poyato (M=53)

Fig. 5. Example of a large curve, shape of a dog. The length of the digital curve is N=458.

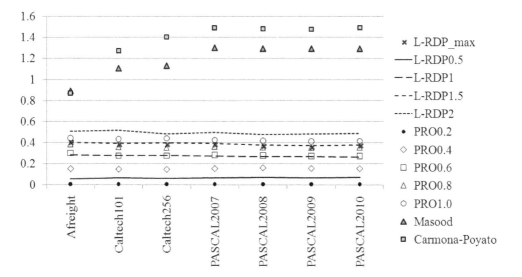

Fig. 6. Precision measure $\left(\varepsilon'_p\right)_{\text{Dataset}}$ for various datasets obtained by different algorithms.

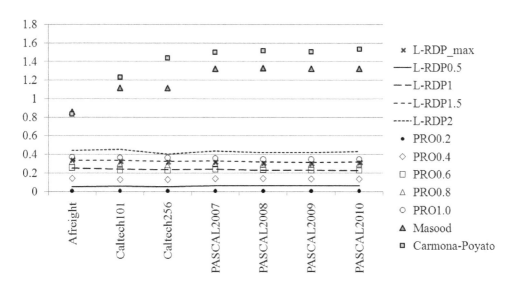

Fig. 7. Reliability measure $\left(\varepsilon_r\right)_{\text{Dataset}}$ for various datasets obtained by different algorithms.

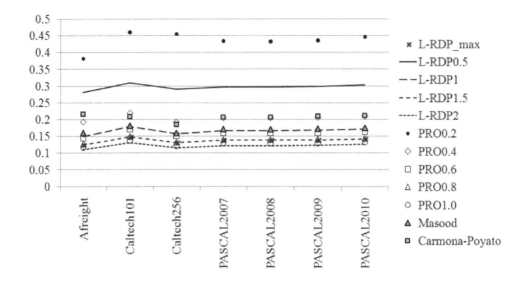

Fig. 8. Average dimensionality reduction for various datasets obtained by different algorithms.

6. Conclusion

Polygonal approximation of digital curves is an important step in many image processing applications. It is important that the fitted polygons are significantly smaller than the original curves, less sensitive to the digitization effect in the digital curves, and good representations of the curvature related properties of the digital curves. Thus, we need methods to deal with the digitization and consider both local and global properties of the fit.

First, we show that the maximum deviation of a digital curve obtained from a line segment has a definite upper bound. We show that this definite upper bound can be incorporated in a polygonal approximation method like L-RDP for making it parameter independent. Various results are shown to demonstrate the effectiveness of the parameter independent L-RDP method against digitization, dimensionality reduction, and retaining good global and local properties of the digital curve. In the future, we are hopeful that this error bound shall be incorporated in various recent and more sophisticated polygonal approximation and give a good performance boost to them, while making them free from heuristic choice of control parameters.

Second, we show that global and local properties of the fit are in contradiction with each other in general. We propose precision measure for measuring the local quality of fit and reliability measure for measuring the global quality of fit. Using them we show that better local fits are achieved by considering small edges of the polygons, while better global fit is achieved by making the edges of the polygon as long as possible. Further, we show that most contemporary measure of quality of fit are either directly related to precision or correspond to the local nature of fit. Since these measures are used in most contemporary algorithms, most of them concentrate on improving the local quality of the fit only. However, as demonstrated by the upper bound of the maximum deviation due to digitization, it may not be worth to reduce the precision below a certain level, since it is difficult to predict if the actual deviation is below the error bound due to digitization, some form of noise, or due to the nature of the curve. In our knowledge, only Carmona-Poyato includes reliability (though indirectly) in its algorithm [Carmona-Poyato, *et al.*, 2010].

We also propose line fitting algorithm that specifically optimize the curves for increasing both precision and reliability simultaneously. We hope that these measures are paid attention to by the research community and better algorithms for polygonal fitting are developed, which provide good local as well as global fit. In the future, it shall be useful to further improve the design of the precision and reliability measures such that they are more representative of the quality of fit. Such improvements in design will also influence the quality of polygonal approximation achieved by the polygonal approximation methods.

7. References

Acton, F. S. (1984). *Analysis of straight-line data*. New York: Peter Smith Publisher, Incorporated.

Arcelli, C., & Ramella, G. (1993). Finding contour-based abstractions of planar patterns. *Pattern Recognition, 26*(10), 1563-1577.

Bhowmick, P., & Bhattacharya, B. B. (2007). Fast polygonal approximation of digital curves using relaxed straightness properties. *IEEE Transactions on Pattern Analysis and Machine Intelligence, 29*(9), 1590-1602.

Carmona-Poyato, A., Fernández-García, N. L., Medina-Carnicer, R., & Madrid-Cuevas, F. J. (2005). Dominant point detection: A new proposal. *Image and Vision Computing, 23*(13), 1226-1236.

Carmona-Poyato, A., Madrid-Cuevas, F. J., Medina-Carnicer, R., & Muñoz-Salinas, R. (2010). Polygonal approximation of digital planar curves through break point suppression. *Pattern Recognition, 43*(1), 14-25.

Carmona-Poyato, A., Medina-Carnicer, R., Madrid-Cuevas, F. J., Muoz-Salinas, R., & Fernndez-Garca, N. L. (2011). A new measurement for assessing polygonal approximation of curves. *Pattern Recognition, 44*(1), 45-54.

Chung, K. L., Liao, P. H., & Chang, J. M. (2008). Novel efficient two-pass algorithm for closed polygonal approximation based on LISE and curvature constraint criteria. *Journal of Visual Communication and Image Representation, 19*(4), 219-230.

Chung, P. C., Tsai, C. T., Chen, E. L., & Sun, Y. N. (1994). Polygonal approximation using a competitive Hopfield neural network. *Pattern Recognition, 27*(11), 1505-1512.

Davis, T. J. (1999). Fast decomposition of digital curves into polygons using the Haar transform. *IEEE Transactions on Pattern Analysis and Machine Intelligence, 21*(8), 786-790.

Debled-Rennesson, I., Rémy, J. L., & Rouyer-Degli, J. (2005). Linear segmentation of discrete curves into blurred segments. *Discrete Applied Mathematics, 151*(1-3), 122-137.

Douglas, D. H., & Peucker, T. K. (1973). Algorithms for the reduction of the number of points required to represent a digitized line or its caricature. *Cartographica: The International Journal for Geographic Information and Geovisualization, 10*(2), 112-122.

Everingham, M., Gool, L. V., Williams, C. K. I., Winn, J., & Zisserman, A. (2007). The PASCAL Visual Object Classes Challenge 2007 (VOC2007). http://www.pascal-network.org/challenges/VOC/voc2007/workshop/index.html

Everingham, M., Gool, L. V., Williams, C. K. I., Winn, J., & Zisserman, A. (2008). The PASCAL Visual Object Classes Challenge 2008 (VOC2008). http://www.pascal-network.org/challenges/VOC/voc2008/workshop/index.html

Everingham, M., Gool, L. V., Williams, C. K. I., Winn, J., & Zisserman, A. (2009). The PASCAL Visual Object Classes Challenge 2009 (VOC2009). http://www.pascal-network.org/challenges/VOC/voc2009/workshop/index.html

Everingham, M., Gool, L. V., Williams, C. K. I., Winn, J., & Zisserman, A. (2010). The PASCAL Visual Object Classes Challenge 2010 (VOC2010). http://www.pascal-network.org/challenges/VOC/voc2010/workshop/index.html

Fei-Fei, L., Fergus, R., & Perona, P. (2007). Learning generative visual models from few training examples: An incremental Bayesian approach tested on 101 object categories. *Computer Vision and Image Understanding, 106*(1), 59-70.

Griffin, G., Holub, A., & Perona, P. Caltech-256 object category database. available at: http://authors.library.caltech.edu/7694

Gritzali, F., & Papakonstantinou, G. (1983). A fast piecewise linear approximation algorithm. *Signal Processing, 5*(3), 221-227.

Kanungo, T., Jaisimha, M. Y., Palmer, J., & Haralick, R. M. (1995). Methodology for quantitative performance evaluation of detection algorithms. *IEEE Transactions on Image Processing, 4*(12), 1667-1674.

Kolesnikov, A. (2008). *Constrained piecewise linear approximation of digital curves*, Tampa, FL.

Kolesnikov, A., & Fränti, P. (2003). Reduced-search dynamic programming for approximation of polygonal curves. *Pattern Recognition Letters, 24*(14), 2243-2254.

Kolesnikov, A., & Fränti, P. (2005). Data reduction of large vector graphics. *Pattern Recognition, 38*(3), 381-394.

Kolesnikov, A., & Fränti, P. (2007). Polygonal approximation of closed discrete curves. *Pattern Recognition, 40*(4), 1282-1293.

Latecki, L. J., Sobel, M., & Lakaemper, R. (2009). Piecewise linear models with guaranteed closeness to the data. *IEEE Transactions on Pattern Analysis and Machine Intelligence, 31*(8), 1525-1531.

Lavallee, S., & Szeliski, R. (1995). Recovering the position and orientation of free-form objects from image contours using 3D distance maps. *IEEE Transactions on Pattern Analysis and Machine Intelligence, 17*(4), 378-390.

Leung, M. K. (1990). Dynamic two-strip algorithm in curve fitting. *Pattern Recognition, 23*(1-2), 69-79.

Lowe, D. G. (1987). Three-dimensional object recognition from single two-dimensional images. *Artificial Intelligence, 31*(3), 355-395.

Marji, M., & Siy, P. (2004). Polygonal representation of digital planar curves through dominant point detection - A nonparametric algorithm. *Pattern Recognition, 37*(11), 2113-2130.

Masood, A. (2008). Dominant point detection by reverse polygonization of digital curves. *Image and Vision Computing, 26*(5), 702-715.

McCarter, G., & Storkey, A. (2003). Air Freight image sequences. http://homepages.inf.ed.ac.uk/amos/afreightdata.html

Mokhtarian, F., & Mackworth, A. (1986). Scale-based description and recognition of planar curves and two-dimensional shapes. *IEEE Transactions on Pattern Analysis and Machine Intelligence, PAMI-8*(1), 34-43.

Pavlidis, T. (1976). Use of algorithms of piecewise approximations for picture processing applications. *ACM Transactions on Mathematical Software, 2*(4), 305-321.

Perez, J. C., & Vidal, E. (1994). Optimum polygonal approximation of digitized curves. *Pattern Recognition Letters, 15*(8), 743-750.

Phillips, T. Y., & Rosenfeld, A. (1987). A method of curve partitioning using arc-chord distance. *Pattern Recognition Letters, 5*(4), 285-288.

Prasad, D. K., Gupta, R. K., & Leung, M. K. H. (2011). An Error Bounded Tangent Estimator for Digitized Elliptic Curves *Lecture Notes in Computer Science* (Vol. 6607, pp. 272-283): Springer Berlin / Heidelberg.

Prasad, D. K., & Leung, M. K. H. (2010a). *An ellipse detection method for real images*. Paper presented at the 25th International Conference of Image and Vision Computing New Zealand (IVCNZ 2010).

Prasad, D. K., & Leung, M. K. H. (2010b, 14-17 November). *Error analysis of geometric ellipse detection methods due to quantization*. Paper presented at the Fourth Pacific-Rim Symposium on Image and Video Technology (PSIVT 2010), Singapore.

Prasad, D. K., & Leung, M. K. H. (2010, 26-28 Feb). *A hybrid approach for ellipse detection in real images*. Paper presented at the 2nd International Conference on Digital Image Processing, Singapore.

Prasad, D. K., & Leung, M. K. H. (2010c, 26-29 Sept). *Reliability/Precision Uncertainty in Shape Fitting Problems*. Paper presented at the IEEE International Conference on Image Processing, Hong Kong.

Prasad, D. K., & Leung, M. K. H. (2012). Methods for ellipse detection from edge maps of real images. In F. Solari, M. Chessa & S. Sabatini (Eds.), *Machine Vision*: InTech.

Prasad, D. K., Leung, M. K. H., Cho, S. Y., & Quek, C. (2011a, 28-30 Nov.). *A parameter independent line fitting method*. Paper presented at the Asian Conference on Pattern Recognition (ACPR), Beijing, China.

Ramer, U. (1972). An iterative procedure for the polygonal approximation of plane curves. *Computer Graphics and Image Processing, 1*(3), 244-256.

Ray, B. K., & Ray, K. S. (1992). An algorithm for detection of dominant points and polygonal approximation of digitized curves. *Pattern Recognition Letters, 13*(12), 849-856.

Rosin, P. L. (1997). Techniques for assessing polygonal approximations of curves. *IEEE Transactions on Pattern Analysis and Machine Intelligence, 19*(6), 659-666.

Rosin, P. L. (2002). Assessing the behaviour of polygonal approximation algorithms. *Pattern Recognition, 36*(2), 505-518.

Salotti, M. (2002). Optimal polygonal approximation of digitized curves using the sum of square deviations criterion. *Pattern Recognition, 35*(2), 435-443.

Sankar, P. V., & Sharma, C. U. (1978). A parallel procedure for the detection of dominant points on a digital curve. *Computer Graphics and Image Processing, 7*(4), 403-412.

Sarkar, D. (1993). A simple algorithm for detection of significant vertices for polygonal approximation of chain-coded curves. *Pattern Recognition Letters, 14*(12), 959-964.

Sato, Y. (1992). Piecewise linear approximation of plane curves by perimeter optimization. *Pattern Recognition, 25*(12), 1535-1543.

Sklansky, J., & Gonzalez, V. (1980). Fast polygonal approximation of digitized curves. *Pattern Recognition, 12*(5), 327-331.

Strauss, O. (1996). *Reducing the precision/uncertainty duality in the Hough transform.* Paper presented at the Proceedings of the IEEE International Conference on Image Processing.

Strauss, O. (1999). Use the Fuzzy Hough transform towards reduction of the precision/uncertainty duality. *Pattern Recognition, 32*(11), 1911-1922.

Tomek, I. (1975). More on piecewise linear approximation. *Computers and Biomedical Research, 8*(6), 568-572.

Wall, K., & Danielsson, P. E. (1984). A fast sequential method for polygonal approximation of digitized curves. *Computer Vision, Graphics, & Image Processing, 28*(2), 220-227.

Wang, B., Shu, H., Shi, C., & Luo, L. (2008). A novel stochastic search method for polygonal approximation problem. *Neurocomputing, 71*(16-18), 3216-3223.

Comparison of Border Descriptors and Pattern Recognition Techniques Applied to Detection and Diagnose of Faults on Sucker-Rod Pumping System

Fábio Soares de Lima, Luiz Affonso Guedes and Diego R. Silva
Universidade Federal do Rio Grande do Norte - UFRN
Brazil

1. Introduction

Due to high competition and the need to meet deadlines, modern industries with focus on market demand high availability and reliability of their equipment. With this view, in the last years the maintenance activity has undergone several changes which have led to an evolution in the standpoint of organization and planning of its execution. According to Kardec & Nascif (1998), the direct causes for this development are:

- The quick increase of the amount and the diversity of physical elements that compose varied equipment of process plants that must be kept available;
- Most complex engineering projects;
- New methods for maintenance activity;
- New approaches about the maintenance organization and their responsibilities.

The concept of predictive maintenance has emerged as a result of these demands. Predictive maintenance is the regular monitoring of operating condition (variables and parameters) - the performance - from a device or process that will provide the necessary data to ensure the maximum allowed interval between repair and better intervention planning.

Historically, the first method of artificial elevation that was used in the oil industry was the sucker-rod pumping. Its importance is reflected in the number of installations found on industry, being the most widely elevation method used around the world. Its popularity is related to low cost of investments and maintenance, flexibility of flow and depth, good energy efficient and the possibility of operating with fluids of different compositions and viscosity in a wide temperature range.

The main advantages of Sucker-rod Pumping are: the simplicity of operation, maintenance and design of new installations. From normal conditions can be used until the end of productive life of a well and the pumping capacity can be modified, depending on the changes of the well's behavior. However, the main advantage of this method relates to the lower cost/production throughout the productive life of the well.

This method is the most common way of artificial elevation (Alegre, Morooka & da Rocha, 1993; Schirmer & Toutain, 1991). It is estimated that 90% of artificial elevation in the world use the system of mechanical pumping (Nazi & Lea, 1994; Tripp, 1989). In Brazil, 64% of the total production is obtained through the mechanical pumping (de Oliveira Costa, 1994). In practice, the monitoring of the mechanical pumping system status is done by reading a card, called dynamometric card. With this card you can know about the condition of the pump located at the bottom of the well. The dynamometric card consists of a graph that relates the charge and the position. This graph reflects the current conditions of pumping (Barreto et al., 1996; Rogers et al., 1990). Thus, the card may take various formats during well's production and represent situations of normal operation or indicate a possible irregularity in mechanical pumping system.

The process of identifying situations of abnormal operation of the mechanical pumping system becomes, thus, a problem of visual information interpretation (Dickinson & Jennings, 1990). In any case, this approach may be influenced by several factors, such as the behavior of the system itself, because of its complexity, which results in diverse forms of dynamometric cards, beyond the knowledge and experience of the engineer responsible for the well. Besides that, nowadays, each field petroleum engineer is responsible for over one hundred wells equipped with mechanical pumping. In this case, the traditional process of interpretation becomes impracticable in an acceptable time.

1.1 Objectives

This study aims to contribute to the predictive maintenance field through the development of intelligent computing techniques (Russell, 2003) based on digital image processing, capable of preventing damage in a particular equipment or industrial process in a predictive way.

In scientific terms, the main objective is to propose and analyze the performance of nonparametric patterns recognition techniques in the context of fault detection and diagnosis using boundary descriptors and metrics or statistics mathematical tools.

In technological terms, the objective of this study is to contribute to the area of fault automatic detection and diagnosis in dynamical systems, by proposing a new architecture based on visual similarity of signatures (images) that represent operating conditions. This, in turn, will bring benefits that may complement the tools that nowadays operate in industrial parks.

The proposed approach is the automation of fault analysis and diagnosis in dynamic systems, basing on the following points:

- A description model based on knowledge through system signatures, and;
- Fault recognition through metric distances or correlations.

In this study, it was used bottom hole dynamometer cards, because the surface cards incorporate various degenerative effects caused by the spread of the charge along the whole column of rods. These effects make surface cards represent only one well. When the bottom cards are used, it is possible to observe that the standards of the system operation are the same (de Almeida Barreto Filho, 1993).

Additionally, was chosen present a new approach of classification of the failures of sucker-rod pumping. As the fault diagnosis in mechanical pumping system is a recognition process of dynamometric cards references, various studies have been developed based on pattern recognition techniques using neural network or expert systems and have been proposed to improve accuracy and efficiency (Nazi & Lea, 1994) of this kind of diagnosis system (Alegre, A & Morooka, 1993; Alegre, Morooka & da Rocha, 1993; Barreto et al., 1996; Chacln, 1969; Dickinson & Jennings, 1990; Nazi & Lea, 1994; Rogers et al., 1990; Schirmer & Toutain, 1991; Schnitman et al., 2003; Xu et al., 2006). Thus, the approach used is based on pattern

Comparison of Border Descriptors and Pattern Recognition Techniques Applied to Detection and Diagnose of
Faults on Sucker-Rod Pumping System

93

recognition using a distance calculus technique (Euclidean Distance) or a similarity tool (Pearson Correlation).

1.2 Document structure

This study is divided into more five sections. In the following section, the tools used are theoretically justified, discussing the techniques of descriptors based on edges and some tools for calculating distance metrics and statistics. In Section 3, the oil Sucker-Rod Pumping System is presented, being a study case for implementation of the proposal work. Then, in the next section the methodology for detection and recognition of the failure is presented. Section 5 presents the results obtained and finally the conclusions are presented in Section 6.

2. Theoretical basis

2.1 Description of boundary descriptors

The boundary descriptors are mathematic methods that describe a object or a region of figure. The descriptors are separated in two groups (Gonzalez et al., 2003): Descriptors based in contour (border) and Descriptors based in region. The first, it describe the object shape basing in its contour. Now, the region descriptors describe the object inside. The proper descriptor ideal must show the following invariant features:

- Translation;
- Rotation;
- Scale;
- Start Point.

In the diagnose process of faults in the Sucker-rod pumping system through dynamometer cards, the rotation feature is unnecessary, because several faults show the same contour, but they are rotated.

2.1.1 Centroid

The contour descriptor by centroid have main focus to calculate the distance between the card geometric center to several points that compose the card to make a distance set ($D = \{D_0, D_1, ..., D_n\}$). The Equations 1 and 2 show the centroid calculus, where N are the quantity of points that compose the card and the ordered pair, x_c and y_c, represents the centroid.

$$x_c = \frac{1}{N} \sum_{i=1}^{N} x_i \tag{1}$$

$$y_c = \frac{1}{N} \sum_{i=1}^{N} y_i \tag{2}$$

The Equation 3 shows the distance calculus between the centroid and several points.

$$D_i = \sqrt{(x_i - x_c)^2 + (y_i - y_c)^2} \tag{3}$$

So, it can use the distance set like contour feature of dynamometer card.

2.1.2 Curvature descriptor

The curvature descriptor is a simple and easy algorithm to develop and the main purpose is calculate the distance between any point in relation to next point (clockwise or counter-clockwise). The Equations 4, 5 and 6 show the distance calculus.

$$D_x i = (x_i - x_i + 1)^2 \tag{4}$$

$$D_y i = (y_i - y_i + 1)^2 \tag{5}$$

$$D_c = \sqrt{D_x i - D_y i} \tag{6}$$

2.1.3 K-curvature

The K-curvature extractor shows the object contour through of the created angle relation between two vectors. From any initial point, p_i, two points, p_{i+k} and p_{i+2k}, are chosen with a spacing of k values with the purpose to eliminate contour noises. So, two vectors (v and w) are defined. The vector v is formed by points p_i and p_{i+k}, while the vector w is formed by p_{i+k} and p_{i+2k}. The Equation 7 shows the angle calculus between the vectors.

$$\theta = cos^{-1} \frac{v \cdot w}{|v| \cdot |w|} \tag{7}$$

So, $v \cdot w$ is the scalar product between vectors (Equation 8) and $|v|$ and $|w|$ are the norms of vectors (Equation 9 and 10).

$$v \cdot w = v_1 w_1 + v_2 w_2 + ... + v_n w_n \tag{8}$$

$$|v| = \sqrt{v \cdot v} \tag{9}$$

$$|w| = \sqrt{w \cdot w} \tag{10}$$

2.1.4 Fourier Descriptor

The Fourier Descriptor is compact and light algorithm. To develop this algorithm, consider the following points: (x_k, y_k) that represent the object contour coordinates, where $k = 0, 1, 2, ..., N - 1$ and N is the points quantity of border. The Equation 11 indicates the complex function of object contour coordinates.

$$z(k) = (x_k) + j(y_k) \tag{11}$$

In spite of sequence not be important to this descriptor, in this work, x is the position of polish rod and y is the applied system force. The Fourier descriptors (Equation 12) are make applying the Discrete Fourier Transform (DFT) in the Equation 11.

$$F_n = \frac{1}{N} \sum_{k=0}^{N-1} z(k) e^{-\frac{j2\pi nk}{N}} \tag{12}$$

Comparison of Border Descriptors and Pattern Recognition Techniques Applied to Detection and Diagnose of
Faults on Sucker-Rod Pumping System

95

$N = 0, 1, 2, ..., N - 1$ and F_n are transformation coefficient of $z(k)$. The descriptors can be rotation invariants when used magnitudes of transformation, $|F_n|$. The scale can be normalize to divide the magnitudes of coefficient by $|F_1|$.

2.2 Mathematical tools for calculating of similarity

2.2.1 Euclidean distance

The Euclidean distance between two points is the length of the line segment connecting them. In Cartesian coordinates, if $p = (p1, p2, ..., pn)$ and $q = (q1, q2, ..., qn)$ are two points in Euclidean space, then the distance from p to q, or from q to p is given by Equation 13.

$$D = d(p, q) = d(q, p) \tag{13}$$

$$D = \sqrt{(p_1 - q_1)^2 + (p_2 - q_2)^2 + ... + (p_n - q_n)^2} \tag{14}$$

$$D = \sqrt{\sum_{i=1}^{n} (p_i + q_i)^2} \tag{15}$$

2.2.2 Pearson correlation

The Pearson correlation (or "product-moment correlation coefficient", or also "r of Pearson") measure the correlation degree and the direction between two variables of metric scale. This coefficient is represented by r and can be between -1 and 1. So, r can be analyzed in the following manners:

$+1$: It means a perfect correlation and the variables are in the same direction;

-1: It means a perfect correlation too, but, in this analysis, the variables direction is opposite.

0: In this case, the variables does not have a linear dependence.

In other words, the signal of the result correlation shows if the correlation is positive or negative and the proportion variable shows the correlation force.

The Pearson correlation coefficient is calculated according to the next formula:

$$r = \frac{\sum_{i=1}^{n} (x_i - \bar{x})(y_i - \bar{y})}{\sqrt{\sum_{i=1}^{n} (x_i - \bar{x})^2} \cdot \sqrt{\sum_{i=1}^{n} (y_i - \bar{y})^2}}$$

Where $x_1, x_2, ..., x_n$ e $y_1, y_2, ..., y_n$ are measure values both of variables. Moreover, x_n can be written:

$$\bar{x} = \frac{1}{n} \cdot \sum_{i=1}^{n} x_i$$

And y_n can be:

$$\bar{y} = \frac{1}{n} \cdot \sum_{i=1}^{n} y_i$$

These variables (x_n and y_n) are arithmetics meanings, both of variables x and y.

3. Sucker-rod pumping system

The first artificial lifting method was the sucker rod pumping, that appears after the birth of the oil industry. The importance of this method is showed in the number of installations now operating in the world. The Figure 1 presents a Sucker Rod Pumping Unit.

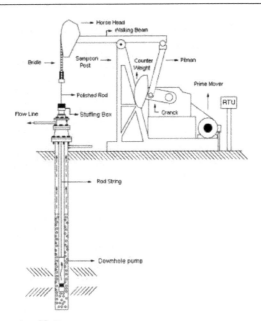

Fig. 1. Sucker Rod Pumping Unit

The great success of the sucker rod pumping system is linked to low cost in investment, maintenance, flow and deep flexibility, good energetic efficiency and the possibility to operate several down-hole conditions.   But, the main advantage is the lowest cost/production relationship during the field production life.

3.1 Components of the sucker rod pumping

3.1.1 Downhole pump

The Downhole Pump is a positive displacement pump - in other words, when the fluid gets in suction, it does not return.

3.1.2 Rod string

The string rod is responsible for providing the surface energy to the downhole pump.

3.1.3 Sucker rod pumping unit

The pumping unit changes the rotation movement of the electric motor in the applied reciprocate movement for polish rod, while the reduction box decreases the rotational speed of the electric motor to allow the pumping speed.

3.1.4 Dynamometer card

A dynamometer card is a graph of effects originated to active charge in the pump during a pump cycle. The Figure 2(a) presents a example of real card.

3.2 Reference card patterns

There are two types of dynamometer cards: the surface and the down-hole card. The charges are recorded in the surface through the dynamometers and in the down-hole through special devices or mathematical models. The dynamometer card is one of main tools to analyze and review the condition of the system. This card is a record of the charges along the rod string path. It is possible to view several conditions of pumping through the dynamometer card. In

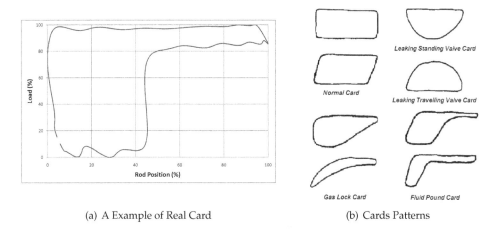

(a) A Example of Real Card   (b) Cards Patterns

this subsection, some Sucker Rod Pumping System cards are presented. Each card showed was chosen based on the main problems of oil fields and they can be found in other previous papers.(dos Santos Côrrea, 1995)

These presented cards (Figure 2(b)) are some reference patterns for the proposed model in the forward section.

3.2.1 Normal operation

The normal pumping pattern is associated with the follow characteristics:

- High volumetric Efficiency;
- Low interference of gas;
- Low or medium suction pressure.

3.2.2 Fluid pound

These patterns are associated with the follow characteristics:

- Low suction pressure;
- Low interference of gas;
- Blocked Pump Suction.

3.2.3 Valve leak

This patterns happen when there is a leak in the down-hole valves (Traveling or Standing valve).

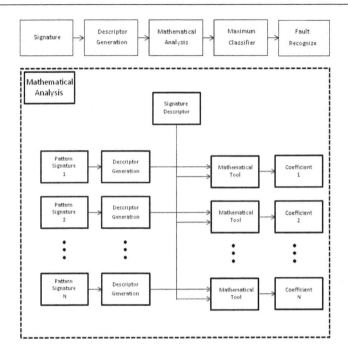

Fig. 2. Stages of Model Proposed

4. Methodology

In this part, it will be presented the used methodology in approximately 1500 dynamometric cards from the sucker-rod pumping system. The current methodology meet four reference cards. Next, the data flow and applied descriptors will be presented.

4.1 Data flow

The used model of data flow is based on selection and processing faults pattern cards. Thus, a border descriptor is generated for each pattern card. After this step, it is repeated for analyze each field card. After the border descriptor of the field card, the Euclidean Distance is calculated with each border descriptor of the pattern cards. The result of each distance calculus is compared in a minimum function. The lower value is linked to the closest pattern of the field card.

The Figure 2 presents an information flow in the proposed model.

4.2 Data acquisition

The data is obtained through the supervisory software. This software gathers the field variables like current, force, horse head position, head pressure, down-hole pressure, among others.

The dynamometer cards are a two dimension graph of force (ordinate axis) *versus* horse head position (abscissa axis). This card consists of one hundred points.

Comparison of Border Descriptors and Pattern Recognition Techniques Applied to Detection and Diagnose of
Faults on Sucker-Rod Pumping System

99

4.2.1 Patterns selection

The pattern cards are selected by an expert engineer. Next, the selected cards are available for system to process. From this moment the treatment is similar to the field card as the pattern cards.

4.2.2 Descriptors generator

After the data acquisition and patterns selection, the cards are processed using the mathematical tool showed in the Section 2.1. Thereby, each field card can be used to calculate the distance with a pattern card that has its own identity.

4.2.3 Calculating of similarity

Any signature can be compared with a pattern through their descriptors using some mathematical tools for calculating distance. Thus, one similarity value (coefficient) is generated for every calculation of distance between one signature and the different patterns.

4.2.4 Minimum classifier and fault recognition

It was necessary to use a classifier to recognize what pattern is closer to the field card. In this study, a simple classifier was used and it is just a maximum function. This function is applied in the generated table in Section 4.2.2. Thereafter, the Euclidean Distance calculus that has the lower value represents the fault.

5. Results

This section is divided in three subsection. The first subsection, the general results are showed and discussed. In the second subsection, each descriptor is tested for invariance of the features needed to Sucker-rod pumping (Scale, Translation and Start point). After, it is showed a modification to improve the performance of recognition. In the last, the consolidate results are presented.

5.1 General results of euclidean distance

The Figures 3, 4, 5 and 6 are the result of pattern recognition analysis with Euclidean Distance. The K-Curvature Descriptor and Fourier Descriptor are the best performance, but in the analysis of Fluid Pound and Gas Lock Pattern, both not show good results.

5.2 General results of pearson correlation

The Figures 7, 8, 9 and 10 are the result of pattern recognition analysis with Pearson Correlation. The Centroid Descriptor and Fourier Descriptor are the best performance, but in the analysis of Fluid Pound and Gas Lock Pattern, both also do not present good results.

5.3 Tests of invariant characteristics

In this subsection, the presented results are about the robustness tests of descriptors in relation to features that must be invariant and for fault recognize on Sucker-rod pumping system. In all the tests, the chosen card represents a fault pattern card. The results are present in the Table 1.

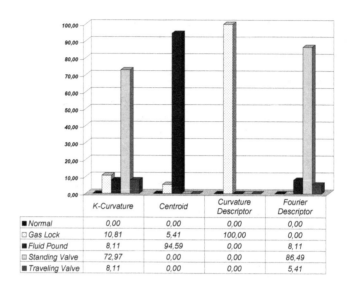

	K-Curvature	Centroid	Curvature Descriptor	Fourier Descriptor
■ Normal	0,00	0,00	0,00	0,00
□ Gas Lock	10,81	5,41	100,00	0,00
■ Fluid Pound	8,11	94,59	0,00	8,11
□ Standing Valve	72,97	0,00	0,00	86,49
■ Traveling Valve	8,11	0,00	0,00	5,41

Fig. 3. Euclidean Distance - Results to Showed Cards of Leaking Standing Valve

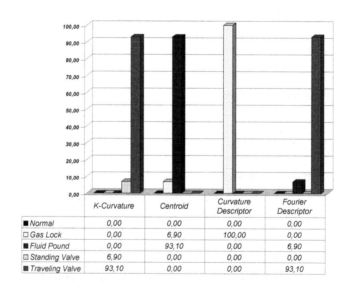

	K-Curvature	Centroid	Curvature Descriptor	Fourier Descriptor
■ Normal	0,00	0,00	0,00	0,00
□ Gas Lock	0,00	6,90	100,00	0,00
■ Fluid Pound	0,00	93,10	0,00	6,90
□ Standing Valve	6,90	0,00	0,00	0,00
■ Traveling Valve	93,10	0,00	0,00	93,10

Fig. 4. Euclidean Distance - Results to Showed Cards of Leaking Traveling Valve

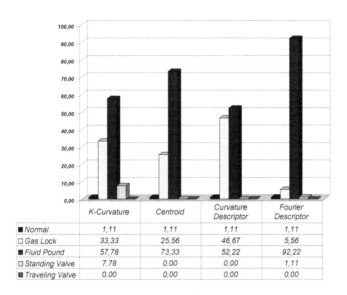

	K-Curvature	Centroid	Curvature Descriptor	Fourier Descriptor
■ Normal	1,11	1,11	1,11	1,11
□ Gas Lock	33,33	25,56	46,67	5,56
■ Fluid Pound	57,78	73,33	52,22	92,22
□ Standing Valve	7,78	0,00	0,00	1,11
■ Traveling Valve	0,00	0,00	0,00	0,00

Fig. 5. Euclidean Distance - Results to Showed Cards of Gas Lock

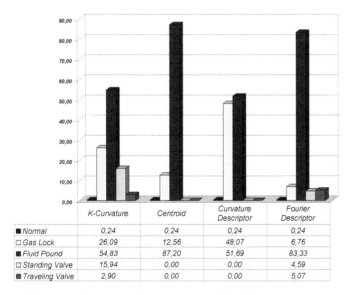

	K-Curvature	Centroid	Curvature Descriptor	Fourier Descriptor
■ Normal	0,24	0,24	0,24	0,24
□ Gas Lock	26,09	12,56	48,07	6,76
■ Fluid Pound	54,83	87,20	51,69	83,33
□ Standing Valve	15,94	0,00	0,00	4,59
■ Traveling Valve	2,90	0,00	0,00	5,07

Fig. 6. Euclidean Distance - Results to Showed Cards of Fluid Pound

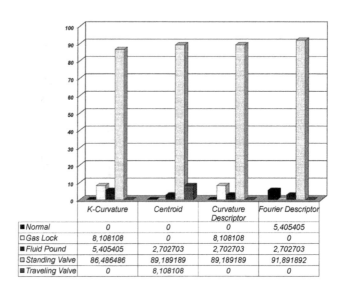

	K-Curvature	Centroid	Curvature Descriptor	Fourier Descriptor
■ Normal	0	0	0	5,405405
□ Gas Lock	8,108108	0	8,108108	0
■ Fluid Pound	5,405405	2,702703	2,702703	2,702703
□ Standing Valve	86,486486	89,189189	89,189189	91,891892
■ Traveling Valve	0	8,108108	0	0

Fig. 7. Pearson Correlation - Results to Showed Cards of Leaking Standing Valve

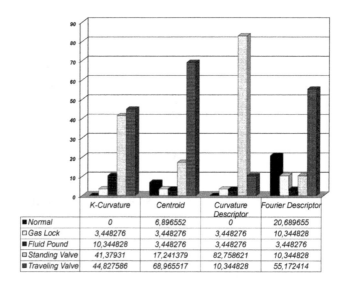

	K-Curvature	Centroid	Curvature Descriptor	Fourier Descriptor
■ Normal	0	6,896552	0	20,689655
□ Gas Lock	3,448276	3,448276	3,448276	10,344828
■ Fluid Pound	10,344828	3,448276	3,448276	3,448276
□ Standing Valve	41,37931	17,241379	82,758621	10,344828
■ Traveling Valve	44,827586	68,965517	10,344828	55,172414

Fig. 8. Pearson Correlation - Results to Showed Cards of Leaking Traveling Valve

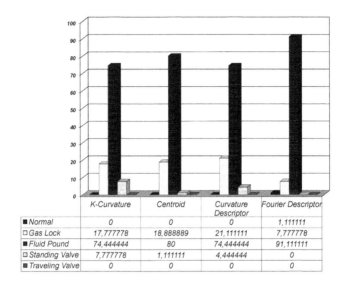

	K-Curvature	Centroid	Curvature Descriptor	Fourier Descriptor
■ Normal	0	0	0	1,111111
□ Gas Lock	17,777778	18,888889	21,111111	7,777778
■ Fluid Pound	74,444444	80	74,444444	91,111111
□ Standing Valve	7,777778	1,111111	4,444444	0
■ Traveling Valve	0	0	0	0

Fig. 9. Pearson Correlation - Results to Showed Cards of Gas Lock

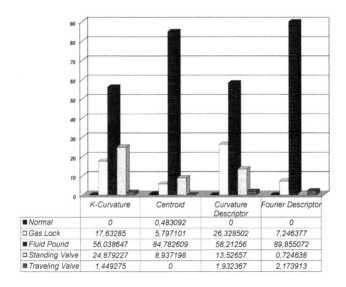

	K-Curvature	Centroid	Curvature Descriptor	Fourier Descriptor
■ Normal	0	0,483092	0	0
□ Gas Lock	17,63285	5,797101	26,328502	7,246377
■ Fluid Pound	56,038647	84,782609	58,21256	89,855072
□ Standing Valve	24,879227	8,937198	13,52657	0,724638
■ Traveling Valve	1,449275	0	1,932367	2,173913

Fig. 10. Pearson Correlation - Results to Showed Cards of Fluid Pound

Descriptors	Translation	Scale	Start Point
Centroid	OK	OK	FAIL
K-Curvature	OK	OK	FAIL
Curvature	OK	OK	FAIL
Fourier	OK	OK	FAIL

Table 1. Invariance Tests

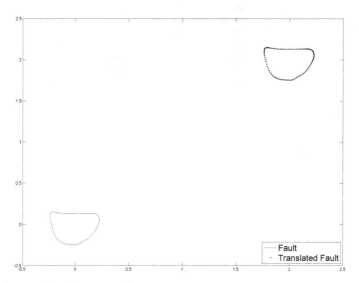

Fig. 11. Used Example to Teste Translation Invariance

5.3.1 Translation invariance

Translation tests, the chosen card was translated as shown in Figure 11. As expected, all descriptors were successful in recognizing.

5.3.2 Scaling invariance

Scaling tests, the chosen card was scaled as shown in Figure 12. And also, all descriptors were successful in recognizing.

5.3.3 Start point invariance

Start point tests, the start point was changed. The Figure 13 shows the both start points (Original Start Point and Modified Start Point) from data acquisition. But now, as can be seen, all descriptors were not successful.

The Fourier descriptor is able to solve this problem. Modifying the Equation 12 to 16 through to calculate of absolute value of Fourier Transform. But, this procedure insert a new problem to recognize of fault that are equal when rotated. It can be seen in the Figure 14 where different faults are recognized as the same when this process is used.

$$F_n = abs\left\{\frac{1}{N}\sum_{k=0}^{N-1} z(k)e^{-\frac{j2\pi nk}{N}}\right\} \tag{16}$$

Comparison of Border Descriptors and Pattern Recognition Techniques Applied to Detection and Diagnose of
Faults on Sucker-Rod Pumping System

105

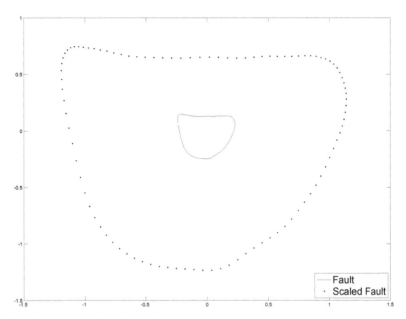

Fig. 12. Used Example to Teste Scale Invariance

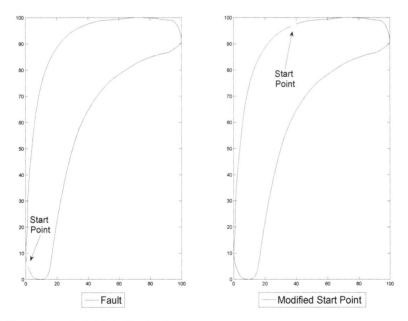

Fig. 13. Used Example to Teste Start Point Invariance

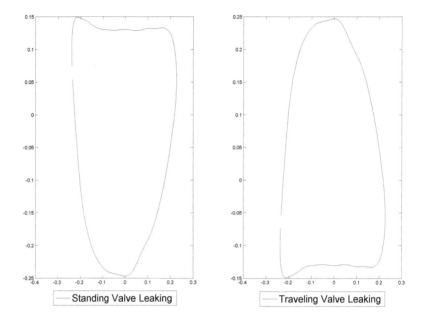

Fig. 14. Examples of Distinct Faults by Rotation

5.4 Proposed modification

To improve the performance of pattern recognizing to Fluid Pound and Gas Lock faults, it is proposed a specialist system that analyze the curvature card. The better curvature that represents a third order function is identified as Gas Lock fault. Look at the results for Euclidean Distance in the Figure 15 and in the Figure 16.

It is possible to observe that the results as the others faults not change its values.

5.5 Consolidate results

The Table 2 presents the consolidate results. Thus, it can be observed that Fourier Descriptor was better than others when used with Euclidean distance and it is as good as the Centroid Descriptor when used with the Pearson Correlation.

Border	Sucess (%)	
Descriptors	Euclidean	Pearson
Centroid	45,91	84,55
K-Curvature	81,49	68,72
Curvature	45,91	62,11
Fourier	86,60	83,12

Table 2. Consolidate Results

Comparison of Border Descriptors and Pattern Recognition Techniques Applied to Detection and Diagnose of
Faults on Sucker-Rod Pumping System

107

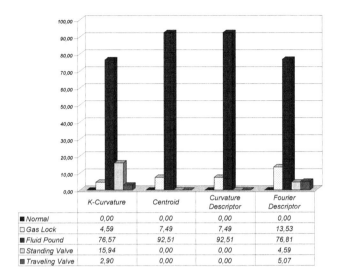

	K-Curvature	Centroid	Curvature Descriptor	Fourier Descriptor
■ Normal	0,00	0,00	0,00	0,00
☐ Gas Lock	4,59	7,49	7,49	13,53
■ Fluid Pound	76,57	92,51	92,51	76,81
☐ Standing Valve	15,94	0,00	0,00	4,59
■ Traveling Valve	2,90	0,00	0,00	5,07

Fig. 15. Modified System - Results to Showed Cards of Fluid Pound

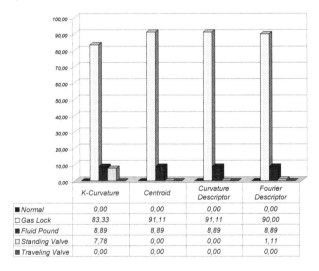

	K-Curvature	Centroid	Curvature Descriptor	Fourier Descriptor
■ Normal	0,00	0,00	0,00	0,00
☐ Gas Lock	83,33	91,11	91,11	90,00
■ Fluid Pound	8,89	8,89	8,89	8,89
☐ Standing Valve	7,78	0,00	0,00	1,11
■ Traveling Valve	0,00	0,00	0,00	0,00

Fig. 16. Modified System - Results to Showed Cards of Gas Lock

6. Conclusion

Nowadays, the quantity of onshore wells using Sucker-Rod Pumping System is higher and it stickles the engineer work. In addition, the difficulty in recognizing a specific card shape augment as the amount of noise increase mainly as a function of well depth.

This study, using the processing image, is suitable for fault diagnosis of Sucker-Rod Pumping System and could help to interpret the down-hole condition of oil well promptly and correctly.

The results presented a high efficiency for processed field cards and seemed to be very robust to inherent problems in the processing images, like rotation, translation and scale. In the future, it is desired to test other recognizing functions and to develop an capable system of identify all faults. It will permit the prediction and the planning of the maintenance, so the field engineer manages his equipments.

7. References

Alegre, L., A, F, D. R. & Morooka, C. (1993). Intelligent approach of rod pumping problems, *SPE - Petroleum Computer Conference* pp. 249–255.

Alegre, L., Morooka, C. & da Rocha, A. (1993). Intelligent diagnosis of rod pumping problems, *SPE - 68th Annual Technical Conference* III: 97–108.

Barreto, F., Tygel, M., Rocha, A. & Morooka, C. (1996). Automatic downhole card generation and classification, *SPE Annual Technical Conference* pp. 311–318.

Chacln, J. (1969). A numerical approach to the diagnosis of sucker rod pumping installations and its verification with downhole pump field measurements, *SPE - Society Petroleum Engineer* .

de Almeida Barreto Filho, M. (1993). *Geração de carta dinamométrica de fundo para diagnóstico do bombeio mecânico em poços de petróleo*, Master's thesis, UNIVERSIDADE ESTADUAL DE CAMPINAS - UNICAMP.

de Oliveira Costa, R. (1994). *Curso de Bombeio Mecânico*, november/1995 edn, PETROBRAS - Petróleo Brasileiro S.A.

Dickinson, R. & Jennings, J. (1990). Use of pattern-recognition techniques in analyzing downhole dynamometer cards, *SPE Production Engineering* pp. 187–192.

dos Santos Côrrea, J. F. (1995). *Sistema inteligente para aplicações de soluções em bombeamento mecânico*, Master's thesis, UNIVERSIDADE ESTADUAL DE CAMPINAS - UNICAMP.

Gonzalez, R. C., Woods, R. E. & Eddins, S. L. (2003). *Digital Image Processing Using Matlab*, Prentice Hall.

Kardec, A. & Nascif, J. (1998). *Manutenção - Função Estratégica*, 1998 edn, QualityMark Editora.

Nazi, G. & Lea, J. (1994). Application of artificial neural network to pump card diagnosis, *SPE Computer Application* pp. 9–14.

Rogers, J., Guffey, C. & Oldham, W. (1990). Artificial neural networks for identification of beam pump dynamometer load cards, *SPE - 65th Annual Technical Conference* pp. 349–359.

Russell, S. (2003). *Inteligência Artificial*, Campus.

Schirmer, G. P. & Toutain, J. C. P. (1991). Use of advanced pattern recognition and knowledge-based system in analyzing dynamometer cards, *SPE Computer Application* pp. 21–24.

Schnitman, L., Albuquerque, G. S. & Corrêa, J. (2003). Modeling and implementation of a system for sucker rod downhole dynamometer card pattern recognition, *SPE - Annual Technical Conference and Exhibition* pp. 1–4.

Tripp, H. (1989). A review: analyzing beam-pumped wells, *JPT* pp. 457–458.

Xu, P., Xu, S. & Yin, H. (2006). Application of self-organizing competitive neural network in fault diagnosis of suck rod pumping system, *Journal of Petroleum Science and Engineering* pp. 43–48.

6

Practical Imaging in Dermatology

Ville Voipio, Heikki Huttunen and Heikki Forsvik
Department of Signal Processing, Tampere University of Technology
Finland

1. Introduction

Visual observation has an important role in dermatology as the skin is the most visible organ. This makes dermatology a good candidate for utilizing digital imaging and automatic diagnostic tools. This chapter illustrates the use of 2D imaging in dermatology by presenting a method for automatization of common allergy testing. The so called "prick test" is the most common diagnostic test for different allergies. It involves measuring the skin response to percutaneously introduced allergens.

If there is a skin reaction against the allergen the blood flow is increased in the area and a wheal is formed. In physical terms, the color of the skin is changed, and a vertical displacement emerges. In this chapter we will concentrate on the color change (erythema) as we are only using 2D without the vertical displacement information.

Several approaches have been proposed to the skin erythema detection. The emphasis is often on detecting signs of melanoma and there exists a lot of literature on melanoma segmentation (Celebi et al., 2009; Gomez et al., 2008; 2007), but only a few studies of measurement of allergic reactions from 2D pictures (Nischik & Forster, 1997; Roullot et al., 2005). There are also some studies which have been performed with 3D imaging (Santos et al., 2008) or other specialized imaging hardware (Wöhrl et al., 2006).

We utilize the inexpensive commonplace 2D digital photography. The key challenges in this approach are the transformation of the color image into a maximal-contrast single-variable (grayscale) image and the interpretation of the wheal dimensions from this transformed image. This chapter is organized so that section 2 discusses the effect of the imaging hardware and camera settings on the medical and scientific imaging. After that we present our algorithm for segmenting the wheal area in Section 3, which is based on our earlier paper (Huttunen et al., 2011). Finally, Section 4 discusses the results.

2. Imaging

The easy availability and high quality of digital cameras made them attractive for medical and other scientific use. Purpose-built scientific digital cameras carry typically a tenfold price tag, and the pace of development is very fast in the mainstream digital cameras.

While the actual performance of the inexpensive cameras is usually very good, their image processing chain is not well documented. Scientific cameras are supplied with photometric specifications, and they do not perform any unspecified processing to the image.

Photography-oriented equipment very seldom gives any photometric specifications, and the cameras may perform a lot of unspecified image processing.

The low cost of ordinary digital cameras opens up a large number of new opportunities in medicine. In order to avoid some common pitfalls associated with their use, one should be aware of the typical image processing in the camera. The actual processing varies from one camera to another, and the image processing methods are not published by the manufacturers, but the following sections outline the fundamental limitations and give an overview of the signal processing in a typical digital camera.

The discussion below will concentrate on digital cameras with interchangeable optics (typically SLR, Single Lens Reflex cameras) if not indicated otherwise. The use of compact cameras is usually not recommended in medical or scientific work; SLR cameras provide much better imaging properties and are still affordable.

2.1 Signal path

Finding a simple and accurate definition for a digital camera is difficult, as the use of a camera may range from art to measurement. In the following discussion the digital camera is viewed as *a measurement device measuring the spectral intensity distribution of light arriving from different spatial angles towards the camera.* Thus, in an ideal camera the spectrum of light arriving from each angle to the film plane is recorded.

Evidently, the definition above gives an infinite amount of information and is in contradiction with both the real world situation and physics. In order to understand the practical limitations, we may have a look at the signal path in a digital camera and the limitations imposed by each step in the path (see figure 1).

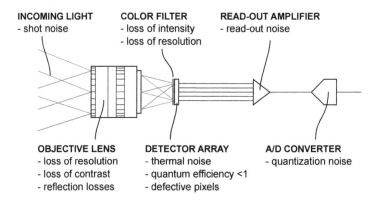

Fig. 1. Signal path in a digital camera and sources of loss of information associated with each step.

The first and a very fundamental reason for loss of information lies in the quantum nature of light. As the light collected by the optical system consists of a number of photons, there is always some statistical noise ("shot noise"). Shot noise is usually the dominant noise source in photography. The signal-to-noise ratio limited by the shot noise is inversely proportional to the square root of the intensity of the light falling onto the detector.

2.1.1 Objective lens

The purpose of the optical system is to direct photons arriving from a certain direction onto the detector plane. There are two physical limitations related to the optical system; limited depth-of-field and diffraction limit. If the optical system is to collect more light, its light collecting area (usually a circular aperture) has to be larger. Inevitably, large aperture makes a shorter depth-of-view, i.e., only objects at a certain limited distance range are in focus (see section 2.3.2). On the other hand, if the aperture is small, the image becomes diffraction limited due to the wave nature of light. In practice, even moderately low cost digital camera systems are often diffraction limited in their behaviour.

The diffraction limit for an optical system is given by the Rayleigh's criterion:

$$d = 1.22\frac{\lambda f}{D},\tag{1}$$

where d is the smallest resolvable detail on the image plane, λ wavelength, D the size of the entrance pupil (aperture), and f the focal length of the objective. For a typical digital camera with a typical objective f/D is in the range of 2..20. The wavelength of green light is roughly 500 nm, and the pixel size of a SLR digital camera is typically approximately 5 micrometers, and hence the resolution becomes easily diffraction limited when $f/D > 8$.

The discussion above is somewhat simplified in two respects. First, the Rayleigh's criterion is somewhat arbitrary, it actually refers to the distance between the center and the first minimum of the Airy disk (a diffraction pattern arising from an aperture), and has its roots in astronomy. Two sharp spots of light can be resolved even when they are closer than the Rayleigh's criterion, so the criterion is more a rule of thumb than an exact measure (Hecht, 1987). Second, in practice the objective may not be diffraction limited at or close to its largest aperture setting.

The optical system may also lose some light due to absorption and reflection losses. While the absolute amount of light lost this way is usually rather small, these losses may be seen as uneven illumination across the field (usually less light in the corners) or loss of contrast when there are very brightly illuminated areas in the image.

2.1.2 Color filters

Virtually all consumer digital still cameras are color cameras. As the light-sensitive pixels in the image detector cannot detect the color of the incoming light, a color filter is required[1]. The color filter represents a major loss of light, as the photons of mismatching energies ("wrong color") are absorbed.

The color filters are laid out so that neighboring pixels have different filters in front of them. There are numerous different filter patterns, both the layout and the actual colors of the filters

---

[1] There is one notable exception to this rule; Sigma Corporation Foveon X3 sensors have three photosensitive sensors overlaid on top of each other, which in principle eliminates the filter and losses associated to it. Also, many digital video cameras employ a color-separation beamsplitter which directs different wavelengths to three separate image sensors.

vary. Probably the most common of these patterns is the Bayer pattern where a 2x2-pixel block has one red, one blue, and one green filter (see Figure 2). The choice of the filter pattern and color is a compromise between spatial resolution, light collecting efficiency, and color reproduction. There are even some cameras which have four color filters (RGBE, E for emerald) to increase the color sensitivity.

It should be noted that whatever the filter pattern, the color reconstruction (demosaic) filter is not a trivial one. If the maximum resolution is desired, the filter needs to identify edges by combining information from several pixels. This requires non-linear processing and is prone to creating artefacts.

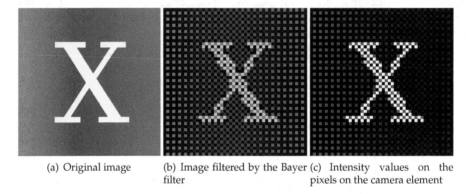

(a) Original image   (b) Image filtered by the Bayer   (c) Intensity values on the
                           filter   pixels on the camera element

Fig. 2. Color reproduction in a Bayer filter.

It is important to note that color cameras are essentially very crude three-channel filter spectrometers; the full spectrum of visible light is reduced to three values. The spectral properties of the color filters are usually not disclosed, and in this way the color information given by a digital camera can usually be interpreted only in a relative manner.

Color is not a physical property of light, it is a property of the human visual system. There are three different types of color sensitive cone cells in the human retina. One cell type is sensitive to longer wavelength (red), the other to medium wavelengths (green), and the third type to short wavelengths (blue). The RGB system for color pictures is adopted with the idea that each of the primary colors corresponds to one type of cone cells.[2]

If the transmission properties of the color filters in a digital camera differ from those of the retinal cone cells, the color space as seen by the digital camera is not the same as seen by the human eye. There may be metameric colors (colors which look the same to a human observer but have different spectral distribution) which a camera may be able to distinguish, and vice versa. There is no simple way to describe these relations without knowing the actual filter characteristics of the color filters in the camera, and even then the practical implications are not necessarily evident.

---

[2] While a RGB image sensor can cover the full range of colors seen by the human eye, the same does not apply to reproducing the color. Mixing light of any three colors can never produce the full range (gamut) of colors which the human eye can see.

2.1.3 Image detector

After going through the color filters, the light is detected by a CCD (Charge-Coupled Device) or a CMOS (Complementary Metal Oxide Semiconductor) array camera. The difference between the two technologies is rather subtle, in both devices a photon hitting a detector cell has some probability of generating a charge carrier which is trapped in the pixel. This probability depends on the sensor and the wavelength of the incident photon and is called the quantum efficiency (QE).

The actual quantum efficiencies of real-world cameras are trade secrets, but Farrell et al. (2006) suggests that the quantum efficiency of a digital SLR pixels is around 0.65, but as the fill factor (proportion of active pixel area to the total sensor area) is only around 50 %, the total QE is approximately 1/3.

The pixel size limits the spatial resolution of the image. However, this is not usually the most limiting factor, as the physical and practical limits of the optics already limit the resolution. Also, making small pixels may reduce the fill factor and increase the relative read-out noise. The choice of pixel size is a compromise between dynamic performance and resolution of the sensor (Farrell et al., 2006). In practice, there are very few situations in medical imaging where a larger number of pixels would be beneficial.

Once the light has been captured by a sensor pixel, it is read out, amplified and quantized by an AD (analog-to-digital) converter. The pixel itself has some temperature-dependent thermally induced noise. Usually this noise is significant only with long exposure times (such as in astrophotography). The pixel readout noise is a source for constant noise which is not dependent on the illumination. Thus, it is usually significant only with low illumination levels (deep dark areas or very low light).

Also, the conversion gain from stored charge carriers to a voltage signal varies from one pixel to another. There may even be hot (always at full output) or dead (always at zero) pixels due to manufacturing defects in the sensor array. Hot pixels may be such that they show only at very long exposure times.

2.1.4 AD conversion

While the number of bits in the AD converter seems to be a an important marketing feature for some digital cameras, the quantization noise of the AD converter is typically far below the other noise sources (readout in the dark area, shot noise in the highlight areas). The maximum dynamic intensity range offered by a 14-bit AD converter is $1 : 2^{14} = 1 : 16384$, whereas the typical maximum dynamic range of the sensor limited by other factors is roughly 1:2000.

Practically all digital cameras offer the possibility to change the sensitivity (ISO number) of the camera. However, this choice does not change the sensitivity of the photosensitive elements. Instead, it either changes the amplification of the analog signal between the camera element and the AD converter or is purely a digital multiplication. As these operations do not change the fundamental noise sources (shot noise, thermal noise, readout noise), it is better to increase the illumination instead of increasing the sensitivity setting.

In this signal chain from the spatial distribution of light to bits from the sensor it is important to note that many of the limitations are fundamental physical limitations (shot noise, depth-of-view, diffraction limit). The camera technology is very good even at today's level, and the room for improvement is rather limited.

2.2 Digital camera signal processing

Before the image from the sensor is available as an image file, it undergoes several digital processing steps. There are at least three different goals in this processing:

1. Correcting image defects
2. Improving the visual appearance of the image
3. Making the image technically easier to use

No image processing can increase the amount of information in the image. Some of the image processing steps may be useful in scientific imaging, but others may make the image less useful in further image processing. At this point the purpose-built scientific cameras are usually more faithful to the actual scene. The image processing steps and algorithms in each individual camera type are proprietary, but there are some general steps which are almost unavoidable:

- Pixel-to-pixel non-uniformity (fixed noise) compensation
- Dead pixel elimination
- Demosaicing (color reproduction)

After these processing steps the result is a RGB image in a linear color space. This is usually the most useful image form for further image processing. Many digital cameras provide such an image under the name "RAW". However, the raw image format is manufacturer-specific, usually does not have any demosaicing applied, and may or may not compensate for dead pixels. The RAW formats are seldom officially published, but there are utilities such as `dcraw` (Coffin, 2011) which can be used to convert the images to some format easier to handle with image processing software.

One attempt to standardize the varying RAW file formats is the DNG ("digital negative") format by Adobe (Adobe Systems Incorporated, 2009). The DNG specification gives an overview of different aspects of RAW images. Despite this attempt, using the RAW images may be slightly challenging in practice.

In everyday photography, the images are usually processed in-camera with at least the following steps:

- Noise reduction
- Illumination correction (white balance)
- Sharpening
- Color space conversion to a non-linear one
- Compression

The purpose of this processing is to make the image look visually pleasing and occupy small space. Unfortunately, these steps reduce the information available in the image. The goal of color space conversion and compression is to reduce the number of bits without removing visually important information. For example, the very commonly used JPEG (ECMA, 2009) image compression reduces the chrominance (color) information more than the luminance (brightness) information, as the human visual system is more sensitive to luminance changes.

The camera image processing may be aware of certain optical properties of the objective lens, e.g., chromatic aberration, geometric aberrations, vignetting (loss of light at the corners), and may perform corrective operations.

For machine vision applications, there are two possibilities when choosing the file format. If a single camera type is used, then using RAW files of that camera preserves as much information as possible. If there is no control over the camera type, then setting the camera to produce JPEG files with as little processing (sharpening, noise reduction, compression) as possible gives a reasonably standardized result.

It should be noted that even the RAW images from the camera may be compressed images. An analysis of dcraw's source code reveals, for example, that some RAW files have the AD outputs further quantized. Whether or not such operations actually reduce any useful information from the image is unknown, as their effect may remain below the noise level.

The example images used in this chapter have been compressed in-camera with a moderate JPEG. This approach is not optimal, and some of the noise visible in Figure 6 is likely to be compression artefacts. Note that all color space transformations tend to emphasize the compression noise, because JPEG is designed for good visual appearance in the RGB color space.

One additional concern is storing the images for long-term use. JPEG images can most probably be read a long time in the future as it is the most common photographic image file format at the moment. The less common RAW formats may be difficult to interpret in the decades to come, as none of the formats has gained significantly larger popularity than the others. In medical applications the images may be stored in the DICOM (NEMA, 2011) format. This does not change the work flow in the digital camera in any way, and the DICOM format offers a number of different lossy and lossless data encoding schemes, whose suitability depend a great deal on the imaging application itself. However, the use of DICOM does not necessarily mean the images will be completely future-proof, as the standard and its use evolve.

2.3 Photographic setup

Designing a suitable photographic setup is very important in scientific or medical photography. The arrangement of the photographic setup has usually much more impact on the usability of the image than differences between different cameras.

The purpose of photographic imaging in dermatology is to measure the spectral reflectance of skin at different points in the area of interest. The accuracy of this process depends on a large number of parameters related to the illumination, setup geometry, optics, camera settings, and the camera itself.

A diagram of the photographic setup used in our project is shown in figure 3. The forearm of the patient is supported so that it does not move during the test. The support is built to

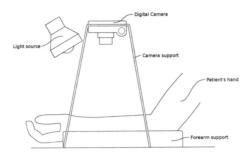

Fig. 3. The photographic setup for the skin prick test.

eliminate unnecessary muscular strain, as the test takes a half an hour to complete. The light falls from the direction of the camera to eliminate shadows. While the basic structure of the test setup is well-suited to the application, the illumination can be improved. Especially, the spectral properties of the light source were suboptimal, as there was little short wavelength (blue) radiation in the illumination.

2.3.1 Illumination

Illumination has an extremely important role. There are three main aspects to be taken into account in designing the lighting:

1. amount of light
2. spectral properties of the illumination
3. geometric properties of the illumination

In practice, the requirement for a correct amount of light translates to the requirement of having enough light. Insufficient illumination decreases the amount of information in the photograph either as a loss of resolution or as an increase of noise. (In some rather rare cases one should also pay attention to the effect of the light or thermal radiation onto the tissue illuminated.)

The way colors are formed in a digital camera actually means that the camera measures the product of the spectrum of the illumination, spectral reflection of the target, and spectral transmission of the camera color filters. This process naturally loses most of the spectral reflection information of the target, and accurate measurement of color-related quantities is difficult in digital photography.

Table 1 summarizes the typical spectral properties of some illuminants. The variation within each technology is usually significant, and if reliable color reproduction is required, the light source has to be chosen and calibrated carefully. It should also be noted that changing the camera type changes the camera filter absorption spectrum and thus the color reproduction.

In most cases the color of the illuminant can be sufficiently compensated for by the white balance compensation. The light reflected off a white or neutral gray target should result

Lamp type	Spectral properties
Incandescent lamp	Smooth spectrum, low intensity in the blue (short wavelength) region (tungsten halogen lamps have more blue emission)
Fluorescent tube	Usually a spectrum consisting of a large number of separate narrow peaks
Photographic flash	Several rather narrow peaks
Monochromatic LED	A single peak with a typical peak width of 20 nm
White LED	Either a single narrow blue peak and a wide yellow peak ("white LED") or three narrow separate peaks (combination of R, G, and B LEDs). The color may depend on the radiation angle.

Table 1. Typical spectral properties of different light sources

in a RGB value with equal amount of each of the components. If this is not the case, the components have to be adjusted by a multiplication:

$$\begin{pmatrix} R_{corr} \\ G_{corr} \\ B_{corr} \end{pmatrix} = k \begin{pmatrix} 1/R_{gray} & 0 & 0 \\ 0 & 1/G_{gray} & 0 \\ 0 & 0 & 1/B_{gray} \end{pmatrix} \begin{pmatrix} R \\ G \\ B \end{pmatrix}, \qquad (2)$$

where X is the uncorrected value for color X, X_{gray} the uncorrected value for the gray surface illuminated with the same illuminant, X_{corr} the corrected value, and k a normalizing factor. If the automatic white balance setting offered by the camera is used, the camera algorithms try to find the optimal correction coefficients. This process is based on typical photographic scenes, and it may result in unexpected correction results in scientific photography. It should be noted that the white balance correction is often quite significant especially in the blue channel.

Most cameras try to convert the information from the image sensor to the commonly used sRGB color space. This conversion usually involves using a 3x3 matrix multiplication from the camera RGB to the sRGB color space. The conversion may be beneficial for human viewing, but after it has been performed, the white balance equations above do not hold true. For an in-depth discussion of white balance, see Viggiano (2004).

Film-based medical photography used to have some applications with monochrome film and an external filter to enhance the contrast of specific features. In general, this method cannot be substituted with digital color photography and digital post processing, as the transmission properties of the filters do not match those of the color filters of the camera. The solution is to use a filter in front of the color camera, filter the light source, or use a (quasi-)monochromatic light source.

The geometric properties of the illumination have a lot of impact on the contrast of the image. The illumination may create shadows or specular reflections (bright spots) which are usually undesired, but in some cases they may be useful in detecting feature outlines or surface normal directions. In general, a point-like light sources give more contrast and more shadows and specular reflections than area sources.

There is very little in the camera or in the image processing that can be done to compensate for a bad illumination geometry. However, if shininess or specular reflections are the only problems in otherwise good photographic setup, a polarizing filter may help, as it blocks the light reflected at certain angles.

2.3.2 Camera settings

There are essentially four independent settings in the camera which can be adjusted:

1. focal length
2. focus
3. aperture
4. exposure time

The focal length together with the image sensor size determine the field of view. In a given photographic setup the position of the camera is usually fixed, so that an objective with a suitable focal length needs to be used. In general, objectives with fixed focal length exhibit better optical performance than zoom objectives. The optimal distance between the target and the camera depends on the application, but usually very short focal lengths (wide field of view) are to be avoided, if possible. Figure 4 illustrates the effect of focal length on the perspective of the image.

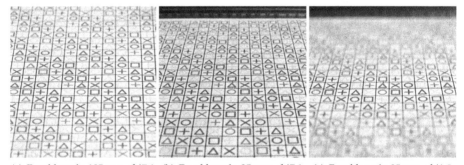

(a) Focal length: 105 mm, $f/7.1$ (b) Focal length: 35 mm, $f/7.1$ (c) Focal length: 35 mm, $f/1.8$

Fig. 4. Effect of focal length and aperture changes. The perspective distortion is much smaller at a longer focal length, and the depth of field is shorter with larger aperture (small f-number). The target and the imaging angle are the same in all images.

The digital cameras offer a selection between automatic or manual focus setting. If the imaging setup is fixed, the manual focus setting is preferred, as the autofocus algorithms are tuned to everyday photography, and the scenes in medical or scientific imaging are different.

The aperture (or entrance pupil) of the optics describes the size of the light collecting area of the objective. A large aperture collects more light and is thus useful in low-light situations. However, the depth of field (useful focus range) is very short at a large aperture (see figure 4). Also, at the large end of the aperture range the image resolution may suffer due to practical limitations. On the other hand, very small apertures have more diffraction, and this may slightly deteriorate the image resolution, as well. The optimal choice of the aperture depends on the application, and finding it may require some experimenting.

It should be noted that comparing the actual light collecting aperture of different cameras is not straightforward. The aperture size is usually given as the f-number (or $f/\#$), so that the actual aperture size in physical units is the focal length divided by the f-number. Thus, a large f-number indicates a small aperture, and the f-number itself is not meaningful unless the focal length is known. Even in digital cameras with interchangeable lenses the aperture area may vary in the range of 1:4 with the same field of view and aperture number.

The exposure time is perhaps the simplest adjustment. The longer the exposure time, the more photons reach the imaging element. Usually the shortest exposure times available in digital cameras are below one millisecond, and the longest times in the order of dozens of seconds. In practice, the short end of the exposure range is not very useful in medical photography, as there very seldom is enough light. On the other hand, exposure times above 1/60 s are prone to movements in the image. The amount of movement depends very much on the actual application, sometimes much longer exposure times are useful.

In some cases the dynamic range of the scene surpasses that of the digital camera. The dynamic range of a digital camera is typically approximately 1:2000. If this is not sufficient for some reason, it is possible to take several shots of the same scene with different exposure times. This technique is called bracketing, and the imaging method carries the acronym HDR (High Dynamic Range). The Achilles' heel of HDR is the time difference between different shots, which usually makes it impossible to apply to moving objects.

3. Wheal shape and size recognition

The skin prick test is widely used in allergy testing. As the test results in local skin reactions (wheals) around a well-defined test site, it lends itself well to computer-based interpretation.

3.1 Medical background

The skin prick test is a well-known and well-established method for quantitative measurement of allergic reactions (Oppenheimer et al., 2011). An allergen is introduced percutaneously; a drop of allergen solution is dropped onto the skin, and the skin is then punctured by a small blade designed for this purpose. If there is an allergic reaction, a wheal will emerge.

3.1.1 Skin reactions

If an allergen is introduced percutaneously, and there are IgE antibodies to that allergen, an inflammatory reaction will arise. Two different types of cells are involved in the process, basophils and mast cells. These cells release chemicals associated with inflammation, such as cytokines and histamines. These chemicals then mediate processes such as vasodilatation (expansion of the blood vessels) and increased permeability of the blood vessel walls.

The result of these processes is redness and heating due to increased blood flow and swelling due to leakage of fluid into the surrounding tissues. In the case of the prick test the reaction is localized around the prick site and produce an approximately circular wheal. In practice, the shape of the wheal may vary a lot depending on the structure of the surrounding tissue.

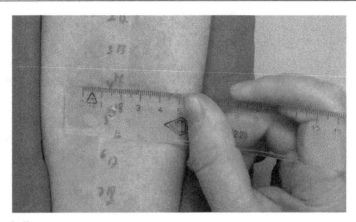

Fig. 5. Manual allergy measurement.

The prick test has some shortcomings. The magnitude of the skin response varies from one patient to another. For example, with young patients the size of the wheal becomes larger as the patient grows (Meinert et al., 1994). Also, the correlation between the actual allergic reactions and the skin reactions is not always very good, and there are several practical factors which may change the results (Haahtela et al., 2010).

3.1.2 Prick testing in practice

In practice, the prick test is used to test several allergens at the same time. To facilitate this, a suitable even skin area is required, the most common such area being the inner forearm. The number of allergens tested at the same time varies, but typically the inner forearm can carry 20 pricks.

The results are read some 15 to 20 minutes after the prick. The time is sufficient for the reaction to emerge but not long enough to let the symptoms fade. There is some evidence that if the time is too long, the reliability of the test may suffer (Seibert et al., 2011). However, the actual development of the inflammation reaction as a function of time is not generally known, as there have not been any suitable tools for measuring it. One of the aims of our research is to introduce these tools, as a series of photographs reveals the development of the wheal as a function of time.

There are different readout methods in use worldwide. In many cases the results are evaluated pseudo quantitatively by visual inspection only. Seibert et al. (2011) argue that the most reliable way of testing is to measure the size of the wheal, as the visual estimation has been shown to be highly variable.

When the wheal size is measured, there are several different ways of doing it. Traditionally, the practitioner uses a ruler to manually measure the size of the wheal. The test procedure assumes an elliptic shape, with possible elongated branches (called *pseudopodia*) disregarded and the result of the measurement is the mean of the major and minor axes of the imaginary ellipse (Santos et al., 2008). There is also a good correlation between the length of the long axis and the area of the wheal, but the mean method should yield even better results.

The practice of measuring the wheal vary. The practitioner may use a transparent ruler and slightly press the wheal to see the outline, or she may try to use the color change only. An illustration of the measurement is in Figure 5, where the application of pressure can be seen. Our computerized interpretation method uses the color change only, and the wheal is always interpreted as an ellipse.

One of the challenges in skin prick testing is the difference of reactions between different individuals. A common way to account for this is to use histamine as one of the test allergens. It is not an allergen, but it always causes an inflammatory reaction, which can be used as a reference of the individual reaction. Saline solution can also be introduced as a zero control which should not cause any reaction. We used both a zero reference and histamine reference in our study.

3.2 Wheal extraction by grayscale transformation

The problem of finding the area within a wheal in a photograph carries some challenges. The color of the skin varies from one person to another, and the skin does not have an even color. The wheal edges are not sharp, so a threshold has to be defined. Naturally, the first step in finding out the wheal area is to convert the RGB image into a single-variable (grayscale) image. Preferably, the method should be adaptive, as the range of skin colors and illumination variations is large.

Among the earlier studies in the field, Roullot et al. (2005) considers seven well known color spaces and compares the separability of the reaction from the background using a training database. As a result, they discover that the optimal dimension among the color spaces is the a^*-component of the $L^*a^*b^*$ color space. Using the extracted a^*-component, they use simple thresholding for segmenting the wheal.

Nischik *et al.* (Nischik & Forster, 1997) also discover the $L^*a^*b^*$ color space most suitable for the wheal segmentation and use the standard deviations of the L^* and a^* components as the features for classification. The classifier is trained to separate between foreground (the wheal) and the background (healthy skin) using manually generated training data. The classifier output determines directly the boundary between the two regions.

Recent work by Celebi *et al.* consider finding optimal color transformation for extracting the foreground (Celebi et al., 2009). Although the paper concentrates on melanoma segmentation, the principle is applicable for other skin diseases, as well. The paper searches for optimal linear combination of the RGB-components, such that the output maximizes the separability of the foreground and background. The foreground and background are determined in each iteration using Otsu thresholding. Thus, the algorithm iterates all projections defined on a finite grid, and tests their performance by measuring the Fisher ratio of the foreground and background (which are determined using Otsu thresholding).

The method of Celebi et al. (2009) is an unsupervised method, which attempts to find the best projection without any user manual assistance. However, in our work we study the case, in which the user points the approximate center of the wheal. From the practical point of view this is acceptable, because it requires less work than the manual measurement. However, we plan to automate the detection of the wheal location in the future. Note also that in the

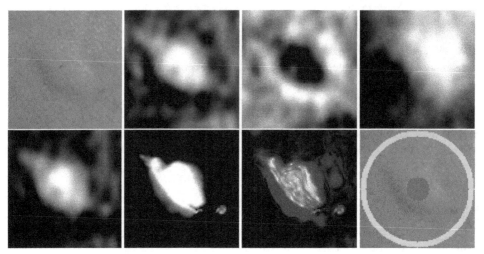

Fig. 6. The projection of the wheal in RGB color space. The original RGB image is shown in Figure (a), and (b) shows the hue component, (c) the a^* component of the $L^*a^*b^*$ color space and (d) is the projection proposed in Celebi et al. (2009). Optimal Fisher discriminant projection is shown in Figure (e), and the results of its kernelized version are shown in figures (f) and (g) using RBF kernel with bandwidth σ selected using Silverman rule of thumb and with fixed $\sigma = 0.5$. The training sets are obtained from areas shown in (h), where the blue center is the foreground sample region and the green circle is the background sample region.

temporal direction, clicking the last image in the time series is enough for determining the wheal location in all pictures, if temporal motion compensation is used.

The key problem when searching the borders of the wheal is the poor contrast between the wheal and skin. An example of a wheal is illustrated in Figure 6 (a). Although the wheal borders are barely visible, the shape becomes highlighted when mapped into grayscale in a suitable manner. Well known mappings for skin color processing include the hue component of the HSV color space (Figure 6 (b)) and the a^* component of the $L^*a^*b^*$ color space (Figure 6 (c)). In all projections, we have smoothed the RGB image by convolution with a disc shaped window of radius 5. However, these are more or less arbitrary, and variability in skin color and allergic reaction strength may decrease their applicability. Instead, training based projections may improve the separation further, and make it more invariant for all patients. An unsupervised method for finding a well-separating projection in terms of the Fisher criterion was proposed by Celebi *et al.* (Celebi et al., 2009), whose result is shown in Figure 6 (d). In this case the coefficients are 1, -0.1 and -0.3 for red, green and blue channels, respectively.

Optimality of the grayscale projection can be studied assuming that we know the approximate location of the wheal. This way we can construct training sets consisting of the wheal area and the surrounding healthy skin, denoted by S_1 and S_0, respectively. With the training sets we can seek for optimal separation in the RGB space in a supervised fashion.

The training set is acquired as follows. When the user has pointed the approximate location of the center of the wheal, a set of RGB values is obtained from the neighborhood. In our experiments, the training set of the wheal (S_1) is obtained inside the circular neighborhood with the radius of 10 pixels. The training set of the healthy skin (S_0) is acquired from pixels that are far away from the center. We have used all pixels located at a radius between 45 and 50 pixels from the center, as illustrated in Figure 6 (h).

The natural tool for optimally projecting the three-dimensions to grayscale is the *Fisher Discriminant*, Fisher (1936). Fisher discriminant finds the projection dimension **w** that maximizes the separability of the classes in terms of the ratio of the between-class-variance and within-class-variance; i.e., the so called Fisher ratio:

$$J(\mathbf{w}) = \frac{\mathbf{w}^T \mathbf{S}_B \mathbf{w}}{\mathbf{w}^T \mathbf{S}_W \mathbf{w}}, \tag{3}$$

where $\mathbf{S}_W \in \mathbf{R}^{3 \times 3}$ and $\mathbf{S}_B \in \mathbf{R}^{3 \times 3}$ are the within-class and between-class scatter matrices, respectively. It can be shown that the optimal direction **w** is given by

$$\mathbf{w} = \mathbf{S}_W^{-1}(\mu_1 - \mu_0), \tag{4}$$

where $\mu_1 \in \mathbf{R}^3$ and $\mu_0 \in \mathbf{R}^3$ are the sample means of S_1 and S_0.

An example of the result of the Fisher discriminant projection is shown in Figure 6 (e).

The FD is a special case of the so called *Kernel Fisher Discriminant* (KFD) (Mika et al., 1999; Schölkopf & Smola, 2001), which is a kernelized version of the standard FD. As all kernel methods, the KFD implicitly maps the original data into a high-dimensional feature space and finds the optimally separating manifold there. Using the implicit mapping via the *kernel trick*, the explicit mapping can be avoided, which allows calculating the FD even in an infinite-dimensional space.

The kernel trick enables better separation between the two classes, which is important because the foreground and the background are typically not linearly separable in the original RGB space. For example, it might be that the foreground is in the middle of two background color regions in the RGB space. One consequence of this is the fact that most authors prefer the $L^*a^*b^*$ color space, because the classes are better linearly separable there. However, the kernel trick makes the color space transformation less significant due to the transformation into a higher dimensional space, where the classes will be better separable almost regardless of the original color space.

Denote the foreground samples by $Y_1 = \{\mathbf{x}_1^F, \mathbf{x}_2^F, \ldots, \mathbf{x}_{N_F}^F\}$, and the background samples by $Y_0 = \{\mathbf{x}_1^B, \mathbf{x}_2^B, \ldots, \mathbf{x}_{N_B}^B\}$, where each sample is a 3-dimensional vector in the RGB space: $\mathbf{x}_k^{F,B} = (r_k^{F,B}, g_k^{F,B}, b_k^{F,B})^T$.

3.3 The Fisher discriminant projection

After the samples from the two classes have been collected, the optimally separating linear transformation is given by projection onto the vector **w** defined by the Fisher discriminant as follows,

$$\mathbf{w} = (\mathbf{C}_1 + \mathbf{C}_0)^{-1}(\mu_1 - \mu_0),$$

where $C_1 \in R^{3 \times 3}$ and $C_0 \in R^{3 \times 3}$ are the sample covariance matrices and $\mu_1 \in R^3$ and $\mu_0 \in R^3$ the sample means of the foreground and background samples, respectively.

3.4 The kernel Fisher discriminant projection

The Fisher discriminant projection is a special case of the kernel Fisher discriminant projection, occurring when the implicit mapping function is $\Phi(x) = x$. The use of more complicated mapping functions allows more complicated separations for the classes. For arbitrary mapping the Kernel Fisher Discriminant extends the FD by mapping the data into a higher dimensional feature space $\mathcal{H}$.

In practice the KFD can be calculated implicitly by substituting all dot products with a kernel function $\kappa(\cdot, \cdot)$. It can be shown, that all positive definite kernel functions correspond to a dot product after transforming the data to a feature space $\mathcal{H}$ with mapping $\Phi(\cdot)$ (Schölkopf & Smola, 2001). The feature space $\mathcal{H}$ can be very high dimensional, and the use of the projection vector w directly may be impractical or impossible. Instead, the famous *Representer theorem* guarantees that the solution can be represented as a linear combination of the mapped samples (Schölkopf & Smola, 2001). Thus, the Fisher ratio in the feature space is based on the weights of the samples α instead of the weights of the dimensions:

$$J(\alpha) = \frac{\alpha^T Q^T S_B^{\Phi} Q \alpha}{\alpha^T Q^T S_W^{\Phi} Q \alpha}, \tag{5}$$

where $\alpha \in R^N = (\alpha_1, \alpha_2, \ldots, \alpha_N)^T$ is the weight vector for the mapped training samples in the matrix $Q = [\Phi(x_1), \ldots, \Phi(x_N)]$, and S_B^{Φ} and S_W^{Φ} are the between-class and within-class scatter matrices in the feature space $\mathcal{H}$, respectively.

Similar solution as the one for the Fisher discriminant in Eq. (4) can be found also for this case (Schölkopf & Smola, 2001). However the inversion becomes more difficult, since the dimension of the weight vector α is now the number of the collected training samples. Therefore, we need a regularization term λI, where λ is a small positive scalar and I is the $N \times N$ identity matrix. Using regularization also improves the robustness of the projection and makes it less likely to overfit, as the solution becomes less sensitive to within-class scatter. In our notation this yields the solution

$$\alpha = (Q^T S_W^{\Phi} Q + \lambda I)^{-1} Q^T (\mu_1^{\Phi} - \mu_0^{\Phi}), \tag{6}$$

where $\mu_1^{\Phi} \in \mathcal{H}$ and $\mu_0^{\Phi} \in \mathcal{H}$ are the sample means of the mapped wheal and skin samples, respectively.

It is straightforward to show, that Eq. (6) can be expressed in terms of dot products and thus the kernel trick (Mika et al., 1999; Schölkopf & Smola, 2001). Also the actual projection of a test sample $x \in R^3$ can be expressed through the kernel as

$$y = \alpha^T Q^T \Phi(x) = \sum_{i=1}^{N} \alpha_i \kappa(x_i, x). \tag{7}$$

To reveal the kernel nature of (6), a part of it is further investigated, giving

$$Q^T S_W^\Phi Q = \sum_{i=0,1} \sum_{x \in \mathcal{S}_i} Q^T (\Phi(x) - \mu_i^\Phi)(Q^T(\Phi(x) - \mu_i^\Phi))^T. \tag{8}$$

Now it is rather clear that (6) can be represented using only dot-products of the mapped samples. Since also the projection of a test sample x to grayscale is expressible as $\alpha^T Q^T \Phi(x)$, the explicit use of mapping function $\Phi(x)$ can be substituted with its dot-products, which in hand are replaceable with Mercer kernels (Mika et al., 1999). This *kernel-trick* removes the curse of dimensionality, ultimately allowing implicit mapping to an infinite-dimensional space. More precise introduction, although with different notation, to KFD by Mika *et al.* is in Mika et al. (1999) and in Schölkopf & Smola (2001).

There are various alternatives for the kernel function $\kappa(\cdot, \cdot)$, among which the most widely used are the polynomial kernels and the Radial Basis Function (RBF) kernel. We experimented with various kernels, and found out that the polynomial kernels do not increase the separation significantly when compared with the linear kernel, which is equivalent to the traditional FD. In other words, all low-order polynomial kernels produce a projection very similar to the first order kernel, shown in Figure 6 (e). However, the separation seems to improve with the RBF kernel

$$\kappa(u, v) = \exp\left(-\frac{||u - v||^2}{2\sigma^2}\right). \tag{9}$$

There are two parameters in the KFD projection with RBF kernel: The regularization parameter λ and the kernel width σ^2. Since there exists a lot of training data in our case, it seems to be less sensitive to the regularization parameter λ than the width σ^2. In our experiments we set the value of $\lambda = 10^{-5}$, and if the condition number of the matrix in Eq. (6) indicates that the matrix is close to singular, the value of λ is increased ten-fold until the inversion succeeds.

Figures 6 (f-g) illustrate the effect of the bandwidth parameter σ^2. Figure 6 (f) uses the bandwidth selected using the so called Silverman's rule of thumb (Silverman, 1986), widely used in kernel density estimation and defined by $\hat{\sigma}_{rot} = 1.06\hat{\sigma}_x N^{-\frac{1}{5}}$, where $\hat{\sigma}_x$ is the sample standard deviation of the data and N is the data length. In the example in Figure 6 (f) the rule of thumb gives $\sigma_{rot} = 1.37$. Figure 6 (g) on the other hand illustrates the result with fixed $\sigma = 0.5$.

It seems that the rule of thumb tends to give too large values for our problem. This can be seen from the visually improved separation which is obtained using a smaller bandwidth, $\sigma = 0.5$, whose result is shown in Figure 6 (g).

3.5 Segmentation of the grayscale image

As the final step of the wheal area segmentation, one has to threshold the grayscale projected image in order to obtain a binary segmentation. The simple approach is to use thresholding. The problem of selecting a proper threshold has been extensively studied, and, e.g., Sezgin et al. (Sezgin & Sankur, 2004) compares 40 selected methods for a set of test images. One of their conclusions is that the best performing method is different depending on the nature of the input grayscale image (e.g., text, natural scenes, etc.). Since one of our goals is to compare different grayscale projections for the wheal detection purpose, we restrict ourselves

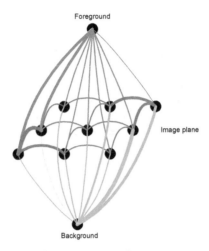

Fig. 7. The graph representation of a 3×3 image plane.

to using only one automatic threshold selection method; the most widely used Otsu method (Otsu, 1979). Without this restriction, we would be comparing all combinations of grayscale projection and thresholding techniques summing up to hundreds of combinations.

As an alternative to grayscale thresholding, we consider a newer approach, the powerful graph cut based segmentation. The idea of using graphs for solving hard optimization problems was originally discovered by Greig *et al.* (Greig et al., 1989), and extended to multilabel problems by Boykov *et al.* (Boykov et al., 2001). A fast implementation was proposed by Boykov *et al.* (Boykov & Kolmogorov, 2004), and their free implementation is widely used, and is the basis for our method, as well.

Graph cuts are a method for efficient minimization of certain energy functionals of the type

$$E[f] = \sum_{p \in \mathcal{P}} D_p(I_p) + \sum_{p,q \in \mathcal{N}} V_{p,q}(I_p, I_q), \tag{10}$$

where $D_p(f_p)$ reflects the distance from the image to be modeled (segmented in our case), and $V_{p,q}(I_p, I_q)$ is the cost assigned to labeling neighboring points differently. In a sense, using graph cuts is *regularized thresholding*, where neighboring points are encouraged to have the same label. In practice, the difference to thresholding is that the resulting labeling has fewer holes. In our case, the graph cut approach for segmentation treats the KFDA-projected grayscale image as a weighted graph, whose nodes represents the pixels and edges the connections between the neighboring pixels. An illustration of this is shown in Figure 7, which represents a 3×3 image, whose nine pixels are considered as nodes of the graph. Each pixel is connected to its closest neighbors, and additionally to two special nodes; *foreground* node and *background* node.

The graph cut method attempts to split the graph into two disconnected parts, such that the foreground and background nodes are in different partitions. The splitting is done with minimal cost, i.e., such that the sum of weights of cut nodes is as small as possible. As a result, the foreground area consists of pixels connected to the foreground node after splitting the graph. Note, that in our case an alternative graph formulation could take advantage of the known foreground and background locations: the background node could be connected only to the borders of the image (which is known to be background) and the foreground node only to the center of the image.

In order to obtain a reasonable segmentation result, the weights are determined according to the following rules. Edges connecting neighboring pixels have a weight inversely proportional to the difference of the grayscale values. This way homogeneous areas (with grayscales close to each other) have large weights and heterogeneous areas (large pixel difference) have small weights. In our case the weight of the edge between pixels p and q with grayscale intensities I_p and I_q is determined by the rule

$$V_{p,q}(I_p, I_q) = 10 \cdot \exp\left(-\frac{|I_p - I_q|}{100}\right). \tag{11}$$

This function satisfies the requirement that far away grayscale values have a small weight while close grayscales obtain a large weight. The exact exponential form and the normalization coefficients of the function were obtained through experimentation, although various other choices were almost equally effective.

The edges connecting the pixels to *foreground* and *background* nodes are determined by the grayscale value. The idea is that the brighter the pixel, the stronger the connection to the foreground node and vice versa. In our case the foreground edge weight for pixel p with intensity $I_p \in \{0, 1, \ldots, 255\}$ was determined by the rule

$$D_f(I_p) = \frac{\gamma}{255 - I_p + 1}, \tag{12}$$

and the background edge weight by the rule

$$D_b(I_p) = \frac{1 - \gamma}{I_p + 1}. \tag{13}$$

The idea is that the foreground connection would be strong, when the pixel value I_p is large (close to 255) and the background connection would be strong, when the pixel value I_p is small (close to 0).

The parameter $\gamma \in [0, 1]$ balances the edge weights and can be used for adjusting the foreground area size. There are closed form solutions for the parameter to obtain a desired the probability of a foreground pixel. However, an easier method is to use binary search over $\gamma \in [0, 1]$ to get a desired ratio of background and foreground sizes. In our case we selected the desired ratio to be equal to that of the Otsu thresholding result.

As the final step, we remove all but the largest object from the segmentation result. This is because sometimes there remain small foreground areas that are due to noise.

3.6 Using a shape model for wheal area detection

The transition from the background (the healthy skin) to the foreground (the wheal) can be quite smooth, and the KFD-projected image may contain several individual foreground

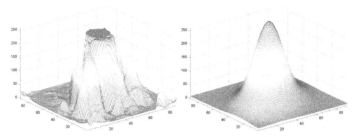

Fig. 8. Left: The grayscale projection data of the wheal in Figure 6 using KFD projection with RBF kernel and $\sigma = 1$. Right: The final result after nonlinear LS fit.

regions although the image has only one wheal. This is mostly due to the noise in the data, whose effect is greatly emphasized by the grayscale projection.

In order to increase the robustness of the segmentation, we fit a shape model for the appearance of the wheal. Since the manual measurement assumes that the wheals are ellipses, an elliptic shape model seems reasonable. Thus, the problem is to find an ellipse that divides the image into two maximally inhomogeneous areas.

Since there are an infinite amount of ellipses, we have to limit the search space somehow. This can be done by fitting a model to the grayscale projection and considering only the isosurfaces of the model. Based on Figure 6, the Gaussian surface seems an appropriate model for the spatial grayscale distribution in this case. Moreover, it suits our assumption of elliptic wheals, because the isosurfaces of the two-dimensional Gaussian are ellipses.

More specifically, the Gaussian model is defined by

$$f(\mathbf{x}; c, \mathbf{x}_0, \mathbf{\Sigma}) = c \cdot \exp\left(-(\mathbf{x} - \mathbf{x}_0)^T \mathbf{\Sigma}(\mathbf{x} - \mathbf{x}_0)\right), \tag{14}$$

where $c \in \mathbf{R}_+$ defines the scale of the Gaussian, $\mathbf{x} = (x, y)^T$ denotes the image coordinates where the the model is fitted, $\mathbf{x}_0 = (x_0, y_0)^T$ denotes the location of the peak of the Gaussian and $\mathbf{\Sigma} \in \mathbf{R}^{2 \times 2}$ is a symmetric coefficient matrix.

The least squares (LS) fit to the grayscale image data is defined by

$$\min_{c, \mathbf{\Sigma}, \mathbf{x}_0} \sum_{k=0}^{N} (z_k - f(\mathbf{x}_k; c, \mathbf{x}_0, \mathbf{\Sigma}))^2, \tag{15}$$

where z_k denotes the grayscale value at image position $\mathbf{x}_k$. Note that the data has to be preprocessed by subtracting the minimum of z_k, $k = 0, \ldots, N$, in order to avoid a constant offset term in the model.

Fitting the Gaussian is a nontrivial problem, although lot of literature on the topic exists (e.g., Brändle et al. (2000)). However, the easiest approach is to use software packages such as Matlab Optimization toolbox to find the optimal parameters.

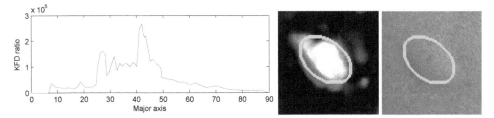

Fig. 9. Left: The KFDR as a function of the ellipse size. Center: The maximally separating ellipse overlaid on top of the corresponding KFD projection. Right: The maximally separating ellipse overlaid on top of original RGB data.

However, in order to ease the task, we first seek for an initial guess for the coefficients by taking the logarithm of the data and the model of Eq. (15):

$$\min_{c, \Sigma, x_0} \sum_{k=0}^{N} (\ln(z_k) - \ln(f(x_k; c, x_0, \Sigma)))^2 = \min_{c, \Sigma, x_0} \sum_{k=0}^{N} (\ln(z_k) + \ln c + (x - x_0)^T \Sigma (x - x_0))^2. \quad (16)$$

This makes the problem linear, and the result can be found in a closed form. However, taking the logarithm increases the importance of the smaller values, and the method essentially fits the model to the noise surrounding the wheal, not the wheal itself. Thus, the resulting solution is used only as the initial guess for the nonlinear LS problem without the logarithm. The nonlinear LS problem is then solved using Matlab Optimization toolbox.

Figure 8 shows the original grayscale data on the left, the result of logarithmic fitting in the center and the result of nonlinear iterative fitting on the right.

The isosurfaces of the Gaussian fit can be used as candidates for elliptic segmentation. As noted earlier, all the isosurfaces are cross-sections of a paraboloid and thus ellipses. Moreover, due to fitting, they most likely have the correct orientation and correct ratio of major and minor axis lengths. Thus, our next goal is to seek for the best elliptic isosurface among them all.

The definition of a good ellipse among the candidates needs some measure of separation between the segmented areas. Recent work by Harchaoui et al. (Harchaoui et al., 2008) considers using the Kernel Fisher Discriminant Ratio (KFDR) for testing the homogeneity between two sets, which coincides well with our use of KFD for grayscale projection in Section 3.2.

In other words, we test all ellipses that are cross sections of the fitted Gaussian and attempt to maximize the KFDR of Eq. (5) with respect to training sets defined by the ellipse. The situation is similar to the grayscale projection, but now we are not looking for a good classifier for the RGB data, but only assessing how well the data *could be classified*. Unlike Section 3.2, the choice of the training samples is now based on the boundaries of the ellipse to be tested.

In a sense, the KFDR homogeneity test attempts to design a classifier to separate the "inside" class and the "outside" class, and the KFDR is a natural measure how well this can be done. Note that this is not equivalent to calculating the variances directly from the projections of

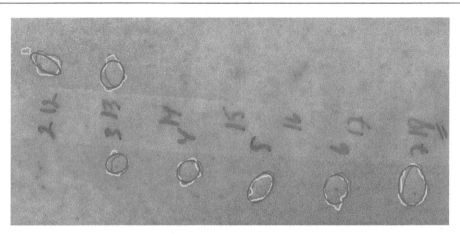

Fig. 10. An example of segmentation result. The red boundary is the result of manual segmentation, while blue and green boundaries represent the result of our method with and without the elliptic shape model, respectively. (Wheals 2, 14, 15, etc. have not been segmented, as there is no detectable allergic reaction at these sites.)

Figure 6, because the projection is calculated separately for the training sets determined by each ellipse candidate.

Sometimes the KFDR separability criterion results in very small ellipses, because a small foreground training set tends to be well separable. As an extreme example, an ellipse containing only a single pixel has extremely good separability assuming no other pixel has exactly the same RGB value. Thus, we decided to modify the criterion by multiplying it with the cardinality of the smaller training set. Alternatively, we could set a minimum size restriction for the ellipse.

An example of the separability test is shown in Figure 9. The figure shows the KFDR between the "inside" class and the "outside" class for ellipses with different radius. It can be seen that the maximal separation is obtained at radius 42, and the corresponding ellipse is illustrated in Figure 9, as well.

3.7 Experiments

The results from the described method are compared to manual wheal segmentations (made by a non-medical expert). The similarity measure used by Celebi et al. (Celebi et al., 2009) compares the *areas* of the segmentations. For our purposes, this is not an appropriate criterion, since ultimately we are interested in the major and minor axes of the wheal. The error in areas increases quadratically with respect to the axes, which is not desirable. Instead, we used the following error criterion between the computer segmentation A and the manual ground truth B:

$$E(A, B) = \frac{\sqrt{\text{Area}(\text{OR}(A, B))} - \sqrt{\text{Area}(\text{AND}(A, B))}}{\sqrt{\text{Area}(B)}}, \tag{17}$$

where $\text{OR}(A, B)$ consists of pixels segmented as foreground in A or B, and $\text{AND}(A, B)$ of foreground pixels in both A and B. Moreover, $\text{Area}(A)$ is the number of foreground pixels in A. The favourable property of Eq. (17) is that it increases linearly with respect to the error in major and minor axes. For example, it can be shown that the error measure for concentric circles with radii $r + a$ and $r - a$ are equal if the true radius is r. This is not the case with the error of (Celebi et al., 2009).

Examples of segmentation results are illustrated in Figure 10. The figure shows the result of manual segmentation (red) compared with the result of the proposed method with (blue) and without (green) the shape model. Table 2 represents the average errors with different grayscale transformations. The test data consists of seven wheals including those shown in Figure 10. The five first columns represent different KFD projections designed using training data, while in the last two columns the projection is designed in an unsupervised or *ad hoc* manner.

From the results, one can see that the $L^*a^*b^*$ color space produces the smallest errors. This is in coherence with the results of earlier studies (Nischik & Forster, 1997; Roullot et al., 2005), who have also discovered the importance of the a^* component in skin color analysis. However, the difference between color spaces is not that significant, especially when using a Gaussian kernel for the KFD. For example, in the case of Gaussian kernel with bandwidth $\sigma = 1$, all errors are close to each other, and visual inspection of the results reveals that there are no gross errors. The lesser importance of the initial color space when using the Gaussian KFD kernel is natural, because the three-dimensional data is mapped to an infinite dimensional space, where the colors are most likely separable regardless of the initial color space.

Another interesting observation is the worse than expected performance of the elliptic shape model. In many cases its use increases the error. However, this is partly due to the fact that the manually segmented wheals are not ellipses, so the elliptic model can not reach zero error even in theory. The best cases are the ones where the true wheal is ellipse-shaped with no elongated pseudopodia, e.g., the 2nd and 3rd wheals from the right in Figure 10. In all other cases the wheal shape is more irregular, and the shape model results in the largest inscribed ellipse. However, there is some randomness in the results due to the small N. We plan to

		Gaussian $(\sigma = 0.5)$	Gaussian $(\sigma = 1)$	Gaussian $(\sigma = \sigma_{rot})$	Linear kernel	2. order kernel	Celebi method	Ad hoc
With Otsu Thresh	RGB	0.3668	0.2393	0.1912	0.2567	0.2723	1.3710	1.0297
	$L^*a^*b^*$	0.2505	0.1861	0.2811	0.2382	0.2925	1.0788	0.9835
	HSV	0.2177	0.2176	0.5129	0.2733	0.2563	1.5259	0.7424
With Graph Cuts	RGB	0.3660	0.2406	0.1915	0.2545	0.2714	1.3759	1.0307
	$L^*a^*b^*$	0.2508	0.1855	0.2813	0.2364	0.2926	1.0810	0.9844
	HSV	0.2176	0.2169	0.5129	0.2714	0.2570	1.5260	0.7422
With Shape Model	RGB	0.4769	0.2479	0.2289	0.4821	0.2143	1.3588	0.4291
	$L^*a^*b^*$	0.2325	0.2388	0.2335	0.1894	0.2240	1.1731	1.4467
	HSV	0.2472	0.2300	0.7174	0.4852	0.3815	1.3465	0.8816

Table 2. The comparison of automated wheal measurement methods in terms of the error of Eq. (17). Each row defines an initial color space, each column corresponds to a grayscale transformation. The last column corresponds to a manually designed transformation based on what looks good. In the RGB case, the *Ad Hoc* transformation is the difference $G - B$, in the $L^*a^*b^*$ case it is the a^* component, and in the HSV case the H component.

study the performance with larger N and compare them with the manual results of a trained physician.

4. Conclusions

This research projects shows one possibility to automatize a simple dermatological examination. While the results obtained are not perfect, they are very promising. Automatization gives several benefits in the case of the prick test, as it eliminates the inter-observer variance and offers a way to study the immune reaction as a function of time.

The method shown above is semi-automatic in the sense that the user has to input a point close to the center of the wheal. This is not a major obstacle in practice, as the prick test can be performed so that the centers are known. Another possibility is to use some easily recognizable markings on the skin so that the centers can be found automatically.

Finding the size of a wheal is a surprisingly complicated task. The wheal edges are not sharp, and the contrast between the wheal and its surroundings is very low. The skin color is not constant, it varies significantly not only between individuals but also between different areas of the skin of an individual.

Our algorithm for determining the wheal size has several steps. First, the image is transformed into a grayscale image by using the KFD (Kernel Fisher Discriminant) projection. Although the linear kernel with the $L^*a^*b^*$ color space resulted in best results in this study, we anticipate that the flexibility of the Gaussian kernel would be useful with larger amount of patients (e.g., with different skin colors).

At this point there are two different methods for finding out the wheal size and shape. The first method segments the wheals using either straightforward thresholding or the Graph Cut method to determine which pixels in the image belong to the wheal. It seems that the performance of the segmentation approaches is equally good. The second method finds the ellipse which has the highest KFDR (Kernel Fisher Discriminant Ratio) between the pixels inside and outside of the ellipse.

It is not clear which of the methods is best in practice. The Graph Cut method gives irregular wheals, and the results are close to those obtained with manual segmentation. On the other hand, the medical practice uses one or two diameters of the wheal, and it in unclear whether or not any protruding features of the wheal should be included. Choosing between these two methods will require a large number of images, as the differences are not very large.

The images used in developing the algorithms were not of the highest quality. They were taken with a relatively old digital camera, and we earned during the process that there were significant compression artefacts in the images, which is clearly visible in the grayscale images. The use of a more modern camera without compression should reduce both compression artefacts and image noise significantly and thus improve segmentation results. This, also, is a topic for further research.

One should also note that the above methods generalize to other multichannel segmentation methods than RGB segmentation. Using alternative wavelengths might help the segmentation, and any combination of input images is possible. Another alternative is to generate artificial input channels, e.g., by filtering the RGB channels using different preprocessing methods. As the results show, there is a difference in results when using different color spaces as the input. Thus, one might anticipate that adding artificial channels produced by different filters may also be of help in the segmentation.

5. References

Adobe Systems Incorporated (2009). *Digital Negative Specification version 1.3.0.0.*

Boykov, Y. & Kolmogorov, V. (2004). An experimental comparison of min-cut/max-flow algorithms for energy minimization in vision, *Pattern Analysis and Machine Intelligence, IEEE Transactions on* 26(9): 1124 –1137.

Boykov, Y., Veksler, O. & Zabih, R. (2001). Fast approximate energy minimization via graph cuts, *Pattern Analysis and Machine Intelligence, IEEE Transactions on* 23(11): 1222 –1239.

Brändle, N., Chen, H., Bischof, H. & Lapp, H. (2000). Robust parametric and semi-parametric spot fitting for spot array images, *ISMB-2000 8th Intl. Conf. on Intell. Syst. for Mol. Biol.*, pp. 1–12.

Celebi, M., Iyatomi, H. & Schaefer, G. (2009). Contrast enhancement in dermoscopy images by maximizing a histogram bimodality measure, *16th IEEE Int. Conf. on Image Proc. (ICIP)*, pp. 2601–2604.

Coffin, D. (2011). dcraw source code.
    URL: *http://www.cybercom.net/ dcoffin/dcraw/dcraw.c*

ECMA (2009). *Technical Report TR/98 JPEG File Interchange Format (JFIF)*.

Farrell, J., Xiao, F. & Kavusi, S. (2006). Resolution and light sensitivity tradeoff with pixel size, *SPIE Electronic Imaging '2006 Conference*.

Fisher, R. (1936). The use of multiple measurements in taxonomic problems, *Annals of Eugenics* 7: 179–188.

Gomez, D., Butakoff, C., Ersboll, B. & Stoecker, W. (2008). Independent histogram pursuit for segmentation of skin lesions, *IEEE Trans. Biomed. Eng.* 55(1): 157–161.

Gomez, D. D., Clemmensen, L. H., ll, B. K. E. & Carstensen, J. M. (2007). Precise acquisition and unsupervised segmentation of multi-spectral images, *Comp. Vis. and Image Understanding* 106(2-3): 183–193.

Greig, D. M., Porteous, B. T. & Seheult, A. H. (1989). Exact maximum a posteriori estimation for binary images, *Journal of the Royal Statistical Society.* 51(2): pp. 271–279.

Haahtela, T., Petman, L., Järvenpaa, S. & Kautiainen, H. (2010). [Quality to allegy testing and interpretation of its results], *Duodecim* 126: 529–535.

Harchaoui, Z., Bach, F. & Eric, M. (2008). Testing for homogeneity with kernel fisher discriminant analysis, *Adv. in Neural Inf. Proc. Syst. 20*, MIT Press, Cambridge, MA, pp. 609–616.

Hecht, E. (1987). *Optics*, 2nd edn, Addison-Wesley, chapter 10.2.6.

Huttunen, H., Ryynänen, J.-P., Forsvik, H., Voipio, V. & Kikuchi, H. (2011). Kernel fisher discriminant and elliptic shape model for automatic measurement of allergic reactions, *in* A. Heyden & F. Kahl (eds), *Image Analysis*, Vol. 6688 of *Lecture Notes in Computer Science*, Springer Berlin / Heidelberg, pp. 764–773.

Meinert, R., Frischer, T., Karmaus, W. & Kuehr, J. (1994). Influence of skin prick test criteria on estimation of prevalence and incidence of allergic sensitization in children, *Allergy* 49: 526–532.

Mika, S., Ratsch, G., Weston, J., Scholkopf, B. & Mullers, K. (1999). Fisher discriminant analysis with kernels, *Proc. IEEE Neural Netw. for Signal Process. IX*, pp. 41–48.

NEMA (2011). *Digital Imaging and Communications in Medicine (DICOM)*.

Nischik, M. & Forster, C. (1997). Analysis of skin erythema using true-color images, *IEEE Trans. Med. Imag.* 16(6): 711–716.

Oppenheimer, J., Durham, S. & Nelson, H. (2011). Allergy diagnostic testing.
URL: *http://www.worldallergy.org/professional/allergic_diseases_center/allergy_diagnostic/*

Otsu, N. (1979). A threshold selection method from gray-level histograms, *Systems, Man and Cybernetics, IEEE Transactions on* 9(1): 62–66.

Roullot, E., Autegarden, J.-E., Devriendt, P. & Leynadier, F. (2005). Segmentation of erythema from skin photographs for assisted diagnosis in allergology, *Pattern Rec. and Image Anal.*, Vol. 3687 of *Lecture Notes in Computer Science*, Springer Berlin / Heidelberg, pp. 754–763.

Santos, R., Mlynek, A., Lima, H., Martus, P. & M, M. (2008). Beyond flat wheals: validation of a three-dimensional imaging technology that will improve skin allergy research, *Clin. Exp. Dermatol.* 33(6): 772–775.

Schölkopf, B. & Smola, A. J. (2001). *Learning with Kernels: Support Vector Machines, Regularization, Optimization, and Beyond*, 1st edn, The MIT Press.

Seibert, S. M., King, T. S., Kline, D., Mende, C. & Craig, T. (2011). Reliability of skin test results when read at different time points, *Allergy Asthma Proc* 32: 203–205.

Sezgin, M. & Sankur, B. (2004). Survey over image thresholding techniques and quantitative performance evaluation, *Journal of Electronic Imaging* 13(1): 146–168.

Silverman, B. (1986). *Density Estimation for Statistics and Data Analysis*, Chapman-Hall.

Viggiano, J. A. S. (2004). Comparison of the accuracy of different white balancing algorithms as quantified by their color constancy, *Sensors and Camera Systems for Scientific, Industrial, and Digital Photography Applications V: Proceedings of the SPIE, volume 5301*.

Wöhrl, S., Vigl, K., Binder, M., Stingl, G. & Prinz, M. (2006). Automated measurement of skin prick tests: an advance towards exact calculation of wheal size, *Experimental Dermatology* 15(2): 119–124.

7

Temporal and Spatial Resolution Limit Study of Radiation Imaging Systems: Notions and Elements of Super Resolution

Faycal Kharfi, Omar Denden and Abdelkader Ali
Neutron Radiography Department/Nuclear Research Centre of Birine,
Algeria

1. Introduction

The characterization of a radiographic imaging system response in terms of spatial and temporal resolution is a very important task that allows the determination of this system limits and capability in the investigation and visualization of very fast processes and of very small spatial details. Thus, the spatial and temporal resolutions limits are very important parameters of an imaging system that should be taken into consideration before the examination of any static object or dynamic process. The objectives of this chapter are the study and determination of radiation imaging system response in terms of spatial and temporal resolution limits and the application of super-resolution (SR) methods and algorithms to improve the resolution of captured neutron images or video sequences. The imaging system taken as example and being studied is a high-sensitivity neutron imaging system composed of an LiF+ZnS scintillator screen (0.25 mm thick), an Aluminium-coated mirror and a Charged Coupled Device (CCD) camera (2×10^{-5} lx at F1.4).

The proposed approach and procedure for spatial resolution and system response determination is based on the establishment of the Modulation Transfer Function (MTF) using standard slanted edge method with the most appropriate algorithm selected according to previous studies. Temporal resolution study and characterization is a more complicated task that requires well understanding of video sequence capture process. In this chapter the limit of temporal resolution allowing minimum motion blur is studied according to a selected dynamic process capture and examination under different exposure conditions. Due to physical constraints (low L/D collimation ratio and weakness of neutron beam) and instrumental limitations of the used imaging system, the captured images or neutron video can be of low resolution. To overcome this limitation, super resolution methods and algorithms are applied to improve space-time resolution. The most used methods are: the iterative variation regularization methods, the methods based on information combing from low resolution frames, the methods of motion compensation and the SR filters.

All the mentioned procedures and approaches above are still available for any similar X-ray or Gamma imaging systems based on the same examination principle of radiation transmission. These methods and procedures are used to judge the ability of such imaging system to produce spatial (internal details) and temporal (dynamic) properties of any moving object or dynamic process under examination.

This chapter is divided into three main parts. In the first one, the MTF determination is presented by proposing an accurate edge identification method and a line spread function under-sampling problem-resolving procedure. The proposed method and procedure were integrated into a MatLab code. The source code can be requested to the author of this chapter. In the second section, induced motion blur when a moving object is examined is studied as a function of video capture frame rate. This approach allows us to determine suitable exposure conditions and therefore the temporal resolution that enables an optimum image quality with minimum motion blur and noise and acceptable contrast. Finally, notions and elements of super resolution are presented in the last section with some interesting examples. The examples of resolution enhancement presented in this chapter concern a water flow process examined with the described neutron imaging system. Experimental results on real data sets confirm the electiveness of the proposed procedures and methodologies. All experiments were performed at the neutron radiography facility and laboratory of the Algerian Es-Salam research reactor.

2. Temporal and spatial resolution limit study of a radiographic imaging system

2.1 Spatial resolution limit determination

Spatial resolution limit is a very important parameter of an imaging system that should be taken into consideration before the examination of any object. In this first chapter part, we propose the determination of a neutron imaging system's response in terms of spatial resolution. The proposed procedure is based on establishment of the Modulation Transfer Function (MTF). The imaging system being studied is based on a high sensitivity CCD neutron camera ($2x10^{-5}$ lx at f1.4). The neutron beam used is issued from the horizontal beam port (H.6) of the Algerian Es-Salam research reactor. Our contribution in this field is in the MTF determination by proposing an accurate edge identification method and a line spread function undersampling problem-resolving procedure. These methods and procedure are integrated into a MatLab program (code). The methods, procedures and approaches proposed in this work are available for any other neutron imaging system and allow the judgment of the ability of a neutron imaging system to produce spatial properties of any object under examination.

The Modulation Transfer Function is a common metric used to quantify the spatial resolution in the system response. Traditional methods for MTF measurements were initially designed for devices forming consecutive images that can give erroneous MTF results, due to the fact that the sampling of digital devices is not properly taken into consideration. The slanted edge method, which is analogous to the impulse response determination for an electronic system, is a common technique used for the measurement of an accurate MTF because it requests a relatively simple experimental arrangement. In neutron imaging, this technique consists of imaging a thin and sharp slanted-edge onto the detector. The edge target must be made from a strong neutron absorbing material such as Gadolinium. The ISO 12233 standard presents the general methodology for MTF measurement based on this technique (Jespers et al., 1976). An interesting algorithms comparison work used for MTF measurement based on slanted-edge technique is presented in reference (Samei, et al., 2005).

The first goal of this chapter is to apply this methodology and to overcome some under-sampling and slanted edge identification difficulties, to establish an accurate MTF curve to be used for the determination of the system response and the effective spatial resolution limit of the neutron imaging system being studied (Domanus, 1992). The components of this imaging system are placed in an aluminium light tight box (175 mm x 105 mm x 120 mm) positioned vertically by a holder fixed on the metallic table of the neutron radiography facility. The camera consists of a 250 μm thick LiF–ZnS scintillator, a front-surfaced Al/SiO$_2$ mirror and a high sensitivity Sony CCD camera with 2×10^{-5} lx (at f1.4) as the minimum required illumination (Figure 1). It has a bit depth of 8 bits. The camera was manufactured and assembled by "Neutron Optics", France (www.NeutronOptics.com). According to the manufacturer specifications, this system has a maximum intrinsic spatial resolution of 200 μm (171.5 μm calculated). All necessary experiments were performed at the neutron radiography facility of the Es-Salam research reactor (Kharfi, et al., 2005). To achieve this task, a MatLab code was developed.

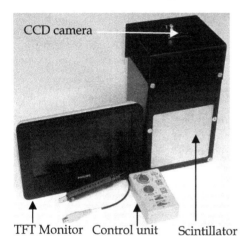
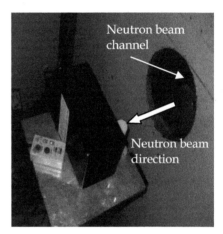

Fig. 1. The neutron imaging system studied.

2.1.1 Theoretical approach and experimental procedures

An MTF is the spatial frequency response of an imaging system. It characterizes the image sharpness produced by such systems. There are many methods allowing the determination of this function. One of them, based on analysis of a slanted-edge image of a suitable target, is used in this work. The methodology followed is described by the ISO 12233 standard. The advantages of this method are the simplicity and the minimal arrangement required during the experimental phase. The MTF curve is calculated from the Line Spread Function (LSF). LSF is computed by taking the first derivative of the Edge Spread Function (ESF). The ESF represent the pixel response in terms of gray levels along a line(s) perpendicular to the edge. Fourier transformation and subsequent normalization procedures are then applied to the LSF to compute the MTF (Estribau & Magnau, 2004). The MTF describes the amplitude or relevant contrast by which sine functions of different frequencies are moderated by an imaging system. It gives a measurement of the degradation when transferring data of the "physical" object to becoming an image. An MTF value of 1 indicates that the full amplitude is transferred by the imaging system, while a MTF value of 0 indicates that no signal at all is transferred. In neutron imaging, an object can be represented in spatial domain by a 3D distribution function of neutron attenuation coefficients, a distribution of materials densities or any suitable distribution, and in the frequency domain by a distribution of frequencies that represent fine (high frequency) and coarse (low frequency) details. A good MTF must be sensitive to any change in the system input frequencies of the target or the examined object. For our case, the MTF deviation from the ideal value of 1 is due to: 1) the scintillator/mirror/CCD detector combination, 2) the geometrical exposure conditions, especially the beam divergent angle and the collimation ratio (L/D), and 3) the scattered neutrons. Indeed, a thorough understanding of exposure geometry and conditions, object or target input frequencies transferring and system response theory are very important for the establishment and correct analysis of the MTF obtained.

The slanted-edge method consists of imaging an edge onto the detector, slightly tilted with regard to the rows (or the columns) (Reichenbach et al., 1991). A slanted oriented edge, therefore, allows the horizontal Spatial Frequency Response (SFR) of the system to be obtained. In this case, the response of each pixel line across the edge gives a different ESF, due to the phasing of the pixel centre locations as the edge location changes with each row of pixels. These ESF are under-sampled but it is possible to mathematically increase the sampling rate by projecting data along the edge.

The main steps of the procedure used in this chapter to establish the MTF are the following:

1. Neutron radiography of the target, scanning of all lines and gray levels averaging and adjusting according to open beam and dark current images. This produces the ESF, also called the edge profile function. The distances in pixels are corrected depending on the angle of the edge slope. The edge should be sloped for smooth averaging.
2. Taking the first derivative from the ESF to generate the LSF.
3. Applying a discrete Fourier transform to the LSF. This produces the MTF.

In this chapter, a MATLAB code based on the Slanted-edge method was developed. This program gives users an accurate edge identification application and a procedure for sampling improvement and ESF construction, Line Spread Function computation and MTF determination and plotting with the possibility of changing input data such as region of interest (ROI) dimensions (m lines, n pixels) and pixel size (display monitor). The output data can be directly displayed or saved in Excel formats. The most important functions of this program are:

1. Edge Identification: The initial task in MTF measurement is the identification of suitable edges for analysis. According to detection pixels grid vertical or horizontal axes, the edge must be oriented with a minimum tilt angle for an along scan or cross scan MTF determination (Figure 2). This minimum angle is required as well as sufficient length for suitable ESF construction (Kohm, 2004). It can be easily proven that at least two horizontal pixels should go through along the target edge to guarantee that sub-pixels will be placed on uniform grid after projection for ESF construction (Figure 2). In our case, the target length is 4.5 cm (~240 pixels), thus the minimum required angle is 0.47°. As the orientation of the angle changes, the resolution varies also, becoming either coarser or finer. The candidate edge must also meet contrast and noise requirements for selection (Jain, 1989). This is because, the MTF value obtained with high contrast edge target is always

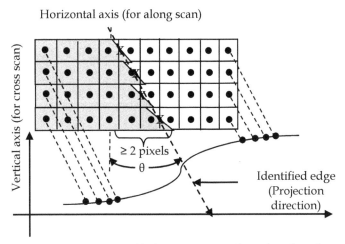

Fig. 2. Sampling improvement by profile line projection after edge identification (for clarity just first and last points are presented).

larger than that obtained with lower contrast target for a given spatial frequency; therefore, when the MTF of a system is presented, the contrast of the line pair used to measure the MTF should be given (Williams, 2004). In our case the maximum contrast of the target image obtained is 37.68% calculated by Michelson formula (Michelson, 1927). Noise can also affect contrast transfer and overall detection capability of imaging system. Therefore, the measured MTF by the used slanted edge method will be biased. The use of multiple lines of profile (m lines) for data improving can reduce the source of error but will usually not eliminate it completely (Burns, 2000). For practical purpose, different tilt angles (θ) varying from 1° to 5° were tested allowing relatively high and low resolution ESF generation. Before starting using our program for edge identification and MTF establishment, a Sobel edge detection operator followed by thresholding and binary morphological processing (filtering) is used to identify edge with the proper (real) orientation (θ_p) for a verification purpose (Figure 3). A value of θ_p of 0.95° was found for a tested tilt angle (θ) of 1° that prove the good target fixing and correct geometrical exposure conditions. After this verification, the image of the target obtained is first read and displayed in a suitable format (.bmp) by the developed program. The edge locations were accurately determined for each lines of profile of the selected ROI. An initial estimate of the location and angle of the edge is then determined by performing a least squares regression of selected points along the edge. The approximate equation of the identified edge average straight line is given by:

$$Y = ax + b \tag{1}$$

With:

$$a = \frac{\left(\sum_{i=1}^{m} x_i y_i\right) - \left(\sum_{i=1}^{m} x_i\right)\left(\sum_{i=1}^{m} y_i\right)}{m\left(\sum_{i=1}^{m} x_i^2\right) - \left(\sum_{i=1}^{m} x_i\right)^2}, b = \frac{\left(\sum_{i=1}^{m} x_i^2\right)\left(\sum_{i=1}^{m} y_i\right) - \left(\sum_{i=1}^{m} x_i\right)\left(\sum_{i=1}^{m} x_i y_i\right)}{m\left(\sum_{i=1}^{m} x_i^2\right) - \left(\sum_{i=1}^{m} x_i\right)^2} \tag{2}$$

Where:
m = number of data (line number of the selected ROI);
X_i = row number;
Y_i = sub-pixel edge position.

Fig. 3. Result of Sobel edge detection operator followed by thresholding and binary morphological processing (filtering) to identify the proper edge orientation ($\theta_p \sim 0.95°$, for $\theta = 1°$).

2. Sampling improvement and Edge Spread Function Construction: The ESF is the system response to the input of an ideal edge. As the output of the system is a sampled image, the fidelity of the edge spread function using a single line of image data is insufficient for MTF analysis. Aliasing due to under sampling in the camera, along with phase effects and the angle of the actual edge with respect to the sampling grid will cause variable results for a single line. The phase effects and edge angle may be exploited, however, to provide a high fidelity measurement of the ESF. Construction of the ESF is graphically represented in Figure 2. The edge is identified in the image as described above. A line is then constructed perpendicular to the edge. For a given line of image data, each point around the edge transition is projected onto the perpendicular line. This process is then repeated for each subsequent line of image data along the edge. The difference in sub-pixel location of the edge with respect to the sampling grid for different lines in the image results in differences in the location of the projected data point onto the perpendicular. This yields a high fidelity representation of the system response to an edge. Small changes in the edge angle used during construction of the super-sampled edge affect the quality of the resulting ESF. The angle is systematically adjusted by small increments of 0.25° around the initial estimate (5°) which is equivalent to one pixel shift of one edge extremity in left or right direction for an along scan. The resulting curve fit (equation) is used to refine the edge angle estimate for the final ESF construction. After the individual ESF data points have been determined, the data must be conditioned and re-sampled to a fixed interval. In general, the angle of the edge with respect to the sampling grid does not produce uniformly distributed data points along the perpendicular to the edge. Also, with longer edges, many data points may be located in close proximity to one another. Suitable 3 order polynomial data fitting is used to re-sample the data to uniformly spaced sample points. More sophisticated fitting algorithm is presented in reference (Cleveland, 1985).

To avoid data interference when performing projection operation, it is important that the selected tilt angle θ (projection angle) obeys the following condition:

$$an\ \theta \geq \frac{P_w}{N_{pl}P_h} \tag{3}$$

Where: P_w is the detected pixel width, P_h is the detected pixel height and N_{pl} is the number of selected profile lines.

The slanted-edge target used is a 25 μm thick foil of Gadolinium which is a highly neutron absorbing material allowing the production of suitable images with the necessary contrast between dark and light parts (edge). The used tilt angles are: 1° for the Sobel edge detection test and 5° for the MTF determination. To check the dependence between tilt angle and MTF result, some others target tilt angles, of values less than 10°, were tested.

The main characteristics of the neutron imaging system studied are presented in the following table (table.1).

Detector element	Sony ICX419ALL, ½ inch interline transfer CCD image sensor
Number of pixels	752(H) x 582 (V), 512x512 used
Unit cell size	8.6 μm x 8.3 μm
Minimum illumination	0.00002 lx. F1.4
Shutter speed or frames rate	Hi: 1/50, 1/125, 1/250, 1/500, 1/1000, 1/2000 sec
	LO: 1, 2, 4, 8 , 16, 32, 64, 128, 256 frame(s)
Manual gain control	8-38 dB
Dynamic range	Relatively Wide at standard imaging conditions
Bit depth	8 bits (255 levels)
Neutron Scintillator	250 μm LiF –ZnS, green emission (~520nm)
Mirror	Front-surfaced Al/SiO$_2$-mirror; optical flatness 2λ/25mm; reflectivity 94%
Signal to noise ratio	52 dB

Table 1. Main characteristics of the neutron imaging system studied.

Neutron radiography image were captured at the neutron radiograph facility of Es-Salam research reactor under neutron beam intensity of 1.5×10^6 n/cm^2/s and with a collimation ratio (L/D) of ~125. The exposure time to the neutron beam was 15 seconds. Selected camera gain was 18 dB. After target image capture, the developed code performs the following operations for MTF computation and plotting:

1. Target image reading in suitable format:
2. ROI selection, 240 lines x110 pixels were chosen from the image of the target. The main criteria for ROI selection are: 1) the width (n pixels) of the ROI must perfectly cover the edge area; 2) the length of the ROI (m lines) should be selected as long as possible to ensure the reduction of noise and low-frequency MTF estimation errors.
3. Edge identification and estimation of the real tilt angle. Edge positions were determined on a line-by-line (ESFs) basis using pixel profile information. For each single blurred line of profile (ESF) a simple digital differentiation is applied to detect maximum slope. The sub-pixel edge points are determined by fitting a cubic polynomial equation to the edge data using four values around the maximum slope point. Then, the zero crossing location of the second derivative of the polynomial coefficients indicates the curve inflection point,

which is assumed as the sub-pixel edge location. Finally, all the ESFs sub-pixel edge locations are forced to be a straight line by assuming that the edge is a straight line. This is done by fitting a line through the sub-pixel edge locations obtained from the previous step and then declaring the actual edge locations to be on the line. The least-squares approach for finding a straight line involves determining the best approximating line when the squared error of the sum of squares of the differences between the edge points on the approximating line and the given edge point values is minimized. All these operations are performed automatically by the developed program

4. Sampling improvement by determination of sub-sampling factor and ESF generation using data projection technique on an orthogonal line to the detected edge. Before data projection, the aligned edge data of every line of profile (ESF) taken from the ROI of the image target is interpolated with a cubic splines. Then all the ESFs are splined using the function spline.m of MATLAB. And finally, the averaged of splined ESFs is determined;

5. ESF data selection between 10% and 90% around edge area in the interval between maximum and minimum gray levels values (Fig.6 (b)) to avoid unnecessary frequencies considering when applying FFT;

6. Fitting a 3 order polynomial equation to average ESF data;

7. Numerical differentiation of fitted ESF curve allowing the determination of LSF;

8. Fast Fourier Transform of LSF with the application of Hamming FFT-window;

9. MTF plotting after normalization of FFT magnitude.

2.1.2 Example of practical application and experimental results

In order to characterize the imaging system being studied, the proposed procedure and developed code were used. The effective spatial resolution was determined for a recommended MTF value of 0.1 (*MTF10*). MTF10 is a value corresponding to the average human eye's separation power (resolution). Another very interesting MTF characteristic is MTF50 corresponding to a value of 0.5 of MTF (Nyquist Frequency) that provides the limit between an under-sampled and poor displayed image (very low frequencies) and an optimally sampled and well-displayed image (medium and high frequencies). The neutron image obtained of the examined edge target is shown in figure 4. Figure 5 represents the main window (screen shot) of the developed program used for MTF computation. The spatial resolution limit (R_l) of our system is calculated in mm by the following expression:

$$R_l = \frac{1\,[\mathrm{lp}]}{2\,\mathrm{MTF10}[\frac{\mathrm{lp}}{\mathrm{mm}}]} \tag{4}$$

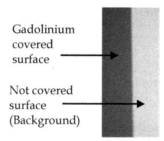

Gadolinium covered surface

Not covered surface (Background)

Fig. 4. Target neutron radiograph.

MTF Determination Program -Slanted-Edge Method-

File name: target1 .bmp

pixel size (mm):   0.2

Calculation basis: ⊙ From a single line   ○ From a Surface (ROI)

number of lines: 1   + add   left   1   high   1

    width   20   high   30

Recalculate

Replot MTF   5   ☐ Plot on the same graph

Data Saving in Excel Format

ESF: ESF_1   .xls   Save

LSF: LSF_1   .xls   Save

MTF: MTF_1   .xls   Save

Fig. 5. Screen shot of the developed MatLab program (code).

Results for the main steps of MTF determination performed by the developed program such as edge identification, profile line superposition and interpolation (ESFs) and data projection by SPLINE function are presented in figures 6(a) and 6(b).

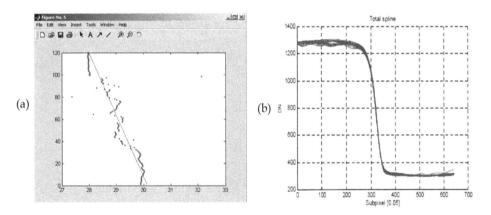

Fig. 6. (a) Example of edge identification by the developed code: after original image pixel decomposing into small intervals (polynomial fit steps), accurate edge location is detected in each horizontal line of profile across the edge and an average straight line of all detected locations is determined (least-squares) allowing thus data projection to improve ESF sampling (SPline), (b) Superposed profile lines using SPLINE function of MatLab.

Finally, the proposed code plots the MTF of the studied imaging system (Figure 7). The analysis of this MTF curve allows the characterization of spatial response of this system and the determination of spatial resolution limit.

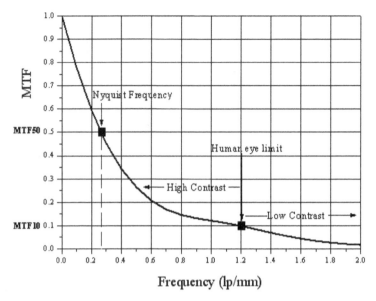

Fig. 7. MTF of the studied neutron imaging system.

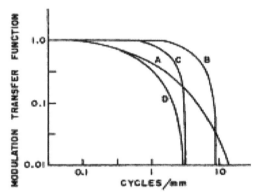

Fig. 8. MTF curves for components of a radiographic imaging system and the composite MTF for the entire system introduced for comparison purpose. A: MTF for the screen-film combination, B: MTF for a 1 mm focal spot with 90 cm between the focal spot and the object and 10 cm between object and film, C: MTF for 0.3 mm motion of the object during exposure, D: Composite MTF for the entire imaging system (Hendee & Ritlenour 2002).

When critically examining the obtained MTF, the following remarks and conclusions can be drawn:

1.   The interesting and best exploited region of MTF is in the interval between the Nyquist frequency and the human eye's resolution. We can see that the MTF curve obtained

drop rapidly in this region. This is not a good characteristic of the imaging system studied because it allows a fair contrast image display when compared to other imaging systems with MTF dropping gradually (Figure 8). The CCD camera, in such a case, presents optimum separation ability (resolution) and, in term of gray levels (contrast), it reproduces fairly the image of the target.

2. The spatial resolution limit at MTF10 that correspond to an MTF of 0.1 is equal to 1.2 lp^1/mm. This value is equivalent to 416 µm (according to equation 6) and is a very significant and an effective one because it is greater than the value of the intrinsic spatial resolution of ~200 µm of the studied imaging system. Deviation from the intrinsic resolution is due to many reasons and factors that are the following:

   1. The geometric properties of the neutron radiography facility: In our case, two parameters are dominant:

      a. The L/D neutron collimation ration (~125): for a practical case of Objetc-to-detector distance (L_f) of 5 cm, the induced geometrical Unsharpness ($Ug=L_f/(L/D)$) due to the beam spread when a point is projected at the same edge position is equal to 400µm.

      b. The scintillator thickness: for scintillator-based converter system, the first source of blur is spreading of emitted light within the scintillator material. The spreading is determined by the material's thickness and by the design of the scintillator in terms of its crystal structure and its neutron absorptive and light emission properties.

      Despite all these constraints, the geometric blurring can be minimized by reducing the object-to-image detector distance as much as possible (e.g., contact), and by increasing the collimator inlet aperture-to-object distance (L) to a suitable level not affecting the neutron beam intensity considerably.

   2. The imaging technique: indeed indirect-conversion method of the used image detector can scatter light over several pixels, further limiting the effective resolution of the system, more so than indicated by pixel size alone (intrinsic resolution).

   3. Optical properties: the intrinsic resolution can often be degraded by other factors which introduce blurring of the image, such as improper focusing and light reflection by the mirror.

However, one cannot isolate spatial resolution effects on neutron image quality from effects due to quantum mottle and electronic noise under typical digital image acquisition conditions.

2.2 Temporal resolution

2.2.1 Temporal resolution estimation

The temporal resolution is determined by the frame rate and by the exposure-time of the camera. These limit the maximal speed of dynamic events that can be well captured by the neutron camera. Rapid dynamic events that occur faster than the frame rate of CCD cameras are not visible (or else captured incorrectly) in the recorded video sequences. There are two typical visual effects in video sequences which are caused by very fast motion (Shechtman,

---

[1] lp : line pairs or cycle.

2005). One effect (motion blur) is caused by the exposure-time of the camera and the other effect (motion aliasing) is due to the temporal sub-sampling introduced by the frame rate of the camera. In our case of neutron imaging, only motion blur is of interest. It occurs when the camera integrates the light coming from the scene (scintillator) during the exposure time in order to generate each frame. As a result, fast moving objects produce a noted blur along their trajectory, often resulting in distorted or unrecognizable object shapes. The faster the object moves, the stronger this effect is, especially if the trajectory of the moving object is not linear (Shetchman et al., 2002). To quantify this motion blur and therefore to determine the temporal resolution limit, we proceed as follows: the neutron imaging video of a rotating cadmium indicator is captured for different rotational speeds (0.0017, 0.45, 1.2 and 1.65 RPS[2]) and different frame rates (Figure 9). The indicator used is a thin 7.9 mm wide cadmium blade. It was put into rotational motion by a speed controlled electrical motor. Video sequences (Vid. Seq.) for different indicator rotational speeds are captured under the following conditions (table 2):

	Frame rates (fps[3])	Neutron beam intensity	Camera Gain	Exposure time (s)
Vid. Seq.1	12.5	1.5×10^6 n/cm^2/s	22 dB	90'
Vid. Seq.2	25	1.5×10^6 n/cm^2/s	22 dB	90'
Vid. Seq.3	50	1.5×10^6 n/cm^2/s	22 dB	90'
Vid. Seq.4	125	1.5×10^6 n/cm^2/s	22 dB	90'
Vid. Seq.5	250	1.5×10^6 n/cm^2/s	38 dB	90'

Table 2. Experimental video sequences capture conditions.

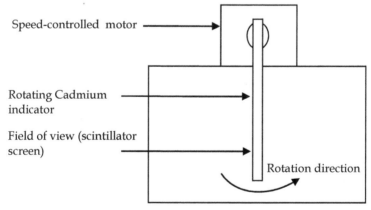

Fig. 9. Experimental arrangement for induced motion blurs characterisation.

The video sequences obtained are examined with suitable image processing and analysis software (Image J). The used CCD neutron camera integrates light coming from the scintillator screen during the exposure time in order to generate each frame. The software

---

[2] RPS : rounds per second.

[3] fps: frames per second.

enables the calculation of the motion blur B using equation (5) for each video sequence obtained. The motion blur in this case is considered as the width (in pixels) of the shade involved behind the rotating indicator appearing in each frame. This width is measured at the middle of the indication on a selected frame. The data obtained allows us to determine the effective limits of temporal resolution for each rotational speed.

$$B = I_{wi} - I_{wr} \left[\frac{L_f}{L} \left(1 - \frac{D}{I_{wr}} \right) + 1 \right] \tag{5}$$

where: I_{wr} is the real indicator width (7.9mm), I_{wi} is the indicator width measured on the obtained image, L_f is the distance between the indicator position and the scintillator screen (10.5 mm), L is the distance between the collimator inlet aperture and the indicator position (2500.5 mm), D is the collimator inlet aperture diameter (20 mm).

2.2.2 Experimental results

Selected frame from captured video sequences is presented in figure 10. Preliminary analysis of the video sequences obtained shows that the temporal resolution is affected principally by motion blur and not by motion-based aliasing.

Fig. 10. Selected frame showing the indicator position and motion blur width taken from selected video sequence captured with a frame rates of 12.5 fps and for a cadmium indicator's rotation speed of 0.45 RPS.

Motions blur variation as a function of frame rate is presented in figure 11. Graphs 1 and 2 correspond to indication rotation speeds of 0.45 and 1.2 RPS respectively.

On graphs 1 and 2, we can easily verify that motion blur decrease when the frame rate is increased up to critical values where it became constant. It was observed that the critical points are located at 12.5, 50, 125 and 250 fps on the frame rate axis for, respectively, 0.0017, 0.45, 1.2 and 1.65 RPS of the cadmium indicator rotation speeds. These critical points correspond to the temporal resolution limits that retain motion blur at a minimum although with low image dynamic range. Results of temporal resolution limits for different rotational speeds are shown in figure 12.

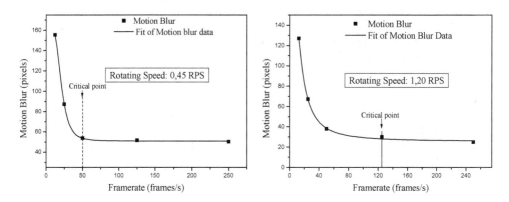

Fig. 11. Motion blurs variation of video sequences in function of frame rates for two rotation speeds of the cadmium indicator.

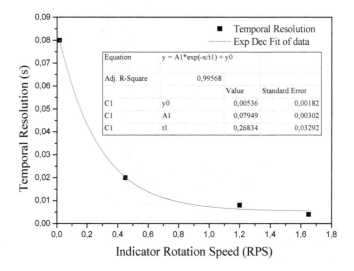

Fig. 12. Temporal resolution limits as a function of indicator rotation speed. The temporal resolution limit allowing optimum image quality in term of motion blur, with, certainly a low dynamic range, presented in this figure are for specific exposure and image capture conditions, namely: a neutron beam intensity of 1.5×10^6 n/cm^2/s, a camera signal gain of 22 dB and 38 dB (last point).

As we can see in figure 11, the temporal resolution limit is closely related to the indicator rotational speed. These values give an idea about the optimal frame rate that must be selected to avoid motion blur but not necessarily the most suitable for optimum frame exposure. With low frame exposure contrast and dynamic range can be seriously affected especially when the neutron beam intensity is low. Finally, it's very important to mention that the video sequence captured are, relatively, not rich in terms of gray levels digitalization and contrast because of the limited dynamic range and bit depth (8 bits) of the imaging system being studied. In this work, it is obvious that, the image quality is analyzed and judged regarding to the performance of the imaging system used for neutron video capture. In order to improve the video image quality it is recommended to increase the neutron beam intensity at the sample level to the maximum and to use a CCD camera with a high bit depth (+14 bits).

3. Criteria for best video capture results and application of super resolution in neutron imaging

Dynamic process imaging using a neutron beam is a very powerful and interesting investigative tool as far as light materials, elements and substances such hydrogen, water lubricants and some other relevant materials are concerned. The neutron imaging system that is most utilised is based on a CCD camera (charged coupled device) and scintillator screen. Because of the complexity and large number of operations necessary for capturing dynamic processes with any neutron digital imaging system (neutron camera), specific optimum experimental conditions and procedural accuracy are required. The sequence of events required to capture a single image with a full-frame CCD camera system is summarized in reference (SIT Technical Note, 1994).

In neutron imaging with CCD-based neutron camera, there are several camera operating parameters that modify the readout stage of image acquisition and have an impact on image quality (Spring, K. R. et al., www.microscopyu.com/articles/digitalimaging/ccdintro.html). The two most important ones are the frame rate (FRM) and the gain (G). The frame rate (also referred to as the readout rate) of most scientific-grade CCD cameras is adjustable. The maximum achievable rate is a function of the processing speed of the camera electronics, which reflects the time required to digitize a single pixel. Applications aimed at tracking rapid kinetic processes require fast readout and frame rates (FRM) in order to achieve adequate temporal resolution. In certain situations, a video rate of 30 frames per second or higher is necessary. A second camera acquisition factor, which can affect image quality because it modifies the CCD readout process, is the electronic gain (G) of the camera system. The gain adjustment of a digital CCD camera system defines the number of accumulated photoelectrons that determine each gray level step distinguished by the readout electronics, and is typically applied at the analogue-to-digital conversion step.

In this work, video sequence quality in terms of contrast, resolution and noise are studied and the most suitable conditions for the flow process examination are determined as a function of the neutron beam intensity. The second objective of this work is the application of a post acquisition super resolution (SR) processing procedures to improve the quality of the neutron video obtained. The neutron imaging system used is the same as described before.

3.1 Neutron video capture conditions study

According to previous work results, it was demonstrated that the optimum acquisition parameters for a water flow process capture are respectively: 12.5 fps as a capture frame rate (display 29.97 fps, MPEG-1 format) and a selected value of 22dB as a signal gain for the case of the imaging system being used (Kharfi et al, 2011). In this work the captured video images have been analyzed in terms of contrast, noise and resolution according to the neutron beam intensity. This is to check the effect of the neutron beam intensity on the image quality. The quantification of contrast, noise and resolution of the neutron video captured is based on histogram and edge profile analysis. Indeed, understanding image histograms is probably the single most important element in the analysis of images or video sequences from a digital CCD camera. A histogram can tell us whether or not the image has been properly exposed, and what adjustments will work best. Noise is the most important variable that can strongly affect the quality of a digital image or video. In this work, only gamma radiation noise (impulse noise) that appears in images as undesirable white spots is considered. The gamma noise can be estimated through the statistical measure called the "standard deviation," which quantifies the typical variation that a pixel gray-scale value will have from its mean and "true" value. This concept can also be understood by looking at the histogram for a carefully selected bright region of interest (ROI) on a frame arbitrarily selected from the video sequence obtained.

A histogram can also describe the amount of contrast. Contrast is the difference in brightness between light and dark areas in a frame. In this work, the maximum contrast is estimated according to Michelson formula given by Eq.5 (Michelson, 1927):

$$C = \frac{I_{max} - I_{min}}{I_{max} + I_{min}} \qquad (6)$$

with I_{max} and I_{min} representing the highest and lowest luminance of the analyzed image.

In neutron imaging, it is common that not all important image quality criteria can be simultaneously optimized in a single image, or a video. Obtaining the best images within the constraints imposed by a particular process or experiment typically requires a compromise between the listed criteria, which often exert contradictory demands (Anderson, 2009). In order to study the influence of the neutron beam intensity on the neutron video quality, capture of time-lapse sequences of water and car engine oil flows inside a metallic container system is performed. Several videos are captured under different experimental neutron exposure conditions of the flow process. Details and conditions of video sequences capture are shown in table 3. The experiment setup used consists of two Aluminium compartments which communicate through three holes of 1mm, 1.5 mm and 2 mm in diameters (figure 13).

	Liquid	Neutron beam intensity (n/cm²/s)	Gain (dB)	Capture frame rate (fps)
Video Sequence.1	water	1.6×10^6	22	12.5
Video Sequence.2	water	1.44×10^7	22	12.5
Video Sequence.3	car engine oil	1.6×10^6	22	12.5
Video Sequence.4	car engine oil	4.8×10^6	22	12.5
Video Sequence.5	car engine oil	9.6×10^6	22	12.5
Video Sequence.6	car engine oil	1.44×10^7	22	12.5

Table 3. Experimental video sequences neutron exposure and capture conditions.

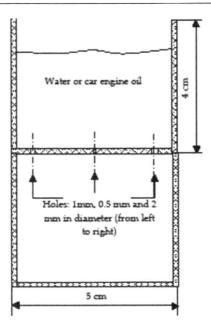

Fig. 13. Experimental system used in the study and visualization of water and car engine oil flow process through three different diameter holes.

3.2 Super resolution video sequence enhancement procedures and algorithms

Super resolution (SR) is a mean of producing a high-resolution (HR) image from one or a set of low-resolution, blurred and noisy images. It represent the capacity to transform noisy and blurred images obtained by low resolution (LR) imaging system (camera) to a higher resolution (HR) image with greater details than those of LR image. Methods of SR are classified coarsely into two categories: (1) The classical multi-images super resolution methods, and (2) Example based super resolution (Irani et al., 1991, Capel, 2004, Farsiu et al., 2004). Practically, classical methods allow small increases in resolution by factor smaller than two (Baker et al., 2002). However, example-based SR methods have been shown to exceed the limits of classical methods (Freeman et al., 2000, Kim et al., 2008). Other more sophisticated methods for image up-scaling based on learning edge models have also been developed and proposed (Sun et al., 2008). To achieve this HR image with classical multi-image super resolution methods, usually, an estimation of an image which minimizes the difference between its projection and each of the low resolution (LR) images through suitable algorithms is performed based on iteration process. LR images must have different sub pixel shifts, so that every image contains new information. To guarantee this last condition, two alternatives are available: 1. Extracting a number of frames from a video that are captured in a very small laps of time, 2. camera is moved from frame to frame, 3. multiple cameras are used in different positions. SR restores HR images from degraded (noisy, blurred and aliased) images. The first step in SR procedure application is the formulation of a model that relates between HR image and LR image. The common used model is given by the following equation (Sroubek & Flusser, 2007, Sung et al., 2003):

$$y_k = D_k B_k M_k x + n_k \qquad (7)$$

Where:
- M_k is the Warp matrix (Translation, Rotation);
- B_k is the Blur matrix ;
- D_k is the Sub sampling matrix;
- n_k is the noise vector ;
- x is the original HR image;
- y_k is the observed LR image.

With this simple formulation, the direct solution estimate can be inaccurate. Robust SR methods can help to improve this solution. The solution estimate in each iteration is updated by a gradient iterative minimization method given by the following expression:

$$x^{n+1} = x^n + \delta \nabla E(x) \qquad (8)$$

where $E(x)$ is the total squared error of resampling the high-resolution image represented by x and δ is a scale factor defining the step size in the direction of the gradient.

$$E(x) = \frac{1}{2} \sum_{k=1}^{n} \| y_k - DB_k M_k x \|_2^2 \qquad (9)$$

The gradient of x is can be given by:

$$\nabla E(x) = \sum_{k=1}^{n} B_k \qquad (10)$$

Robustness is introduced by replacing this last sum of images by the scaled pixel median:

$$\nabla E(x) = n.\,median\{B_k\}_{k=1}^{n} \qquad (11)$$

Some other combinations in addition to the median operator can also be applied to get more suitable and accurate results.

The procedure of SR consists of three stages (Fig.14):

1. registration;
2. interpolation onto HR grid;
3. Removing blur and noise.

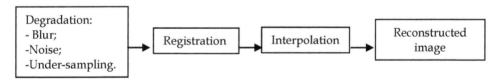

Fig. 14. Model for Super Resolution for observed LR.

The most important SR image reconstruction approaches are the following:

- Non uniform interpolation approach;
- Frequency domain approach;
- regularized SR reconstruction approach;
- Projection onto convex sets approach;

-   Maximum likelihood projection onto convex sets hybrid reconstruction approach;
-   Iterative back-projection approach.

The second objective of this work is the application and testing of SR procedure based on robust method on a neutron imaging video in order to improve their quality in term of spatial resolution by reducing the motion blur and also in term of noise. For such a purpose, we have adapted a Robust SR procedure described in (Zomet et al., 2001) in a MATLAB code to improve the quality and resolution of neutron video obtained. This method is an Iterated Back Projection one that computes the gradient, which is not given by the sum of all errors, but by the median of all errors. This brings robustness against outliners in the LR images.

For practical purpose, the video frames are, first, rearranged into sets of frames (5 frames in each one). Then, the SR procedure mentioned above is applied on each set of frames separately with an interpolation factor of 2 (figure 15). For each set of frame, the motion

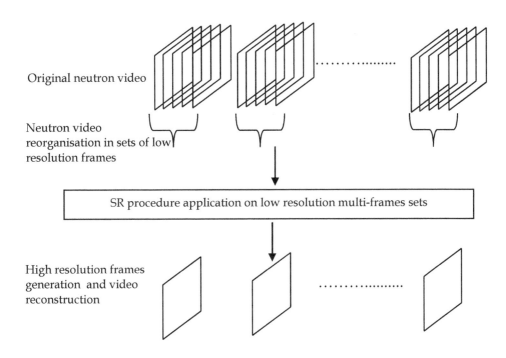

Fig. 15. Neutron video reorganisation in sets of multi-frames, SR procedure application on low resolution frames, high resolution frames generation and high resolution neutron video reconstruction.

estimation that is necessary for the application of this SR method is performed with Vandewalle et al (2006) algorithm. This method uses the property that a shift in the space domain is translated into a linear shift in the phase of the image's Fourier Transform. Similarly, a rotation in the space domain is visible in the amplitude of the Fourier Transform. Hence, the Vandewalle et al. motion estimation algorithm computes the images' Fourier Transforms and determines the 1-D shifts in both their amplitudes and phases. One advantage of this method is that it discards high-frequency components, where aliasing may have occurred, in order to be more robust. When all the frames sets are processed, the HR frames generated are used for a high resolution neutron video reconstruction and displaying with a standard speed of 25 fps or 30 fps (figure 14). To guarantee a best result with this proposed procedure, the capture frame rate of the examined dynamic process must be higher than the displaying one which is generally selected equal to 25 or 30 fps, depending on the used standard. The robust method applied to improve spatial resolution is based on pixel interpolation and super-sampling. The presented example in this chapter will not claim for completeness. The field of neutron imaging is experimental and seems to change with every new system built and CCD camera used for the examinations.

It is very important to mention that the capture frame rate must be accuracy selected to guarantee the optimum exposure of each frame to the neutron beam that is necessary for the well perception of the dynamic process being examined regarding its speed. The spatial resolution limit of the imaging system must be also taken into consideration. In our case the selected video capturing speed (frame rate) of 12.5 fps is sufficient to ensure the optimum visualization of the studied dynamic process. The rearrangement of the obtained video into frames sets of 5 frames doesn't affect the video quality. This is because our imaging system has a spatial resolution limit of ~ 400 μm and the average speed of the studied flow is about 0.095 m/s. According to these data, the equivalent video frame rate after SR procedure application, which is equal to the ratio of the average speed and the spatial resolution limit values, is approximately equal to ~2.35 fps. This effective frame rate when multiplied by 5 must give a value that is in the order of the selected video capture frame rate of 12.5 fps (5x2.35=11.75). Indeed, the selected capture frame rate and the number of frames in each set ensure the optimum visualization of studied flow process.

3.3 Results and discussions

3.3.1 Best video capture practical conditions establishment

Selected frames from the video sequences obtained are presented in figure 16 and 17. Selected region of interest (ROI) of 40x30 pixels are indicated by dashed and white squares. These regions indicate where gray levels measurements are performed that allow the calculation of necessary standard deviation for the estimation of noise and the necessary maximum and minimum gray levels values for the determination of contrast. A summary of the results obtained is given in table 4 based on histogram analysis. The variation of contrast and noise as a function of neutron beam intensity is shown in figure 18(a) and 18(b).

From the results obtained, we can first observe that at the maximum neutron beam intensity of 1.44 x 10^7 n/cm^2/s, the video sequence obtained is the best one in terms of contrast and

Fig. 16. Frames taken respectively from video sequence 1 and 2 of the water flow process for a frame rate of 12.5 fps, a Gain of 22 dB and a respectively neutron beam intensity of 1.6 x 10^6 n/cm²/s and 1.44 x 10^7 n/cm²/s (from the left).

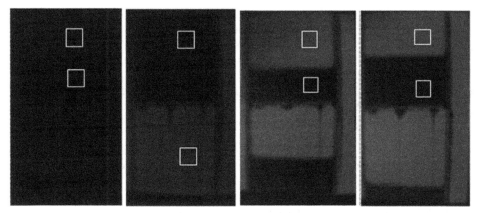

Fig. 17. Frames taken respectively from video sequence 3, 4, 5 and 6 of the car engine oil flow process for a frame rate of 12.5 fps, a Gain of 22 dB and a respectively neutron beam intensity of 1.6 x 10^6 n/cm²/s, 4.8 x 10^6 n/cm²/s, 9.6 x 10^6 n/cm²/s and 1.44 x 10^7 n/cm²/s (from the left to the right).

Video Sequences	liquid	Thermal noise (std.dev)	Contrast
Video Sequence.1	water	1.58	0.184
Video Sequence.2	water	1.52	0.409
Video Sequence.3	car engine oil	1.35	0.164
Video Sequence.4	car engine oil	2.35	0.376
Video Sequence.5	car engine oil	4.05	0.426
Video Sequence.6	car engine oil	1.89	0.446

Table 4. Summary of results obtained.

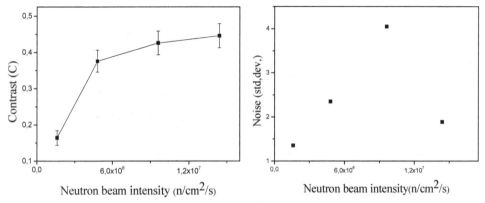

Neutron beam intensity (n/cm^2/s)   Neutron beam intensity(n/cm^2/s)

Fig. 18. (a: left). Contrast variation as a function of neutron beam intensity, (b: right). Random distribution of noise as a function of neutron beam intensity.

noise. Thus, a value of a neutron beam intensity of 1.6×10^6 n/cm^2/s is not enough to produce a well perceptible neutron image with a wide dynamic range in this case of studied flow process. The contrast was found proportional to the neutron beam intensity but after a value of $\sim 1 \times 10^7$ n/cm^2/s it becomes almost constant (kharfi et al., 2011). The impulse noise that affects the video sequences has a random distribution as a function of the neutron beam intensity. The optimum exposure and acquisition parameters that allow capturing a high quality neutron video sequence for this case of flow process examination are the following (table 5):

parameters	Neutron beam intensity	Capture Frame rate	Gain
Optimum value	1×10^7 n/cm^2/s	12.5 fps	22 dB

Table 5. Optimum video capture parameters.

In this work, it was established that the best video sequences 2 (water) and 6 (oil)) were obtained with a frame rate of 12.5 fps and a gain of 22 dB for a neutron beam intensity 1.44×10^7 n/cm^2/s. These exposure and capture video condition have guaranteed 256 digitized levels (full dynamic range). These video sequence are well exposed, the different phases of the flow process (continuous flow, drops) are well perceptible. These video can be well exploited in study the flow process phases and the drops shape as a function of hole diameter. The flow speed as a function of pressure and hole diameter can be also measured. Thus, the neutron video sequences obtained are rich in information and can be used for a wide variety of applications and purposes in the domain of fluid flow analysis. A future works will be focused on the exploitation of such video sequence information for a specific flow analysis.

3.3.2 Practical example of video capture and Super Resolution image quality improvement

According to the above results, video sequence 5 captured at a neutron beam intensity of 4.8×10^6 n/cm^2/s is the highly noised one. A selected LR frames set is taken from this video sequence. A frame from this set is shown in figure 19 with its corresponding FFT[4] and

---

[4] FFT : Fourier Fast Transform.

histogram. The FFT is used to show the frequency support of the noisy and low resolution original frame and the histogram can inform us about sampling, gray levels distribution and noise affecting this frame. The SR algorithm and method described above is applied with an interpolation factor of 2 to improve the quality of this frame after a shift estimation.

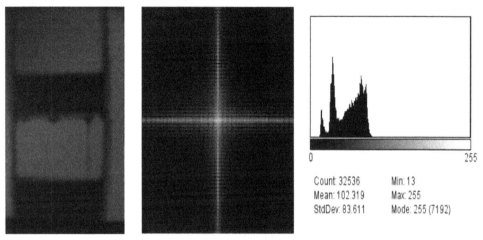

Count: 32536   Min: 13
Mean: 102.319   Max: 255
StdDev: 83.611   Mode: 255 (7192)

Fig. 19. One of the five LR frame selected from a set after arrangement of obtained neutron video in a number of frames sets and its corresponding FFT and histogram.

Example of generated high resolution frame result after the SR method application is shown in figure 20 with the corresponding FFT and histogram.

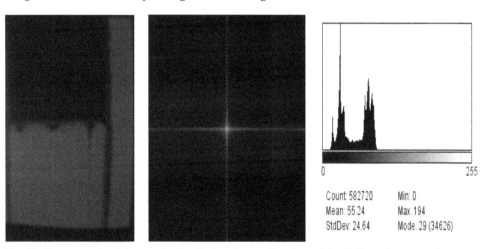

Count: 582720   Min: 0
Mean: 55.24   Max: 194
StdDev: 24.64   Mode: 29 (34626)

Fig. 20. Super resolved frame obtained after the application of the Robust Super resolution method on a set of low resolution frames arbitrary selected from the obtained neutron video of the flow process and its FFT and Histogram. When comparing FFT and histograms, we can easily verify that the sampling and resolution are improved and the noise (standard deviation) is significantly reduced.

From the HR frames obtained by SR procedure, a new high sampled and lowly noised neutron video is reconstructed. Although the neutron images (frames) processed through the proposed SR method are originally of optimum quality because a prior good selection of suitable video capture parameters was performed, the application of such SR method can reduce noise and improve the sampling of the obtained images and therefore allow the possibility to exploit theses images quantitatively. Because of the high sampling performance of the used CCD camera, not all SR methods are suitable for neuron images and video enhancement. The methods if well adapted and applied can contribute to improve the quality of neutron images and video suffering from motion blur with high efficiency.

4. Conclusions

Ultimately, the MTF is one component in characterizing the overall image quality performance of an imaging system. A robust method for estimating the MTF of high sensitivity neutron imaging CCD camera is presented. Longitudinal scan MTF results for the neutron imaging system are provided. Although the ISO 12233 slanted edge methodology was originally designed mostly for digital still camera MTF evaluation, it can successfully be applied to our neutron imaging system characterization. The weak dependence on tilt angle for values of less than $10°$ (the standard recommendation is $5°$) allows the alignment constraints to be relaxed. The use of a standardized target and a specifically developed program allows MTF data to be easily and quickly obtained from a single target image. The ISO slanted-edge technique is seen to be a valuable alternative for fast and efficient MTF measurements, allowing the determination of spatial response and effective spatial resolution of the neutron imaging system being studied.

The approach followed and the experimental procedures for temporal resolution limit determination were found to be very suitable and allowed the production of very accurate data. Although, our neutron camera can operate under high frames rates, the temporal resolution is limited and cannot exceed some values which are conditioned by the intensity of the neutron source, the performance of the imaging system and the speed of the dynamic process under examination. The study of temporal resolution limits for the case of higher indicator's rotational speeds (1.2 and 1.65 RPS) demonstrates that, in order to get the best visualization conditions, the frame rate must be increased. Practical tests reveal that this last operation may cause contrast degradation and brightness loss in the frames of the neutron video produced. This, because of the limited dynamic range - due to the limited neutron beam intensity- and the small bit depth of the imaging system used.

Results of flow processes studied by imaging with our neutron imaging system demonstrate that different capture conditions situations often produce completely different neuron video results in terms of noise and contrast. A small number of CCD performance factors and camera operating parameters such as frame rate and signal gain dominate the major aspects of digital image quality in neutron imaging; and their effects overlap to a great extent. The neutron beam intensity was also demonstrated as an important exposure parameter that can modify completely the quality of neutron image in terms of contrast and dynamic range. A flux of $\sim 1\text{x}10^7$ $b/cm^2/s$ was found enough to produce a high contrast image with a maximum dynamic range. For our case of flow process, frame rates of 12.5 fps with a signal gain of 22 dB were found as optimum video capture conditions. The super resolution method tested in this work proves that it is possible to improve the quality of the neutron video sequence with a post processing procedures. Here it is very important to mention that the post processing procedures must be well selected to avoid unnecessary processing.

5. References

Crow, L. (2009). Neutron detectors for imaging. In: *Neutron imaging and applications* Anderson, I.S., McGreevy, L. M., Biheux, H. Z., pp.(47-66) , Springer Science, ISBN: 978-0-387-78692-6.

Baker, A., Kanade, T. (2002). Limits on super resolution and how to break them, *IEEE Transactions on Pattern Analysis and Machine Intelligence (PAMI)*, 24(9), pp.(1167-1183).

Burns, P.D. (2000). Slanted-Edge MTF for Digital Camera and Scanner Analysis, *Proc. IS&T 2000 PICS Conference*, pp. (135-138).

Capel, D.P. (2004) *Image mosaicing and super resolution.* Springer-Vergla, ISBN: 1852337710.

Cleveland, W. (1985). *The Elements of Graphics Data,* Ward Worth, Belmont, CA, USA.

Domanus, J.C. (1992). *Practical Neutron Radiography*, Kluwer Academic Publishers, Dordrecht, Holland.

Estribau, M., Magnau, P. (2004). Fast MTF measurement of CMOS images using ISO 12233 Slanted-edge methodology, *Proceedings of the Society of Photo-optical Instrumentation Engineers (SPIE), vol.5251*, 2004, pp.(243-252), Bellingham, WA, USA, ISBN:0-8194-5135-5.

Farsiu, S., Robinson, M.D., Elad, M., Milanfar, P. (2004). Fast and robust multiframe super resolution. *IEEE Transactions in image processing*, vol. 13, No 10, pp. (1327-1344).

Freeman, W.T., Pasztor, E., Carmichael, O.(2000). Learning low-level vision, *International Journal of Computer Vision (IJCV)*, 40, No.1, pp.(25-47), Kluwer Academic Publishers.

Hendee, W.R., Ritlenour, E.R. (2002). *Medical imaging physics.* Wiley-LISS, New York.

Irani, M., Peleg, S. (1991). Improving resolution by image registration. *Graphical Models and Image Processing*, 53, pp. (231-239).

Jain, A. (1989). *Fundamental of Digital Image Processing*, Prentice Hall, Englewood Cliffs, NJ, USA.

Jespers, P. G., Van de While, F., White, M. H. (1976). *Solid State Imaging*, Noordhoff International Publishing, pp. (485-522).

Kharfi, F., Abbaci,M., Boukerdja, L. Attari, K. (2005). Implementation of Neutron Tomography around the Algerian Es-Salam Research Reactor: preliminary study and first steps, *Nuclear Instrument and Methods in Physics Research, vol. A542*, pp. (213-218).

Kharfi, F., Denden, O., Ali, A. (2011). Implementation and characterisation of new neutron imaging system for dynamic processes investigation at the Es-Salam research reactor, *Journal of Applied Radiation and Isotopes*, 69, pp.(1359-1364).

Kim, K., Kwon, Y. (2008). *Example-based learning for single image super resolution and JPEG artifact removal.* Max Planck Institute for Biological Cybernetics, Technical Report TR-173.

Kohm, K. (2004). Modulation Transfer Function measurement method and results for the ORBVIEW-3 high resolution imaging satellite, *Proceedings of ISPRS annual conference*, Istanbul, Turkey, 2004.

Michelson, A. (1927). *Studies in Optics.* U. of Chicago Press, USA.

Reichenbach, S.E., Park, S.K., Narayanswaury, R. (1991). Characterizing digital image acquisition devices, *Optical Engineering, 30*, pp.(170-177).

Samei, E., Buhr, E., Granfors, P., Vandenbroncke, D., Wang, X. (2005). Comparison of edge analysis techniques for the determination of the MTF of digital radiographic systems, *Phys. Med. Biol. 50*, No.15, pp. (3613–3625).

Shechtman, E., Caspi, Y., Irani, M.(2005). Space-Time Super-Resolution, *IEEE Transactions on Pattern Analysis and Machine Intelligence (PAMI)*, Vol.27, No.4, pp.(531-545).

Shetchman, E., Capsi, Y., Irani, M. (2002). Increasing Space-Time resolution in video, *Proceedings of the 7th European Conference on Computer Vision (ECCV)*, Springer-Vergla, vol.890, Issue 5, pp. (753-768), ISBN: 3540437452.

SIT Technical Note. (1994). *An introduction to scientific imaging charge coupled devices*, Scientific Imaging Technologies. Inc, Beaverton, Oregon, USA.

Spring, K. R., Fellers, T.J., Davidson, M. W. *Introduction to charge coupled devices (CCDs)*, www.microscopyu.com/articles/digitalimaging/ccdintro.html.

Sroubek, F., Flusser, J. (2007). Multiframe blind deconvolution coupled with frame registration and resolution enhancement. *IEEE Transactions on Image Processing*, vol. 16, No. 9, pp. (2322-2332).

Sun, J., Xu, Z., Shum, H. (2008). Image super-resolution using gradient profile prior, *Proceedings of the IEEE conference on Computer Vision and Pattern Recognition (CVPR)*, pp.(1-8), ISBN: 978-1-4244-22425.

Sung Cheol Park, S.C., Park, M. K., Kang. M. M. (2003). Super resolution image reconstruction, a technical overview, *Signal Processing Magazine, IEEE*, Volume 20, Issue 3, May 2003, pp. (21 – 36).

Vandewalle, P., Süsstrunk, S., Vetterli, M. (2006). A Frequency Domain Approach to Registration of Aliased Images with Application to Super-Resolution. *EURASIP Journal on Applied Signal Processing (special issue on Super-resolution)*, Vol. 2006. Article ID 71459, 14 pages.
www.NeutronOptics.com

Williams, D. (2004). Low-Frequency MTF Estimation for Digital Imaging Devices Using Slanted Edge Analysis, *Proc. SPIE-IS&T Electronic Imaging Symposium*, SPIE vol. 5294, pp. (93-101), 2004.

Zomet, A., Rav-Acha, A., Peleg, S. (2001). Robust Super-Resolution, *Proceedings of the international conference on computer vision and pattern recognition (CVPR)*, Hawaii, USA, December 2001, vol.1, pp.(645-650).

8

Microcalcification Detection in Digitized Mammograms: A Neurobiologically-Inspired Approach

Juan F. Ramirez-Villegas and David F. Ramirez-Moreno
Computational Neuroscience, Department of Physics,
Universidad Autonoma de Occidente,
Colombia

1. Introduction

A Computer-Aided Diagnosis (CAD) system is a set of automatic or semi-automatic tools developed to assist radiologists in the detection and/or classification of abnormalities presented in diagnostic images of different modalities. Although on the early phase of research and development CAD systems were criticized by some computer scientists; regardless of this criticism, nowadays' experimental evidence indicates that success rates of radiologists increase significantly when they are helped by these systems: In mammography, researchers have reported results from prospective studies on a large number of screenees, regarding the effect of CAD on the detection rate of breast cancer. Although there is a large variation in the results, it is important to note that all of these studies indicated an increase in the detection rates of breast cancer with the use of CAD; as a consequence of this, using CAD contributes to decrease cancer-related deceases due to the early detection of cancer signs.

The idea of developing computer systems to assist physicians in the detection of diseases has been a challenging matter during the last years, specifically on reducing the number of missed diagnosis and the time taken to reach a diagnosis among the different diagnostic image modalities. Moreover, the recent development of full-field digital imaging and picture archiving and communication systems (PACS) have been a catalyst in the increase of such computer systems in developed countries.

Because of the emphasis on screening programs in almost every country, the number of mammograms to be analyzed by the radiologists is enormous but, only a small portion of them are related to breast cancer (Oliver et al., 2010). In addition, a mammographic image is characterized by a high spatial resolution which is adequate enough to detect subtle fine-scale signs such as microcalcifications. Consequently, the analysis of mammographic images is a complex and cumbersome task which requires highly specialized radiologists.

During the last years, the number of papers related to CAD has been augmented due to the increased interest on improving disease diagnosis using different image modalities. As far as the evidence indicates, it appears reasonable to use CAD for screening examinations, provided that large fractions of them give normal results and therefore the task of diagnosis becomes both cumbersome and time-consuming. In addition, the current performance of commercial CAD systems have shown that there is a substantial gain in detection rates as well as an important increase in recall rate, not to mention the overall performance of such systems for the detection of disease signs (e.g., 98% sensitivity at 0.25 false positives per mammographic image, for one of the latest commercial CAD systems) (Doi, 2007).

As far as the literature shows, there seems to be only one attempt to integrate CAD systems into a multi-organ and multi-disease one incorporating all the diagnostic knowledge (Kobatake, 2007). On the other hand, the current status of single-purpose, single-organ CAD systems shows some good examples of commercial and functionally CAD systems for practical and clinical use. In mammography, chest radiography and thoracic CT, a number of commercial systems are available. The former systems include the detection and differential diagnosis of masses and microcalcifications. Furthermore, in chest radiography and thoracic CT, CAD schemes include the detection and differential diagnosis of lung nodules, interstitial lung diseases, and the detection of cardiomegaly, pneumothorax and interval changes (Doi, 2007). Researchers have reported an important reduction in the mean age of patients at the time of detection when CAD was used along with the increase in the detection rates of breast cancer (Cupples et al., 2005), similar results were achieved on the detection rates of lung cancer, colon diseases, intracranial aneurysms, among others (Doi, 2007).

Microcalcification detection has been extensively studied. Yu and Guan, 2000, developed a technique for the detection of clustered microcalcifications. The first part of the algorithm addresses the extraction of features based on wavelet decomposition and gray-level statistics, followed by a neural-network classifier. The detection of individual objects depends on shape factors, gray-level features, and a second neural network as a classification scheme. The algorithm was tested using a set of 40 mammograms and the sensitivity reported was 90% at 0.5 false positive per image.

Christoyianni et al., 2002, proposed a neural classification scheme for different kinds of regions of suspicion (ROS) on digitized mammograms; in this approach the Mini-MIAS database was used to perform the feature extraction and classification stages. The feature extraction stage was based on independent component analysis calculation in order to find a set of regions that generates the mammograms observed. The recognition accuracy for the detection of abnormalities was 88.23% and 79.31% in distinguishing between benign and malignant regions. El-Naqa et al., 2002, used support vector machines to detect microcalcification clusters. The algorithm was tested using 76 mammograms, containing 1120 microcalcifications, and it outperformed several well-known methods for microcalcification detection with a sensitivity of 94% at one false positive.

Vilarrasa, 2006, proposed a variety of visual processing and classification schemes to detect and classify mammary tissue. This group of algorithms employs standard segmentation procedures such as Tukey outlier test, region growing and segmentation via watershed transformation; additionally, a neural classifier is proposed to distinguish between healthy and calcified mammary tissue. The results were not good enough (were not reported due to its poorness), nevertheless, a morphologic filter was used to increase the success rates of the classifier; finally, the system reached 84% sensitivity, 64% specificity and 77.2% accuracy.

Verma et al., 2009, used a novel soft cluster neural network technique for the classification of suspicious areas in digital mammograms; the main idea of the soft clusters is to increase the generalization ability of the neural network; this network used a set of six features and was trained and tested using the DDSM benchmark database and the results showed an accuracy between 79% and 94%. Wei et al., 2009, proposed a microcalcification classification scheme assisted by content-based mammogram retrieval. The algorithm was tested using 200 different mammographic images from 104 cases. This approach used an adaptive support vector machine (Ada-SVM) as classifier which outperformed the classification accuracies given by other classifiers due to the incorporation of proximity information; the reported classification accuracy was 0.82 in terms of the area under the ROC curve.

Tsai et al., 2010, proposed an approach in which suspicious microcalcified regions are separated from normal tissue by wavelet layers and Renyi's information theory. Subsequently, several statistical shape-based descriptors are extracted; principal component analysis (PCA) is used to reduce the dimensionality of the feature space and the data classification is performed by a standard MLP neural network. The maximum performance achieved by this approach was 97.1 at 0.08 false positives.

2. Visual cortex mechanisms: Neurobiological considerations and potential for CAD

Up to this moment, microcalcification detection has been largely studied along with the development of computer vision algorithms. There are many computational approaches which have driven the problem at reasonable cost-effectiveness. Nonetheless, as a matter of fact, neurobiologically-inspired approaches have been rather neglected due to the poor establishment of the relation between cogent neurobiological principles and their potential to visual computer systems development.

Primates' visual cortex is capable to interpret dynamical scenes in clutter, in spite of using several serial visual processes as the attention shifting and saccadic eye movements suggest. As pure parallel processing of visual inputs becomes obscure and cumbersome for the visual cortex machinery, it deals with such task by selecting circumscribed regions of visual information to be processed preferentially and by changing the processing focus over the time course. Up to this moment, there are several approaches for the dynamic routing of visual stimuli and information flow through the visual cortex, which accounts for competitive interactions and dynamical modifications of the neural activity into the ventral and dorsal pathways, and the consequent biasing of these interactions in favor of certain objects of the space into scene-dependent (bottom-up) and/or task-dependent (top-down) strategies (Itti & Koch, 2000). The interactions among these two visual processes have been addressed by many researchers (Fix et al., 2010; Navalpakkam & Itti, 2005; Navalpakkam & Itti, 2002; Walther & Koch, 2006; Serre et al., 2006).

Objects in the visual field must compete for processing within more than 30 different visual cortical areas. As the ability to screen out objects during visual search tasks is contextual and primates often detect a single target in an array of non-targets, detections –for all the effects– depend largely on the correlation between targets and non-targets. According to this biased competition model, the targets and non-targets of a scene compete for processing spaces during visual search. There may be biases towards sudden appearances of new objects in the visual field and towards objects that are larger, brighter, faster moving, etc (Desimone & Duncan, 1995).

Many computational models of human visual search have embraced the idea of a saliency map to accomplish preattentive selection. This representation contains the overall neural activity elicited by the objects and non-objects of the space, which compete for processing spaces in the visual search according to primary visual features such as intensity, orientations, colors and motion. The conformation of feature maps is a consequence of highly structured receptive fields of cells in lateral geniculate nucleus (LGN) and, notably, V1. Certain well-established neurobiological evidence points out the existence of this neuronal map and, on the other hand, some other evidence rejects the idea of a topographical representation standing for the overall saliency of visual stimuli and, therefore, points out the selectivity as a consequence of interactions among feature maps, each codifying the saliency of objects in a specific feature (Itti & Koch, 2000).

Modeling of visual attention mechanisms seems to have reasonably high promise, and its application to microcalcification detection will be the main topic and purpose of this chapter. In this approach we perform pre-processing and post-processing stages using several computer vision algorithms. This allows us to identify the potential of the neurobiologically-inspired visual mechanisms model as part of a CAD scheme. We also give some relevant comparisons in relation to our previous approach (Ramirez-Villegas et al., 2010).

3. The proposed algorithm

The algorithm proposed in this book chapter is illustrated by Figure 1. The overall procedure is divided in six stages: (1) Mammographic images were taken from the Mini-MIAS Database of Mammograms (see sub-section 3.1. for a detailed description of the data); (2) The region of interest (ROI) cropping is accomplished by using the available information on the description section of the database; specifically we took into account the location and the approximate radius of the circle enclosing the abnormalities (microcalcifications); (3) Adaptive histogram equalization and the so-called top-hat algorithm were performed as pre-processing steps in order to enhance the microcalcifications' traces; (4) A pre-attentive bottom-up visual model was implemented in order to preliminarily distinguish between calcified and non-calcified tissue; (5) Tukey outlier test-based segmentation was used to perform the final segmentation of sub-regions via the simulated gaze allocation outcomes obtained in the former step; (6) Finally, a Self-Organizing Map (SOM) neural network was implemented in order to adjust topologically the microcalcifications and to provide a final visual output.

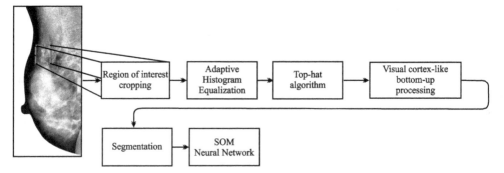

Fig. 1. Overview of the proposed approach.

3.1 Mammographic database

In this work, a total of 23 mammographic images containing microcalcified tissue were taken from The Mini-MIAS Database of Mammograms (Suckling, 1994), which is widely used by researchers to carry out and evaluate their research work before other researchers in the area of CAD of breast cancer. We have used this database in our previous research (Ramirez-Villegas et al., 2010; Ramirez-Villegas & Ramirez-Moreno, 2011). The database provides appropriate details of the pathologies and general characteristics of the mammograms: The MIAS database reference number, character of background tissue (as it can be fatty, fatty-glandular and dense-glandular), class of abnormality (as it can be calcification, well-defined/circumscribed masses, spiculated masses, ill-defined masses, architectural distortion, asymmetry or normal), severity of abnormality (as it can be benign or malignant), the (x,y) image-coordinates of centre of abnormality and the approximate radius (in pixels) of a circle enclosing the abnormality. The resolution of the original images was 200 micron pixel edge so that every image's size was 1024 x 1024 pixels. The images are centered in the matrix.

All ROIs (calcified tissue samples) were selected using the reference given in the description of the database.

3.2 Mammograms enhancement

Enhancement algorithms have been employed for the improvement of contrast features and the suppression of noise (Papadopoulos, 2008). They are commonly used to increase the radiologist's detection effectiveness or as pre-processing stages of CAD schemes. In the preprocessing module, the significant features of the mammogram are enhanced, recovering most of the hidden characteristics and improving the image quality. According to recent findings (Papadopoulos, 2008), the contribution of the preprocessing module in the detection of ability of the CAD system is definite. Consequently, the final outcome of the CAD scheme depends largely on the pre-processing steps.

The pre-processing stage of the current approach is divided in two parts: (1) Contrast enhancement and, (2) microcalcification enhancement by the so-called top-hat algorithm. The usefulness of these methods is reported in the literature along with their potential to enhance signs present in mammographic images.

3.2.1 Adaptive Histogram Equalization (AHE)

In our previous work (Ramirez-Villegas et al., 2010; Ramirez-Villegas & Ramirez-Moreno, 2011), we implemented the Adaptive Histogram Equalization (AHE) as preprocessing stage. According to our findings, this technique can be applied to enhance the high frequency components of the image, i.e., microcalcifications, due to the computations applied to central and contextual region pixels. In order to avoid the noise amplification a contrast limited-equalization can be performed, especially in homogeneous areas. This method exhibits improvements over the Local-Area Histogram Equalization (LAHE), which presents high computational load and noise magnification due to standard histogram equalization computed for each pixel taking into account its neighborhood (contextual region).

In order to decrease the computational load, equalization can be computed only for some pixels (and its context regions), as the image is divided into a mosaic; thereby, the modified pixel is the central pixel, and the others are obtained using a standard interpolation method. In this way, each contextual region will affect, with its equalization, another spatial zone which doubles its length.

The final value of each pixel will be obtained applying the pixel mapping given by

$$L(i) = C\left[E\,N_{--}(i) + (1-E)N_{+-}(i)\right] + (1-C)\left[E\,N_{-+}(i) + (1-E)N_{++}(i)\right],\tag{1}$$

where N_{--} is the mapping of the left superior area, N_{-+} is the mapping of the left inferior area, and so on; and

$$C = \frac{(y-y_-)}{(y_+ - y_-)}, \text{ and } E = \frac{(x-x_-)}{(x_+ - x_-)}$$

3.2.2 Top-hat algorithm

As a matter of fact, background removal and microcalcification enhancing are considered as necessary procedures in many CAD applications, given the initial visibility and detectability of such mammographic signs. Morphological operations can be employed to enhance mammographic images at reasonable computational load-effectiveness. A large class of filters can be represented by mathematical morphology implementing two simple operations: Erosion and dilatation. When the signal of gray levels and the background of an image are constant, a standard image thresholding procedure can be performed to detect objects. Nonetheless, the top-hat algorithm becomes a very good choice when the signal of gray levels of the background is highly sparse, as it is the mammary tissue in a mammographic image.

The top-hat algorithm consists of a standard pixel-to-pixel subtraction of the original image from its opened version. The image opening is defined as the erosion of the image followed by its dilatation. Erosion is the morphologic operation in which a pixel, located at the center of the structuring element, is substituted by the minimum value of the pixels of the neighborhood. Hence, this operation reduces small regions with higher gray levels than those of the structuring element. On the other hand, dilatation is the opposite morphologic operation to erosion; in this case, the pixel located at the center of the structuring element is substituted by the maximum value of the pixels of the structuring element. Consequently, this operation enlarges the regions of the image with high gray levels which did not disappear as a result of the erosion step.

The top-hat algorithm can be formulated as follows:

$$A'(x,y) = A(x,y) - \left[A(x,y) \circ B(x,y)\right],\tag{2}$$

where:

$$A(x,y) \circ B(x,y) = \left[A(x,y) \ominus B(x,y)\right] \oplus B(x,y),\tag{3}$$

is the opening of the image $A(x,y)$ by a structuring element $B(x,y)$, where $\ominus$ and $\oplus$ denote erosion and dilatation, respectively.

As images are functions mapping a Euclidean space E into $\mathbb{R} \cup \{-\infty,\infty\}$, where $\mathbb{R}$ is the set of real numbers, the grayscale erosion and dilatation of $A(x,y)$ by $B(x,y)$ are given, respectively, by:

$$A(x,y) \ominus B(x,y) = \arg\min_{x',y' \in E} \left[A(x',y') - B(x'-x, y'-y) \right], \tag{4}$$

$$A(x,y) \oplus B(x,y) = \arg\max_{x',y' \in E} \left[A(x',y') + B(x-x', y-y') \right], \tag{5}$$

3.3 Background suppression (revised method)

The enhancement stage must be sensitive enough to emphasize small low-contrast objects, while it must have the required specificity to suppress the background. Usually the background corresponds to some smoothed fractions of the image provided by the tissue characteristics and image acquisition process; in consequence, these areas are softened regions of image which give no-relevant information about pathologies in many cases. In our last work (Ramirez-Villegas et al., 2010), the suppression is performed using difference of Gaussians filters according to Eq. (6).

$$I_r(x,y) = I(x,y) - DoG(x,y) \otimes I(x,y), \tag{6}$$

where $I(x,y)$ is the input image, and the additional term of convolution is the filter function. In this way, the convolution term corresponds to a smoothed version of the input image. DoG (Difference of Gaussians) is a linear filter implemented in several artificial vision tasks, which works by subtracting two Gaussian blurs of the image corresponding to different functions widths.

$$DoG(x,y) = A_1 \frac{1}{2\pi\sigma_1{}^2} \exp\left[-\frac{x^2+y^2}{2\sigma_1{}^2} \right] - A_2 \frac{1}{2\pi\sigma_2{}^2} \exp\left[-\frac{x^2+y^2}{2\sigma_2{}^2} \right], \tag{7}$$

The enhancing process with the DoG works in both the spatial and frequency domain. The performance of the filter is conditioned by parameters σ_n and in one case, A_n peaks estimation. In Eq. (7), Standard deviation σ_n is related with lateral inhibition of the filter, while the term which follows A_n peaks normalizes the sum of mask elements to unity in the image processing. Typically these parameters are determined in a heuristic way, according to the desired performance and microcalcifications and image general characteristics. Nevertheless, as a reference method for this research, there are some mathematical expressions (Ochoa, 1996) used to determine the DoG parameters according to microcalcifications' average width and Marr's ratio (Marr, 1982). For reference, an example of the DoG processing is in Figure 2.

As background suppression using DoG filters is a well-known method, it will give us some feedback in order to compare the performance of the current approach and, consequently, to express where it stands relative to the existing literature.

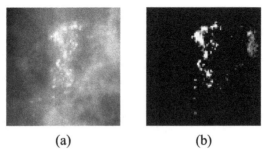

(a)   (b)

Fig. 2. Example of background suppression by DoG: (a) Input ROI; (b) Enhanced ROI.

3.4 Bottom-up processing in visual cortex

The selection of a part of the available sensory information before a detailed processing stage by intermediate and high visual centers is an ability of the visual system of primates. Koch and Ullman (Koch & Ullman, 1985) introduced the idea of a saliency map to accomplish pre-attentive selection. Saliency map can be defined as a two-dimensional representation that represents topographically the saliency of objects in the visual field. The competitive behavior of the neurons in this map gives rise to a single winning location, which corresponds to the most salient object. Subsequently, the next conspicuous locations are attended in order of decreasing saliency, given the prior inhibition to already attended locations.

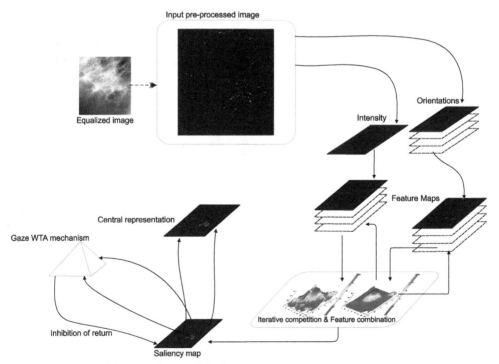

Fig. 3. Overview of the visual cortex-like bottom-up processing step.

Microcalcifications are low-contrast conspicuous locations in a background of distractors (surrounding mammary tissue and noisy regions). The competitive behavior of the neurons in the early stages of visual processing guarantees that there would be a biased competition in favor of certain objects of the space based on certain characteristics which make them 'unique'. But, how do unique features attract attention? Experimental evidence shows that neural structures in Lateral Geniculate Nucleus (LGN) and primary visual cortex (V1) are responsive to features which are common to all objects of the visual field, e.g., intensity, orientation, color opponency, motion, stereo disparity, among others. In this work, we assume that visual input is represented in the form of iconic, topographic feature maps. In order to construct such representations, we use center-surround computations in every feature at different spatial scales and within-feature spatial competition (Itti & Koch, 2000). All the information contained in these maps is combined to obtain a single representation, i.e., the saliency map.

This part of our approach computes saliency using two features studied by Itti et al., 1998, for the formerly visual attention model proposed model of Koch & Ullman, 1985: Intensity and orientation. These features are organized into 30 maps (6 for intensity, 24 for orientation; a detailed explanation of this is given further). These maps are combined using across-scale sums in order to obtain the conspicuity maps, which provide input for a unique saliency map (central representation). Figure 3 illustrates the overview of this processing step.

This model is limited to selective attention given by the properties of the visual stimuli and consequently it does not involve any volition-dependent process (top-down visual processing). Low-level visual features are directly extracted from the input image over different resolution scales using pyramid-like linear filters, i.e., the so-called Gaussian pyramids. This approach consists of successive filtering processes and compression of the input images (Burt & Adelson, 1983). This process is illustrated by the following equations:

$$g_l(i,j) = \sum_{m=-2}^{2} \sum_{n=-2}^{2} w(m,n) g_{l-1}(2i+m, 2j+n), \tag{8}$$

where $0 < l < N_l$ and i, j, $0 \leq i < C_l$, $0 \leq j < R_l$. N_l is the number of levels of the pyramid and, C_l and R_l are the dimensions of the image at the lth level. Finally, w is defined according to Eq. (9) and Eq. (10).

$$w(m,n) = \hat{w}(m)\hat{w}(n), \tag{9}$$

where $\hat{w}$ is a normal and symmetric function:

$$\hat{w}(x) = \begin{cases} b - a/2, & x = -2, 2 \\ b, & x = -1, 1 \\ a, & x = 0 \end{cases} \tag{10}$$

Typically the value of a is 0.4 and the value of b is 0.25, in consequence, the values of $\hat{w}(x)$ are given by Eq. (11).

$$\hat{w}(x) = \begin{cases} 0.05, & x = -2, 2 \\ 0.25, & x = -1, 1 \\ 0.4, & x = 0 \end{cases} , \tag{11}$$

Note that there is a 5x5 pattern of weights w to generate each pyramid array.

In this step, a total of nine spatial scales $\sigma = [0,1,...,8]$ are created using the Gaussian pyramid scheme. This approach yields horizontal and vertical image reduction factors from 1:1 (scale zero) to 1:256 (scale eight) in eight octaves.

Subsequently, each feature is calculated using the center-surround scheme, which is highly related to the visual receptive fields. Such center-surround differences are calculated between coarse and fine resolution scales in every feature: The receptive center corresponds to a pixel at resolution level $c \in \{2,3,4\}$ in the pyramid, and the surround is the corresponding pixel at resolution level $s = c + \delta$, with $\delta \in \{3,4\}$. As a result of the combination between the receptive center and surround resolution levels, we obtain a total of six feature maps.

Intensity contrast is extracted by standard band-pass filtering to calculate center surround differences between the established resolution levels:

$$I(c,s) = |I(c) \ominus I(s)|, \tag{12}$$

where $I(c)$ is the center intensity signal, $I(s)$ is the surround intensity signal and the symbol "$\ominus$" is termed across-scale subtraction, i.e., the point-by-point subtraction of images of different resolutions by interpolation to the finer scale.

Orientation is extracted using standard Gabor pyramids $O(\theta,\sigma)$, where $\theta \in \{0°,45°,90°,135°\}$ (Greenspan et al., 1994). Thereby, orientation contrast is defined as:

$$O(c,s,\theta) = |O(c,\theta) \ominus O(s,\theta)|, \tag{13}$$

where $O(c,\theta)$ and $O(s,\theta)$ are the center and surround orientation signals, respectively.

The local orientation maps $O(c,\theta)$ and $O(s,\theta)$ are computed by convolving the levels of the intensity pyramid with standard Gabor filters (note that this procedure can be performed either in the frequency or spatial domain):

$$O(\sigma,\theta) = \left[I(\sigma) * O_E(\theta) \right]^2 + \left[I(\sigma) * O_O(\theta) \right]^2, \tag{14}$$

where σ is the resolution level, and O_E and O_O:

$$O_E(x,y,\theta) = \exp\left(-\frac{x'^2 + \gamma^2 y'^2}{2\delta^2} \right) \cos\left(2\pi \frac{x'}{\lambda} + \psi \right), \tag{15}$$

$$O_O(x,y,\theta) = \exp\left(-\frac{x'^2 + \gamma^2 y'^2}{2\delta^2} \right) \sin\left(2\pi \frac{x'}{\lambda} + \psi \right), \tag{16}$$

are even and odd Gabor filters, respectively, with aspect ratio γ, standard deviation δ, wavelength λ, phase ψ, and rotated coordinates by θ:

$$x' = x\cos(\theta) + y\sin(\theta), \tag{17}$$

$$y' = -x\sin(\theta) + y\cos(\theta), \tag{18}$$

Once we obtain the 30 feature maps (6 for intensity and 24 for orientation), feature maps of the same type are linearly combined and, consequently, we obtain two conspicuity maps (one for each feature):

$$\overline{I} = \bigoplus_{c=2}^{4} \bigoplus_{s=c+3}^{c+4} N[I(c,s)], \tag{19}$$

$$\overline{O} = \sum_{\theta \in \{0°, 45°, 90°, 135°\}} N\left[\bigoplus_{c=2}^{4} \bigoplus_{s=c+3}^{c+4} N[O(c,s)] \right], \tag{20}$$

The purpose of the function $N(\cdot)$ is to normalize each conspicuity map. The simplest procedure to achieve such normalization is to adjust the dynamic range of the maps. However, it is possible to obtain a normalized map into an iterative or trained way (Itti & Koch, 2000).

All conspicuity maps are linearly combined into one saliency map according to Eq. (21).

$$S = \frac{1}{2}\left[N(\overline{I}) + N(\overline{O}) \right], \tag{21}$$

Finally, as the objects in the space compete for processing spaces during visual processing, the locations in the saliency map representation compete for the highest saliency value into a winner-take-all (WTA) strategy. This means that the next location to be attended (x_w, y_w) is the most salient one in the saliency map; subsequently, the saliency map is inhibited by means of the so-called inhibition of return mechanism, allowing the model to simulate a visual scan path over the whole content of the image.

WTA models have been largely implemented for making decisions from a neurobiologically-inspired perspective (Koch & Ullman, 1985; Itti et al. 1998; Walther & Koch, 2006). It should be noted that in a neuronally plausible implementation, the saliency map could be modeled as a layer of leaky *integrate-and-fire neurons*, as a backwards WTA selection mechanism (Walther & Koch, 2006) or as a layer of neurons with logistic profiles implemented in the form of mean field equations (Ramirez-Moreno & Ramirez-Villegas, 2011). In the case of the leaky *integrate-and-fire neurons*, when a threshold potential is reached, a prototypical spike is generated and the capacitive charge of the neuron is shunted to zero (note that neurons here are RC circuit-based models). Therefore, the synaptic interactions among the units ensure that only the most active location of the saliency map remains and the potential elicited by other locations are suppressed. Similarly, using the mean field approach in a network of neural populations, the WTA approach emerges directly from the competitive behavior of the units, thereby, inhibitory and local excitatory connections among the neurons of the same layer produce the most active location to rise above the other ones (Ramirez-Moreno & Ramirez-Villegas, 2011).

As the main aim of the current approach is not to reproduce the brain dynamics in a one-to-one implementation, we select the most active location in the saliency map in order to define the position where the model should attend; hence, we define the most salient location as follows:

$$FOA_w = \arg\max\left[S(x,y)\right], \tag{22}$$

where FOA_w defines the winning location $(x_w, y_w) \subseteq (x,y)$ and x, y, $0 < x \le N'$, $0 < y \le M'$ in the saliency map of dimensions $N'^* M'$.

Under this strategy, the focus of attention (FOA) is shifted to the location of the winner neuron. Further, local inhibition must be applied in an area in the location of the FOA, in order to allow the system to determine a new winning location and then produce a new attentional shift. In order to reproduce such inhibition of return mechanism, when selecting the most active location in the map, a small excitation is activated in the surrounds of the FOA (Koch & Ullman, 1985), consequently, the shape of the FOA can be approximated to a disk whose radius is fixed according to the microcalcifications' average width (in this work, we compared the performance obtained using radiuses of 2, 3 and 5 pixels); subsequently, such location is inhibited by setting its activity to zero.

3.5 Serial segmentation procedure

Frequently the processing in the collected images is varying in quality (satisfactory quality and poor quality); hence, this establishes some individuality of the grey level contrast (Ramirez-Villegas et al., 2010) provided by the tissue characteristics and image acquisition process. Furthermore, regions of images such as mammograms are suitable to several segmentation algorithms. The image segmentation procedure must be specific enough to avoid false positives in the enhancing process.

In statistical analysis, when outliers are present, the estimates of the data are distorted. Consequently, these estimates are not suitable to make inferences about the data. In this case, these erroneous values should be eliminated for subsequent analysis purposes.

The Tukey outlier test (Hoaglin et al., 1983) assumes that there is no specific distribution of the data series. This method is based on the supposition that any distribution has a group of typical values surrounded by atypical data (i.e., outliers) that exaggerate the histogram length. The larger the sample size, the higher the probability of getting at least one outlier. The Tukey outlier test is based in, at least, two assumptions: (1) that the central part of the distribution contains most of the information of the genuine reference values; and (2) that outliers may be detected as values lying outside limits, taking into account the statistical properties of this central part.

In our work, we implemented this outlier detector as a serial segmentation algorithm using the FOAs determined by the saliency-based bottom-up approach described in Section 3.4. Each serially attended location (i.e., the circumscribed regions used to simulate attentional shifting) is a subset $S'(x,y) \subseteq S(x,y)$; the Tukey outlier test will set aside the observation $S'(x_o,y_o)$ if one of the following conditions is fulfilled:

$$S'(x_o,y_o) < L, \tag{23}$$

where

$$L = \left[q_1 - 1.5(q_3 - q_1)\right], \tag{24}$$

or

$$S'(x_o,y_o) > U, \tag{25}$$

where

$$U = \left[q_1 + 1.5(q_3 - q_1)\right], \tag{26}$$

where q_1 and q_3 denote the first and third quartiles of the sample, respectively. Once the arguments of the above expressions are obtained, pixels above U and below L are considered as outliers of the distribution. As microcalcifications at this stage of the approach appear as highly bright regions with atypical gray level values (outliers in the distribution of the resulting processed image), the segmentation threshold to segment them is equal to U.

From a neural networks perspective, the segmentation procedure proposed in this work can be seen as a hard-limit transfer function node, where:

$$H\left[S'(x,y)\right] = \begin{cases} 1 & S'(x,y) > U \\ 0 & otherwise \end{cases}, \tag{27}$$

Under this scheme, the typical gray values of the distribution are discarded (set to zero) and the others are transferred to the next processing step (SOM neural network).

3.6 Self-organizing map (SOM) neural network

The final stage of the approach reported in this chapter, is the implementation of a SOM neural network in order to topologically adjust the microcalcifications and show the final outcome for diagnosis purposes. Figure 4 illustrates the architecture of the neural network with the saliency map as input.

Self-Organizing Maps (SOM) have been largely implemented for a plethora of tasks, in a very similar way to those which other neural networks have been used to, e.g., pattern recognition, vision systems, signal processing, among others. In SOM-like neural networks, neighboring cells compete through mutual lateral interactions, and develop adaptively into specific detectors of different signal patterns (Kohonen, 1990). Each point of the input data shaping the structure of an N-dimensional space determines the spatial location of the weight of a cell in the network. Consequently, the network would be capable of giving a categorization of the input space.

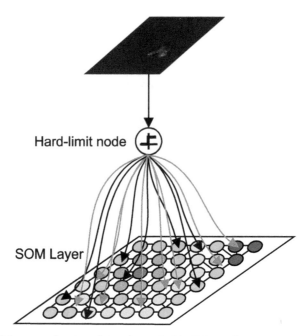

Fig. 4. Scheme of the neural network implemented in this work.

Let $X_i = [x_i, y_i]^T \in S_s(x,y)$ be a two-dimensional input vector in the segmented saliency map. The weight vector of the node j in the SOM layer is therefore denoted by $w_j = [w_{j,1}, w_{j,2}] \in S_s(x,y)$. We define an analytical measure of match between X and w. The simplest way to define the match may be the inner product $X_i^T w_j$; however, the Euclidean distance gives better and more convenient matching criterion (Kohonen, 1990). The Euclidean distance between the input patterns and the vector of weights is defined as:

$$E_{ji} = \left\| w_j - X_i \right\| = \sqrt{\left(w_{j,1} - x_i \right)^2 + \left(w_{j,2} - y_i \right)} \, , \tag{28}$$

The minimum Euclidean distance defines the winner neuron at the current iteration. Hence, there is a single neuron chosen such that:

$$E_c = \arg\min_{j,i} \left(E_{ji} \right) , \tag{29}$$

Lateral interactions among the units are enforced by defining a neighborhood set n', around the winner unit. At each learning step the cells within the neighborhood are updated. Depending on the neighborhood function, the cells outside n' are left intact or almost intact. Such function technically defines the adaptation strength among the neurons of the map. For a closer proximity to the winner node, stronger adaptation strength is elicited by the other nodes. In our work we used an elliptical Gaussian function, which according to our experimentation gave robust solution to the topologic adjustment task:

$$f\left(x,y;\sigma_1,\sigma_2\right) = \frac{1}{2\pi\sigma_1\sigma_2}\exp\left[-\left(\frac{x^2}{2\sigma_1^2}+\frac{y^2}{2\sigma_2^2}\right)\right], \tag{30}$$

The parameters of the function (the Gaussian widths) define the size of the neighborhood. Typically, it changes according to a monotonically decreasing function throughout the whole training procedure. In the current implementation such function for either Gaussian width is given by:

$$\sigma_n\left(t\right) = \sigma_{n,0}\left(\frac{\sigma_{n,f}}{\sigma_{n,0}}\right)^{t/T}, \tag{31}$$

where t represents the current training cycle and T the total number of train cycles. The initial $\sigma_{n,0}$ and final $\sigma_{n,f}$ neighborhood sizes can be estimated according to the map size (the neurons' distribution), the segmented saliency map size or in a heuristic way. It should be noted that a wide initial neighborhood first induces a rough global order in the w_j values after which narrowing the neighborhood improves the spatial resolution of the map.

Finally, the updating process of the weights is given by the following equation:

$$w_j\left(t+1\right) = w_j\left(t\right) + \alpha\left(t\right)f\left(\cdot\right)\left[X_i - w_j\left(t\right)\right], \tag{32}$$

where $\alpha\left(t\right)$ is the so-called adaptation gain $0 < \alpha\left(t\right) < 1$, which is related to the rate at which the network learns the topology of the input space. Typically, this parameter is also described by a monotonically decreasing function. In our work, it has the following form:

$$\alpha\left(t\right) = \alpha_0 + \left(\alpha_f - \alpha_0\right)\left(\frac{t}{T}\right), \tag{33}$$

here, the initial α_0 and final α_f learning rates must be small values and $\alpha_f < \alpha_0$.

For illustrative purposes, a topology adjustment example by a SOM network is given by Figure 5. In this example, the input space is a square-shaped random distribution of points,

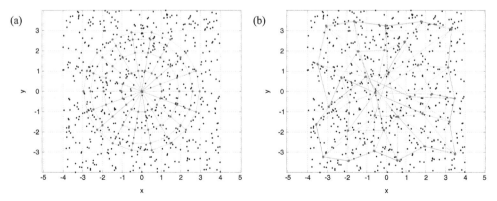

Fig. 5. SOM neural network (two-dimensional circular array) in a squared input space: (a) Initial weights (iteration 0); (b) weights after several training cycles (iteration 100).

while the network (initially) is a circle-shaped array of interconnected units. Note that the weight vectors tend to approximate the density function of the input vectors after a few training cycles (the blue edges indicate that the neurons are neighbors in the grid).

4. Results

As aforementioned, we tested our approach using The Mini-MIAS Database of Mammograms (Suckling, 1994), which is widely used by researchers to carry out and evaluate their research work before other researchers in the area of CAD of breast cancer. From this database, a total of 23 mammographic images made part of our study (those containing microcalcifications). The background and tissue character in the images enabled us to test the algorithm with certain variability of conditions. ROIs were extracted according to the specifications of the database in the form of squared regions enclosing the microcalcification clusters. In some cases calcifications were widely distributed throughout the mammogram rather than concentrated at single sites; in these cases various ROIs of the images containing microcalcifications were extracted. Subsequently, all the processing steps were performed according to Figure 1.

In this section we present the main outcomes of the proposed methodology. In Section 4.1 we give some relevant examples to illustrate how the proposed CAD application operates during mammogram inspection. Similarly, in Section 4.2 we present comparative Free-Response Operating Characteristic (FROC) curves to test the outcome of our methodology varying the radius of the FOAs in the saliency-based bottom-up model. We also conduct relevant comparisons between the proposed algorithm and the DoG approach and additionally, other comparisons are made between the performance obtained in the detection of benign microcalcification signs and the detection of malign microcalcification signs.

4.1 Experimental results

The analysed ROIs containing the microcalcifications in the mammograms vary in radius from 8 to 93 pixels, and the performance of the SOM neural network was achieved in 500 training cycles, in which location of the possibly pathological regions are given as an output.

In Figure 6 and Figure 7, examples of microcalcification detection are presented. Note that after the preprocessing stages (the image histogram equalization and the top-hat algorithm), the saliency-based bottom-up approach reveals the locations of the image which the visual system should attend to. In this case, the visual processing model biases the competition among the different locations of the image in favour of certain objects of the space. The attended conspicuous objects in this case are the microcalcifications present in the mammograms. As the degree of conspicuity of the microcalcifications on the preprecessed images varies, the saliency map activity is somewhat heterogeneous. This illustrates that the neural responses elicited by the objects and the competitive interactions among certain locations in the maps induce one target to rise above the others at a given time instant. In addition, our model incorporates the iterative normalization strategy described by Itti & Koch, 2000, which consists on iteratively convolving the feature maps by a 2D DoG filter, adding the result to the original image and setting the negative results to zero after each iteration. We tested the model with a reduced number of iterations (a maximum of 3 iterations) and a small inhibition factor (between 0 and 1) in order to avoid undesired over-competitive behaviour among the neurons of the map.

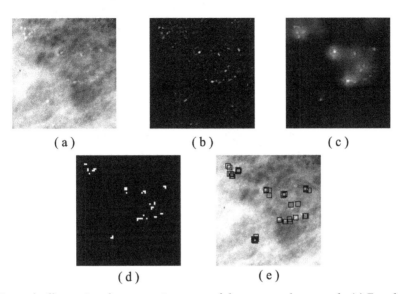

(a)   (b)   (c)

(d)   (e)

Fig. 6. Example illustrating the processing steps of the proposed approach: (a) Equalized ROI; (b) output of the top-hat algorithm; (c) saliency map; (d) segmented image; (e) topologic adjustment of microcalfications by SOM neural network.

Figure 6(d) and Figure 7(d) illustrate the results of the serial segmentation. Note that the specificity of the bottom-up processing increases with the pattern discrimination obtained after the serial calculation of the Tukey outlier test. For these examples the radius of the FOA was 2 pixels. The white locations in Figure 6(d) and Figure 7(d) were those for which the statistical procedure detected at least one outlier. Furthermore, like in many other relevant situations, according to our results, it is hard to find an algorithm that can handle all the possible scenarios and all mammographic images' conditions. In addition, regardless of the distribution of the FOA, in absence of outliers (microcalcifications), the Tukey statistical test provided a low rate of false detections (specificity). We performed extensive experiments to evaluate the serial segmentation algorithm by limiting the maximum number of attended locations by the saliency-based bottom-up model; the algorithm's outcome limiting the number of attended locations did not present large variations as if the attention shifting occurred across the whole saliency map.

Figure 6(e) and Figure 7(e) show the topologic adjustment of microcalcifications performed by the SOM neural network. This performance was obtained by training the network over 500 cycles, in which the locations of the possibly pathological regions were given. Although the topological adjustment made by the SOM network is accurate and suitable for the application, some microcalcifications were not associated because the number of neurons in the input space was limited due to computational load constraints. Further research will be needed to evaluate other schemes in the topologic adjustment task.

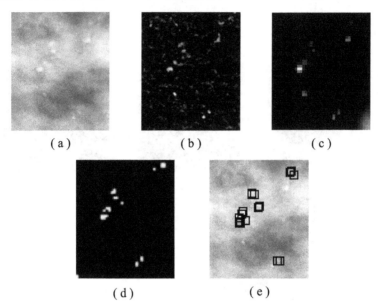

Fig. 7. Example illustrating the processing steps of the proposed approach: (a) Equalized ROI; (b) output of the top-hat algorithm; (c) saliency map; (d) segmented image; (e) topologic adjustment of microcalfications by SOM neural network.

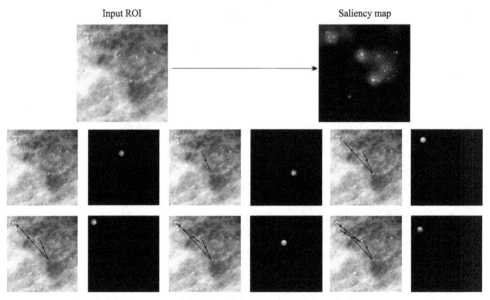

Fig. 8. Example of the operation of the visual saliency model with the mammographic ROI in Figure 6. Note that once the visual machinery model combines the information of the topographic conspicuity maps into the saliency map, the most salient locations of the scene are attended into a serial strategy (the black arrows indicate the spatial shifts of the FOA).

Additionally, Figure 8 illustrates the FOA shifting for the first six attended locations in the saliency map in the example of Figure 6. In this case, the FOA is represented by a disk of radius 2 pixels. In general, although it depends on the ROI size, the processed ROI required approximately from 16 to 300 shifts (with overlapping) to cover all the possible saliency map locations. Since larger ROIs took somewhat longer to be analyzed by the algorithm, in the slowest case the processing steps took approximately one minute to be performed. Furthermore, since mammographic regions could be considered as highly cluttered scenes, the current state of this model reproduces many classical results in psychophysics.

4.2 Performance evaluation

The performance of the proposed system is shown by FROC curves in Figure 9 and Figure 10. A FROC or Free-response Receiver Operating Characteristic curve is the plot of the lesion localization vs. the non-lesion localization, as the threshold to report a finding is varied; FROC curves are mainly implemented to objectively evaluate and analyse image processing algorithms, such as imaging CAD algorithms. Increasing the sensitivity of the algorithm can lead to false positives when reaching the detection of subtle signs. The experimental results of this algorithm were directed to how the proposed algorithm can improve the diagnosis of pathological signs (in this case, microcalcifications). When a microcalcification (or microcalcification cluster) is detected at the approximate position given in the database specifications, we count a true positive (TP). Otherwise, if a microcalcification (or microcalcification cluster) is detected outside the approximate radius indicated in the database, we count a false positive (FP). Furthermore, the malignancy of the pathologies in diagnostic images in different modalities should be one of the main topics in CAD evaluations, as it provides information about how specific are the techniques or approaches in detection of pathologies; thereby they can be characterized by powerful descriptors such as the size of the signs, character of the background tissue, characterization of the abnormality (e. g. single or clustered microcalcifications) and the approximated radius of the pathology in each image.

Figure 9 illustrates the FROC curves for different FOA radiuses. Note that as the FOA becomes narrower, the overall performance of the proposed neurobiologically-inspired algorithm increases. This is an expected effect that emerges from the visual system's features: As the circumscribed region to which attention is directed reduces, the sensitivity of the system increases. Furthermore, this is a convenient strategy when the scenes are too cluttered and consequently, difficult to analyse. The maximum performance reached by the proposed algorithm was approximately 92.0% at one false positive and 100.0% at 1.5 false positives implementing a 2-pixel FOA radius. Note that at this stage, the visual cortex model described in this work is limited to the bottom-up control of attention. Furthermore, we have followed this strategy as our main concern is the localization of the stimuli to be attended, not their identification.

From the FROC curves in Figure 10 and specifically the true positive ratios and the average number of false positives per image, it should be noticed that the pre-attentive bottom-up model outperforms the DoG-based approach. In general, DoG kernels exhibit a medium specificity, which allows the use of a single filter to enhance all the microcalcifications under certain conditions. This means that in order to make the system more robust and make microcalcifications of all sizes detectable, a bank of filters would be needed. Although the

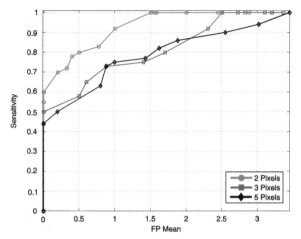

Fig. 9. FROC curves illustrating the performance of the proposed approach for different FOAs' radiuses (in pixels).

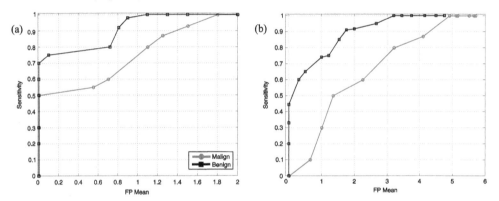

Fig. 10. FROC curves illustrating the performance of (a) the proposed approach; and (b) the DoG approach reported by Ramirez-Villegas et al., 2010, for the malign and benign cases.

performance of the DoG filters could be somewhat limited, DoG filters attenuate (to some extent) adequately the low frequencies, which is highly desirable in some of the processing stages. On the other hand, the proposed approach adapts better to all mammographic conditions given the multi-resolution processing strategy of the visual attention model and the center surround interactions; this makes the model selective enough to enhance the conspicuous locations and suppress low frequency components as well as some high ones in a band pass-like strategy.

5. Discussion, conclusions and perspectives

5.1 Visual cortex mechanisms

Many computational principles regarding bottom-up and top-down visual processing have emerged from experimental and modeling studies. Different features contribute to perceptual saliency and their weighing can be influenced by top-down modulation (Deco & Rolls, 2004; Peters et al., 2005; Serre et al., 2006). There is experimental evidence concerning strong interactions among different visual modalities such as color and orientation for certain visual locations; these interactions are subjected to top-down modulation and training. On the other hand, the most important issue regarding the bottom-up processing is the contrast among features instead of the absolute intensity of each feature. However, the primary visual neurons are not only tuned to some kind of local spatial contrast, but also to neural responses elicited tightly by context, in a structure that extends the range of the classical receptive field.

It is likely that the relative weight of the features which contribute to the most general representation is modulated by higher cortical centers. In this way, the attention process selects the necessary information to discriminate between the distractors and the target as both bottom-up and top-down processes are carried out to analyze the same scene: Here the top-down process is related to previously acquired knowledge that biases the neural processing competition among the objects, therefore the recognition is performed by selecting the next eye movement that maximizes the information gain. The computational challenge, then, lies in the integration of bottom-up and top-down cues, such as to provide coherent control signals for the focus of attention, and in the interplay between attentional orientating and scene or object recognition (Itti & Koch, 2001). As the current approach is familiar only to bottom-up processes, it presents high resemblance and compatibility to integrate top-down processes. Integrating such processes would raise the overall performance of the mammography CAD system.

5.2 Could this approach be extended to mass detection? Through multi-sign detection

Another important issue is the possibility of multi-sign detection, i.e., the detection of multiple signs on the same image modality. Current image processing techniques make the primitive breast abnormalities detection easier (Verma, 2008), nevertheless, the detection of these abnormalities leads to many false detections which depend on the robustness of the vision system (Vilarrasa, 2006; Ramirez-Villegas et al., 2010). On the other hand, the modular architectures of most of such existing systems lead to the necessity of creating separate algorithms for detecting different kinds of cancer signs, e.g., microcalcifications and masses. As these two types of abnormalities are in several ways remarkably different, many researchers have addressed these two diagnostic tasks separately; consequently, the difficulty on detecting cancer rises in direct proportion with the number of implemented algorithms for such tasks (in this case, at least two different processing pathways). Nevertheless, visual attention modeling could be an important step towards the development of a fully-comprehensive CAD system for mammographic image analysis. Up to the knowledge of the authors of this chapter, the potential of such models in the analysis of mammographic images have not been yet issued, nor identified. Theoretically, given the features of the visual processes intended to be modeled, any visual cortex-like model would be capable of helping (to some extent) in the analysis of any diagnostic image.

Figure 11 illustrates an example of how the saliency-based bottom-up model operates for a mammographic image containing a mass.

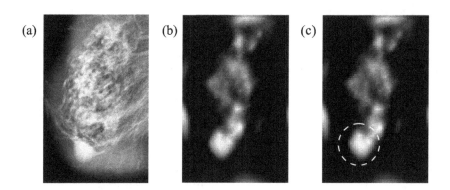

Fig. 11. Saliency-based bottom-up approach in the detection of masses: (a) Equalized image; (b) Saliency map; (c) First attended location by the WTA approach.

5.3 Perspectives: Through multi-organ and multi-disease CAD

There are many computational approaches which have addressed the problem of diagnosis at reasonable cost-effectiveness relation; however, they commonly are single-purpose systems, i.e., their target is the detection of only one disease and one organ. Such schemes are referred to as *abnormality-dependent approaches*. These approaches work well in the case of a single-purpose CAD; nonetheless, it is not preferable to apply such approaches to a multi-disease CAD, given the disproportionately large amount of algorithms that would be necessary to detect every single disease (at least one per disease). The future integration of CAD systems into multi-disease and multi-organ ones ensures its usage in diagnosing a large amount of target diseases with a fully comprehensive and integral architecture. Conversely, the diversity of acquisition conditions and the features of different kinds of diagnostic images pose additional challenges on well-known CAD processing steps such as segmentation, registration and classification, not to mention that the characteristics of abnormal regions on these images depend largely on the type of disease. Therefore, it is desirable to integrate the diagnostic knowledge of various types of diseases into a *universal dictionary of features for diagnosis*.

Some research efforts have been made in improving multi-organ and multi-disease CAD. As a matter of fact, there is a rising interest on integrating such systems into multi-purpose ones. One aspect of this is that cancer, for instance, can spread to other organs in the body. Therefore, if a single-disease CAD can detect cancer, it would be of quite limited use for predicting metastasis and complications related to such cancer detection; moreover, it also would be of little use in order to detect cancer in other organs when such metastasis has occurred.

Conventional single-disease CAD approaches have addressed as many diseases as the number of involved computer vision algorithms to detect them. As a matter of fact, the wide range of conditions and characteristics of images is the most cumbersome issue that abnormality-dependent approaches have to face. Conversely, from the viewpoint of computational efficiency, it is not desirable to have as many diagnosis algorithms as the number of target diseases. It has become obvious that a more straightforward strategy will be needed to overcome the problem of integrating and understanding all the diagnostic knowledge by processing images and extracting candidate regions having structures and/or characteristics that are not normal. Furthermore, the integration and processing of such wide variety of multi-modal medical images need to be assembled and implemented as part of PACS in order to be used in clinical situations.

For instance, in clinical situations, it is important that the sensitivity of the system to be maintained as high as possible, which is achievable using a complex and strongly wired computational model (such as cortex-like models), and not with an unnecessarily increased number of different and complementary CAD schemes. Furthermore, although a fully-comprehensive CAD scheme can be seen as a highly robust and integral software, processing images from so many modalities is time consuming and therefore, it is likely that diagnosis would not be performed in real time; rather than that, image analysis would be performed offline. As a first goal towards the development of a multi-organ and multi-disease CAD, the integration of multi-modal medical images and intelligent assistance in diagnosis of multi-dimensional images has been of great interest (Kobatake, 2007). This task poses additional challenges from the viewpoint of the computational efficiency and the trade-off between the processing efficacy at large datasets and the time taken to reach the diagnosis to support the decision of the physician. Moreover, the analysis of structures is another important issue to consider for the diagnosis of multiple diseases. For example, the thoracic structure contains at least nine different areas of high diagnostic interest (including lung area, trachea and pulmonary vessels) related to at least eight pathology-related signs (large lesions, pulmonary nodules attached to vessels, isolated pulmonary nodules, among others). Therefore, the integrated multi-disease and multi-organ CAD system, in this particular case, would extend the standard lung-cancer detection CAD system, irrespective of the methods used to detect the disease signs.

Finally, beyond the quite simple technical predictions of the authors of this book chapter, comprehensive CAD systems and the potential of cortex-like mechanisms modeling to overcome detection problems and to raise the sensitivity on disease sings detection will contribute dramatically to the development and improvement of the current capabilities of CAD systems.

6. References

Burt, P. J. & Adelson, E. H. (1983). The Laplacian pyramid as a compact image code. *IEEE Trans. Com.*, Vol. 31, No. 4, (April 1983), pp. 532-540, ISSN 0090-6778

Christoyianni, I., Koutras, A., Dermatas, E. & Kokkinakis, G. (2002). Computer aided diagnosis of breast cancer in digitized mammograms. *Computerized Medical Imaging and Graphics*, Vol. 26, No. 5, (September 2002), pp. 309-319, ISSN 0895-6111

Cupples, T. E., Cunningham, J. E., Reynolds, J. C. (2005). Impact of computeraided detection in a regional screening mammography program. *American Journal of Roentgenology*, Vol. 185, No. 4, (October 2005), pp. 944-950, ISSN 1546-3141

Deco, G. & Rolls, E. T. (2004). A neurodynamical cortical model of visual attention and invariant object recognition. *Vision Research*, Vol. 44, No. 6, (March 2004), pp. 621-642, ISSN 0042-6989

Desimone, R. & Duncan, J. (1995). Neural mechanisms of selective visual attention. *Annu. Rev. Neurosci.*, Vol. 18, No. 1, pp. 193-222, ISSN 0147-006X

Doi, K. (2007). Computer-aided diagnosis in medical imaging: Historical review, current status and future potential. *Computerized Medical Imaging and Graphics*, Vol. 31, No. 4-5, (June-July 2007), pp. 198-211, ISSN 0895-6111

El-Naqa, I., Yang, Y., Wernick, M.N., Galatsanos, N.P. & Nishikawa, R.M. (2002). A support vector machine approach for detection of microcalcifications. *IEEE Trans. Med. Imaging*, Vol. 21, No. 12, (Febrero 2003), pp. 1552-1563, ISSN 0278-0062

Fix, J., Rougier, N. & Alexandre, F. (2011). A dynamic neural field approach to the covert and overt deployment of spatial attention. *Cognitive Computation*, Vol. 3, No. 1, (March 2011), pp. 279-293, ISSN 1866-9956

Greenspan, H., Belongie, S., Goodman, R., Perona, P., Rakshit, S., & Anderson, C. H. (1994). Overcomplete Steerable Pyramid Filters and Rotation Invariance, *Proceedings of IEEE Computer Vision and Pattern Recognition*, pp. 222-228, ISBN 0-8186-5825-8, Seattle, WA, USA, June 21-23, 2002.

Hoaglin, D., Mosteller, F. & Tukey J. (1983). *Understanding Robust and Exploratory Data Analysis*, John Wiley & Sons, ISBN 978-0471384915, New York, USA.

Itti, L., Koch, C. & Niebur, E. (1998). A Model of Saliency-Based Visual Attention for Rapid Scene Analysis. *IEEE Trans. Patt. Anal. Mach. Intel.*, Vol. 20, No. 11, (November 1998), pp. 1254-1259, ISSN 0162-8828

Itti, L. & Koch, C. (2000). A saliency-based search mechanism for overt and covert shifts of visual attention. *Vision Research*, Vol. 40, No. 10-12, (June 2000), pp. 1489–1506, ISSN 0042-6989

Itti, L. & Koch, C. (2001). Computational modeling of visual attention. *Nature Reviews Neuroscience*, Vol. 2, No. 3, (March 2001), pp. 194-203, ISSN 1471-0048

Kobatake, H. (2007). Future CAD in multi-dimensional medical images – Project on multi-organ, multi-disease CAD system. *Computerized Medical Imaging and Graphics*, Vol. 31, No. 4-5, (June-July 2007), pp. 258-266, ISSN 0895-6111

Koch, C. & Ullman, S. (1985). Shifts in selective visual attention: towards the underlying neural circuitry. *Human Neurobiol.*, Vol. 4, No. 4, pp. 219-227, ISSN 0721-9075

Kohonen, T. (1990). The self-organizing map. *Proceedings of the IEEE*, Vol. 78, No. 9, (September 1990), pp. 1464-1480, ISSN 0018-9219

Navalpakkam, V. & Itti, L. (2002). A goal oriented attention guidance model. In: *Lecture Notes in Computer Science*, H. Bülthoff, C. Wallraven, S-W. Lee & T. Poggio, (Eds.), 453-461, Springer Berlin/Heidelberg, ISBN 978-3-540-00174-4, Berlin, Germany

Navalpakkam, V. & Itti, L. (2005). Modeling the influence of task on attention. *Vision Research*, Vol. 45, No. 2, (January 2005), pp. 205-231, ISSN 0042-6989

Ochoa, E. M. (1996). *Clustered microcalcification detection using optimized difference of Gaussians (DoG)*. M.Sc. thesis, Dept. of the Air Force, Air Force Institute of Technology, Air University, Ohio, USA.

Oliver, A., Freixenet, J., Martí, J., Pérez, E., Pont, J., Denton, E.R.E. & Zwiggelaar, R. (2010). A review of automatic mass detection and segmentation in mammographic images. *Medical Image Analysis*, Vol. 14, No. 2, (April 2010), pp. 87-110, ISSN 1361-8415

Papadopoulos, A., Fotiadis, D.I. & Costaridou, L. (2008). Improvement of microcalcifications cluster detection in mammography utilizing image enhancing techniques. *Computers in Biology and Medicine*, Vol. 38, No. 10, (October 2008), pp. 1045-1055, ISSN 0010-4825

Peters, R. J., Iyer, A., Itti, L. & Koch, C. (2005). Components of bottom-up gaze allocation in natural images. *Vision Research*, Vol. 45, No. 18, (August 2005), pp. 2397-2416, ISSN 0042-6989

Ramirez-Moreno, D. F. & Ramirez-Villegas, J. F. (2011). A computational implementation of a bottom-up visual attention model applied to natural scenes. *Rev. Ing.*, ISSN 0121-4993 (In press)

Ramirez-Villegas, J. F., Lam-Espinosa, E. & Ramirez-Moreno, D. F. (2010). Microcalcification detection in mammograms using difference of Gaussians filters and a hybrid feedforward-Kohonen neural network. *XXII Brazilian Symposium on Computer Graphics and Image Processing*, 11-15 October, pp. 186-193, ISSN: 1550-1834.

Ramirez-Villegas, J. F. & Ramirez-Moreno, D. F. (2011). Wavelet packet energy, Tsallis entropy and statistical parameterization for support vector-based and neural-based classification of mammographic regions. *Neurocomputing*, ISSN 0925-2312 (In press)

Serre, T., Wolf, L., Bileschi, S., Riesenhuber, M. & Poggio, T. (2007). Robust Object recognition with cortex-like mechanisms. *IEEE Transactions on Pattern Analysis and Machine Intelligence*, Vol. 29, No. 3, (March 2007), pp. 411-426, ISSN 0162-8828

Suckling, J. (1994). The Mammographic Image Analysis Society Digital Mammogram Database. Excerpta Medica, International Congress Series, Vol. 1069, pp. 375-378.

Tsai, N-C., Chen, H-W. & Hsu, S-L. (2010). Computer-aided diagnosis for early-stage breast cancer by using Wavelet Transform. *Computerized Medical Imaging and Graphics*, ISSN 0895-6111 (In Press)

Verma, B. (2008). Novel network architecture and learning algorithm for the classification of mass abnormalities in digitized mammograms. *Artificial Intelligence in Medicine*, Vol. 42, No. 1, (January 2008), pp. 67-79, ISSN 0933-3657

Verma, B., McLeod, P. & Klevansky, A. (2009). A novel soft cluster neural network for the classification of suspicious areas in digital mammograms. *Pattern Recognition*, Vol. 42, No. 9, (September 2009), pp. 1845-1852, ISSN 0031-3203

Vilarrasa-Andrés, A. (2006). *Sistema inteligente para la detección y diagnóstico de patología mamaria*, PhD Thesis, Dept. de radiología y medicina física, Universidad Complutense de Madrid, Madrid, España

Walther, D. & Koch C. (2006). Modeling attention to salient proto-objects. *Neural Networks*, Vol. 19, No. 9, (November 2006), pp. 1395-1407, ISSN 0893-6080

Wei, L., Yang, Y. & Nishikawa, R.M. (2009). Microcalcification classification assisted by content-based image retrieval for breast cancer diagnosis. *Pattern Recognition*, Vol. 42, No. 6, (June 2009), pp. 1126-1132, ISSN 0031-3203

Yu, S., Guan, L. (2000). A CAD system for the automatic detection of clustered
    microcalcifications in digitized mammogram films. *IEEE Trans. Med. Imaging,* Vol.
    19, No. 2, (February 2000), pp. 115-126, ISSN 0278-0062

9

Compensating Light Intensity Attenuation in Confocal Scanning Laser Microscopy by Histogram Modeling Methods

Stefan G. Stanciu[1], George A. Stanciu[1] and Dinu Coltuc[2]
*[1]Center for Microscopy-Microanalysis and Information Processing,
University "Politehnica" of Bucharest
[2]University Valahia of Targoviste
Romania*

1. Introduction

The scientific discipline of microscopy aims to make possible the visualization of objects that cannot be observed by the unassisted human vision system, allowing researchers to enhance their understanding on the morphology and processes which characterize such objects. All microscopy techniques by themselves represent crucial tools for scientists working in various fields of research, and furthermore, when combined with image processing and computer vision algorithms the level of information and the speed at which it can be extracted from microscopy images can be greatly increased.

Confocal Scanning Laser Microscopy (CSLM) is generally considered to be one of the most important microscopy techniques at this time because of the optical sectioning possibilities offered. It is widely accepted that the confocal microscope was invented by Marvin Minsky, who filed a patent in 1957 (Minsky, 1957). However, at that time such a system was very difficult, if not impossible, to implement, due to the unavailability of the required laser sources, sensitive photomultipliers or computer image storage possibilities. The first CSLM system, functioning by using mechanical object scanning, was developed in Oxford in 1975, and a review of this work was later published (Sheppard, 1990). As mentioned above, the architecture of a CSLM system provides the possibility to acquire images representing optical sections on a sample's volume. In order to achieve this, in a CSLM system an excitation source (laser) emits coherent light which is scanned across the sample surface. In reflection mode the light reaching the sample is reflected backwards to the objective, towards a detector. In fluorescence mode the same optical path is used, with the difference being that the reflected light is discarded and the detector collects only the light rays corresponding to the fluorescence emission from the sample. While in conventional microscopy, the detector is subjected to light which is reflected by out of focus planes, resulting in out-of-focus blur being contained in the final image, the architecture of a CSLM system avoids this situation. In order to acquire images corresponding to a certain optical section, a confocal aperture (usually known as pinhole) is situated in front of the detector. More precisely, the pinhole is placed in a plane conjugate to the intermediate image plane and, thus, to the object plane of the microscope. As a result, only light reflected from the focal plane reaches the detector, out-of-focus light being blocked by the pinhole (Fig. 1). The dimension of the pinhole is variable and together with the wavelength which is being used and the numerical aperture of the objective, determines the thickness of the focal plane (Shepard et. al., 1997; Wilson, 2002).

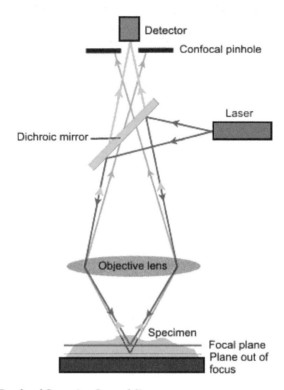

Fig. 1. Principle of Confocal Scanning Laser Microscopy.

The architecture of a CSLM offers specific advantages such as increased resolution and better contrast than conventional microscopy. Meantime, by providing access to images corresponding to optical sections it offers as well significant advantages for people working in fields such as biology, medicine, material science or microelectronics mainly because the CSLM image stacks can be used for 3D reconstructions of the material surfaces (surface topological studies) or of the internal structure of semi-transparent specimens (sub-surface bulk studies) (Rigaut et al., 1991; Sugawara et al. 2005; Liu et al. 1997; Rodriguez et al, 2003; Pironon, 1998). The limits of a CSLM system's performance are essentially determined by the working depth of the high numerical aperture (NA) objective lens which is used in a particular investigation session but also by the properties of other components such as the laser source, the photomultiplier sensitivity or others.

One of the causes that lead to problematic scenarios which can occur during the CSLM investigations sessions is light intensity attenuation. This problem is mainly caused by light scattering and adsorption, light-aberrations or photo bleaching in the case of fluorescence labeled samples. Also, due to the fact that staining thick samples by fluorophores evenly is a difficult task, the intensity attenuation with depth is commonly encountered in CSLM investigations on such samples. The intensity attenuation can be caused also by chromatic or spherical aberrations which may occur due to various properties of the optical elements present in a CSLM system. These aberrations can lead to a distortion of focus, which can further on lead to decrease in the excitation intensity. The attenuation of light can increase with the depth of the imaged focal planes also because of physical phenomena such as scattering and absorption, more precisely due to the fact that the light rays are significantly scattered and absorbed by the atoms and molecules contained in the medium encountered by the light on the path to the targeted focal plane (and on the return path as well). When a dense medium that significantly scatters and absorbs light is present above the region of focus, the image that corresponds to the focal plane will have a lower contrast than the images that are collected from the upper planes. As a consequence, the images within the image stacks captured using confocal optical microscopy will have different intensities depending on the depth at which they have been collected.

Besides absorption and scattering, another phenomenon which can lead to light attenuation and thus affect the CSLM image acquisition is the reflection of the incident laser beam towards a different direction rather than the direction of the objective. When the laser beam encounters a plain surface, it will reflect backwards, in the direction of the objective. When the laser beam encounters an inclined surface instead of reflecting backwards towards the objective, it will reflect in a direction normal to the plane of that surface as illustrated in Fig 2. The light that reaches the detector in the case of the interaction between the laser beam and regions with morphology of this type will have a low intensity. An example on such a scenario can be found in (Stanciu et al. 2010), where CSLM images collected on Photonic Quantum Ring Laser devices that have a deficient aspect due to this situation are presented.

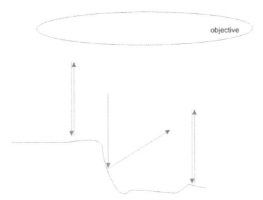

Fig. 2. Scenario in laser scanning microscopy when in certain regions the laser beam is not reflected backwards, towards the objective, due to the sample's geometry.

The intensity attenuation and structural blurring in the image stacks can be the cause of serious problems in the analysis of CSLM images. Problematic situations occur also when trying to use computer vision algorithms designed for tasks such as object & scene recognition or object tracking along with image stacks collected by CSLM. These types of techniques can provide awkward results when the contrast parameters, which are directly dependant to the light intensity, have very different values throughout the series. For example the results that may be achieved by using various thresholding algorithms directly depend on the separability and stationarity of the intensity distributions corresponding to the two classes in the 1D intensity space. In the case of light intensity attenuation, the intensity distributions are non-stationary and non-stationarity reduces the effective separability between the classes, which is likely to lead to segmentation errors (Semechko et al, 2011). In (Sun et al., 2004) is shown that intensity compensation can also enhance the visualization of CSLM data when 3D reconstruction techniques are employed for volume rendering.

In this chapter we overview several recently reported digital image processing techniques that can be used to compensate the effects of light attenuation in CSLM imaging. The techniques that we present in this chapter can be regarded as histogram modeling methods. In order compensate light attenuation, Capek et al. (2006) considered the specification for each frame in the stack of a standard histogram. The standard histogram was computed according to a normalization procedure proposed by Nyul et al. (2000) which consists on matching landmarks in histograms. Stanciu et al. (2010), propose in the same purpose a method based on exact histogram specification. In their method to each of the images in the CSLM stack is exactly specified the histogram of a reference frame. The reference frame is elected by using an estimator which takes into account aspects such as brightness, contrast and sharpness. Semechko et al (2011), propose an intensity attenuation correction method which combines the ones of Capek et al. (2006) and Stanciu et al. (2010). In this method, the authors use as reference the standard histogram proposed in Capek (2006), specify it in its exact shape to the other images of the stack by using the algorithm of Coltuc (2006) and finally nonlinear diffusion filtering is used aiming to suppress noise and homogenize locally over-enhanced image regions. Each of these methods will be presented in detail in the following sections.

2. Intensity attenuation based on histogram normalization & histogram warping

In Capek et al., (2006) a method for the compensation of intensity attenuation based on the warping of the histograms of the individual images in the CSLM stack to a standard histogram is introduced. The standard histogram is constructed such that warping the histograms of the individual images onto it will both preserve the high contrast of the optimally captured sections while in the same time will improve the contrast and the brightness of the low quality images in the stack. The high quality images are most likely to correspond to the topmost layers in the specimen, while the low quality images are most likely to correspond to the deep ones. The computation of the standard histogram is inspired by a procedure for histogram normalization proposed by Nyul et al. (2000) which consists in directly matching landmarks in histograms. Unlike the original approach by Nyul et al.(2000), the method proposed by Capek et al. (2006) searches for the longest distance between two adjacent landmarks in one histogram. The considered landmarks correspond to the minimum intensity, maximum intensity and the n-th percentiles of the image histogram, for $n= \{10, 20,..., 90\}$. This approach is chosen by the authors as maximal distances between landmarks are likely to preserve maximum image contrast. These maximal distances ($M_0, M_1, M_2, \ldots, M_{10}$) are searched in the histograms of all images in the stack and once found are counted up and stretched to cover a grayscale of 256 levels. The breaks between the rescaled maximal distances ($L_0, L_1, L_2, \ldots, L_{10}$) represent the new landmarks of the standard scale (Fig. 3). The landmarks of the standard scale are matched to the landmarks of individual image histograms in order to compute the new intensities of the image pixels and further on the image intensities between the landmarks ($L_0, L_1, L_2, \ldots, L_{10}$) are piece-wise linearly interpolated, as illustrated in Fig. 4. In other words, the normalized histogram is determined by taking for each pair of landmarks the maximal distance and by stretching these distances to cover the graylevel range. Finally, the normalized histogram is specified to each image in the stack by histogram warping. Histogram warping, originally proposed by Cox (1995), is closely related to histogram specification. Instead of transforming a given image to match a given histogram, for histogram warping one should transform two given images in order to achieve the same somehow "intermediate" histogram. In fact, the histogram warping problem consists in deriving the intermediate histogram which can be exactly specified to both images. The complete details of the algorithm presented above can be found in the original publication (Capek et. al, 2006).

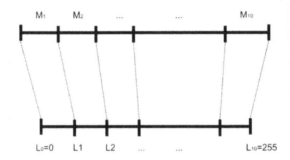

Fig. 3. Mapping of the maximal distances to a standard 256 levels grayscale.

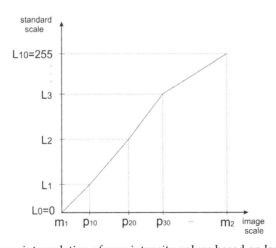

Fig. 4. Piece-wise linear interpolation of new intensity values based on landmark matching.

In Fig. 5 we present a subset of a a stack of images collected by CSLM on a sol–gel matrice sample doped with a photosensitizer, in original aspect and in the aspect resulted after processing by using the algorithm described in this section. The number in the top left corner depicts the numerical order of optical sections in the full series. The distance between sections in the subset is of 1 μm. The image series were collected by using a Leica TCS SP CLSM system, working in reflection workmode (HeNe 633nm). A HC PL FLUOTAR 20.0x objective was used, having a numerical aperture of 0.50.

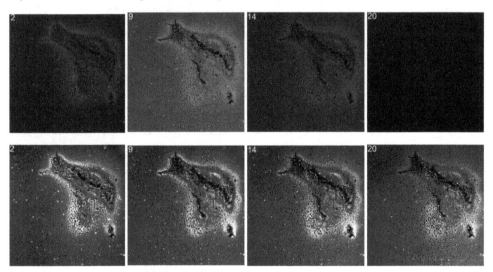

Fig. 5. Subset from CSLM stack collected on sol-gel matrice sample a) in original aspect; b) in an aspect resulted after histogram warping to a normalized histogram

3. Intensity attenuation based on reference frame detection & exact histogram specification

The drawback of the method presented above is a certain over-enhancement which may occur, as in the case of the basic histogram equalization method presented in (Stanciu and Friedman, 2009). If the contrast is increased too match, false contours may appear along with an enhancement of the noise. In order to eliminate these drawbacks, Stanciu et al. (2010) have introduced a different technique based on histogram modeling aiming to compensate the light attenuation in the case of CSLM images. In the proposed method instead of a uniform or a normalized histogram, the histogram of the best visual quality image of the stack is specified to the other images in the stack. This image of best visual quality was entitled the 'reference frame'. The reference frame was elected from among the images that make up the stack based on a procedure that offers automated selection. In order to specify the histogram of the reference frame to the others, the exact histogram specification algorithm introduced by Coltuc et al., (2006) was used instead of the classical histogram specification algorithms. It should be stressed that the approach of Coltuc et al., (2006) provides exact results, while the classical histogram specification as well as the histogram warping method proposed by Cox et al. (1995) provide only approximate results.

As mentioned above, the proposed method relies on specifying the histogram that corresponds to the image of the best visual quality in the series onto the rest of the images in the stack. The reference frame can be selected by visual inspection, with a human operator examining the entire image stack and choosing the best quality frame. Obviously, such an approach is both subjective and time consuming. Therefore, the authors have proposed a procedure that offers the automated detection of the reference frame. In order to automate the reference frame detection, a quality assessment metric is defined, and the reference frame is selected as the one with the best score with respect to the considered metric. The metric that the authors have proposed is based on the evaluation of three attributes which are generally considered as responsible for the quality of a graylevel images. These are: brightness, contrast and contour sharpness.

A good measure of image brightness is the average graylevel of the image. Considering the discrete image $f:[0,M-1] \times [0,N-1] -> [0,L-1]$ and $H=\{h(0), h(1),... h(L-1)\}$ its histogram. The average graylevel, μ_f, can be defined as follows:

$$\mu_f = \frac{\sum_{i=0}^{L-1} ih(i)}{\sum_{i=0}^{L-1} h(i)} = \frac{1}{MN}\sum_{i=0}^{L-1} ih(i)$$

(1)

As the standard deviation measures how widely spread the values in a data set are, it can be regarded as a measure of contrast. If many data points are close to the mean, then the standard deviation is small. By the contrary, if many data points are far from the mean, then the standard deviation is large. Finally, if all data values are equal, then the standard deviation is zero. Obviously the variance is a measure of the contrast, too. The standard deviation has the advantage that, unlike variance, it is expressed in the same units as the data. An unbiased estimate of the standard deviation can be defined as follows:

$$\sigma_f = \sqrt{\frac{1}{MN-1}\sum_{i=0}^{L-1} h(i)(i - \mu_f)^2}$$

(2)

The third factor that we have taken into consideration when designing the reference image estimator is related to the sharpness of the edges contained in the image. An image is generally considered to be of good quality if the objects contained in it can be discerned very clearly. Edges characterize boundaries and represent therefore a problem of fundamental importance in image processing. Edges can be regarded as discontinuities between image regions of rather uniform graylevel or color. Since detecting edges means detecting discontinuities, one can use derivative operators as the gradient or Laplacian. Derivative operators are commonly used as well for focus assessment in microscopy imaging (Osibote et al., 2010) and can be employed in image fusion methods (Stanciu, 2011). We have employed the Sobel edge detector (Gonzales and Woods, 2002) in the design of the automatic reference frame estimator. The Sobel operator uses a pair of 3x3 convolution masks S_x & S_y, with S_x estimating the gradient in the x-direction (columns), while S_y estimating the gradient in the y-direction (rows):

$$S_x = \begin{vmatrix} -1 & 0 & 1 \\ -1 & 0 & 1 \\ -1 & 0 & 1 \end{vmatrix}, \; S_y = \begin{vmatrix} -1 & -1 & -1 \\ 0 & 0 & 0 \\ 1 & 1 & 1 \end{vmatrix} \tag{3}$$

With g_x & g_y being the gradients in x and y direction computed by convolution with S_x, and S_y, respectively, the magnitude of the gradient can be defined as:

$$g = \sqrt{g_x^2 + g_y^2} \tag{4}$$

As an estimate on the sharpness of contours (edges) contained in image f, the mean intensity of its gradient image g, namely μ_g is used.

The three measures discussed above, μ_f, σ_f, and μ_g are normalized in order to take values in [0,1]. Thus, μ_f and μ_g are divided by $L-1$, the graylevel range, and σ_f is divided by $(L-1)^2/12$, i.e., by the standard deviation of a uniform random variable defined on [0,L-1]. Finally, the quality measure for automated detection of the reference frame, q_f is computed as the simple product:

$$q_f = \mu_f \sigma_f \mu_g \tag{5}$$

After computing q_f for all the images in the stack, the image that outputs the highest response to q_f is selected as reference frame. Further on, its histogram is specified to the other images by using the exact histogram specification algorithm of Coltuc et al. (2006). This algorithm is presented in the next part.

Considering $H=\{h(0), h(1),\dots h(L-1)\}$ the histogram to be specified, the exact histogram specification proceeds as follows:

1. The image pixels are ordered in increasing order by using a special strict ordering relation;
2. The ordered string is split from left to right in groups of $h(j)$ pixels;
3. For all the pixels in a group j the jth gray level is assigned, where $j=0,\dots,L-1$.

The definition of the strict order relation is the essential stage of histogram specification. Since image informational content should be preserved, the induced ordering must be consistent with the normal ordering. This means that, if a pixel graylevel is greater than another one with the normal ordering on integers set, it should be greater with the new ordering as well. The new ordering should refine the normal ordering on the set of integers, i.e., equal pixels according to the normal order will be differentiated by the induced ordering. Meantime, in order to avoid noise, the induced ordering should correspond, in a certain way, to the human perception of brightness.

Coltuc et al. (2006) have transferred the problem of ordering on a scalar image to a K-dimensional space by associating a vector to each pixel. The image pixels are ordered by lexicographically ordering the vectors and inducing the same ordering among them. The approach considers a bank of K filters, $\Phi=\{\varphi1, \varphi2,\dots, \varphi K\}$ whose supports W_i, i=1,...,K, are symmetric and obey an inclusion relation: $W_1 \subset W_2 \dots \subset W_K$. The support of $\varphi1$, W_1, is one pixel size. The size of each Wi is kept to a minimum. Each filter extracts some local information about graylevels around the current pixel $f(x,y)$. Furthermore, to each pixel $f(x,y)$ is associated the K-tuple $\Phi(f)(x,y)=\{\varphi 1(f)(x,y), \varphi 2(f)(x,y),..., \varphi K(f)(x,y)\}$. Finally, the new ordering between image pixels is defined by ordering in lexicographic order on the corresponding K-tuple set. A higher value for K is equivalent to a finer ordering. If K is large enough, for natural images a strict ordering is induced. Furthermore, it clearly appears that the inclusion among the filter supports orders the amount of information extracted by each filter. Thus, when i is small, the information extracted is strongly connected to the current pixel. As index i increases, support Wi increases as well and the weight of the current pixel decreases in the filter response. This is a reason for ranking pixels using the lexicographic order starting with the first index. In case of using moving average filters, it appears that an almost strict ordering is obtained for a rather small value of K, i.e., $K=6$. Other linear or nonlinear filters can be used as well (Gaussian filters, median, etc.). Wan and Shi (2007) applied the same idea of ordering, but on the coefficients of the non-decimated wavelet decomposition of the image. A discussion on exact histogram specification can be found also in Bevilacqua and Azzari (2007) while a solution for exact global histogram specification optimized for structural similarity is proposed by Avanki (2009).

In Fig. 6 we present a subset from the stack of images collected by CSLM on a sol–gel matrice sample doped with a photosensitizer (presented in Fig. 5, as well), in original aspect and in the aspect resulted after processing by using the algorithm described in this section.

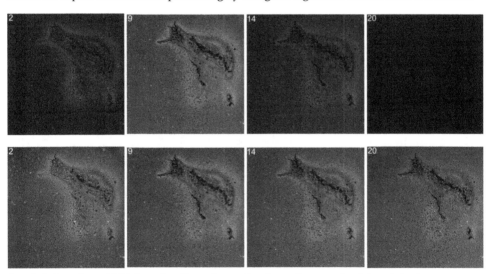

Fig. 6. Subset from CSLM stack collected on sol-gel matrice sample a) in original aspect; b) in an aspect resulted after exact specification of the reference frame's histogram

In Fig. 7, an example of how the histogram of an image is modified upon exact histogram specification and histogram warping is presented. The initial histograms of the 2nd, 9th, 14th, 20th images in the stack; the specified histogram, which is actually the histogram of the 9th image in the stack; and the modality in which histogram warping influences the histogram shape in the case of a particular example (i.e., frame 20) are illustrated. Both the warping model histogram and the histogram resulted after histogram warping are presented. The histogram resulted after exact histogram specification, by using the algorithm of Coltuc et al. (2006), is exactly the same histogram as the specified one, in our case the histogram of the 9th image in the stack. It can be observed very clearly the difference between the results obtained by the three different techniques. The complete details of the method presented in this section can be found in the original publication (Stanciu et al, 2010).

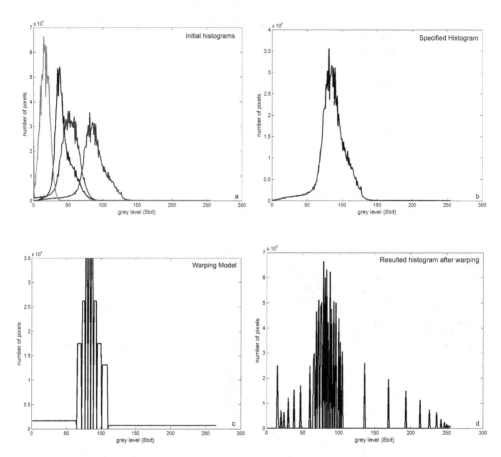

Fig. 7. a) Initial histograms of the 2nd,9th,14th,20th frames corresponding to the sol gel matrice sample; b) specified histogram; c) histogram warping model; d) resulted histogram after warping.

4. Intensity attenuation by exact specification of a normalized histogram and nonlinear diffusion filtering

The third method that we overview is the one of Semechko et al, (2011), who propose a method that performs intensity attenuation correction that combines aspects from the methods of Capek et. al. (2006) and Stanciu et. al. (2010) with nonlinear diffusion filtering. The authors choose to use nonlinear diffusion filtering aiming to suppress noise and homogenize locally over-enhanced image regions. The method overviewed in this section consists in three main steps: calculation of the reference histogram, the exact specification of the reference histogram to all the images taking part of the CLSM stack and diffusion filtering.

The reference histogram is computed by using the method proposed by Capek et al. (2006), taking into account the intensity information of the entire CLSM stack. As detailed in section 2, the first step in computing the normalized histogram involves remapping of intensities of individual CLSM frames so that they cover the same intensity range. The authors regard the resulted reference histogram as a global representation of intensity distribution of the entire volumetric image, without being targeted towards any specific cross section. As the authors experiment on biofilm samples, they consider this approach more appropriate than the one presented in Stanciu et al. (2010), because the proportions of biofilm and fluid may be different in the top and bottom CLSM cross sections that they experiment with. This situation can result in different aspect of the images in the stack depending on the fluid ratio corresponding to a particular optical section.

In the next step, the reference histogram is specified in its exact form to the images that make up the CLSM stack. The algorithm used for the exact histogram specification is the one used also by Stanciu et al. (2010), presented in section 3 of this chapter. The authors justify their choice as regardless of the difference in intensity representation of the materials in lower and upper CLSM cross sections, the pixels that are likely to represent the biofilm will be mapped to higher intensities and pixels corresponding to fluid will be mapped to lower intensities, thus preserving separability of intensity-based representation and enforcing stationarity (Semechko et al, 2011).

In the last step of this method, a diffusion filter is applied to the processed CLSM images in order to suppress any local overenhancement that may occur after the exact specification of the reference frame. In the same time, the diffusion filter can attenuate the noise the CSLM images may contain. The authors justify their choice to use diffusion filtering after the intensity attenuation stage and not before, as in the second case it will cause unequal noise filtering throughout the CLSM stack and will potentially blur structural boundaries in the cross sections most affected by intensity attenuation. With the diffusion being modulated by the magnitude of the intensity gradient (which is related to contrast and hence, to intensity attenuation) between the neighboring voxels, the amount of diffusion will be greater in the bottom cross sections than in the upper cross sections. The authors claim that the gradient magnitude at the biofilm and fluid interface is also likely to be smaller in comparison to the upper cross sections, due to the reduced contrast in the lower cross sections. This approach is meant to avoid changes of structural appearance, which could occur if the gradient magnitude is smaller than the contrast threshold parameter in the diffusion equation used in the nonlinear diffusion filter.

Considering Ω as the image domain and $I(x,0)$: $\Omega \rightarrow$ the original image. The filtered image, $I(x,t)$, was obtained as a transient solution of the diffusion equation :

$$\partial_t I = div(D(\nabla I)\nabla I) \tag{6}$$

In case of inhomogeneous isotropic diffusion, $D(\nabla I)$ is a spatially dependent scalar quantity commonly referred to as diffusivity. The authors of this method chose to compute diffusivity using Tukey's biweight (Black et al, 1998). The complete details of the algorithm presented in this section can be found in the original publication (Semechko et al, 2011)

5. Conclusions

In this chapter three recent methods for the compensation of intensity attenuation in CSLM imaging have been overviewed. The method based on histogram warping requires no interaction with the user and can be performed automatically, but the resulted image stack can be subject to contrast over enhancement. The method based on histogram specification that we have previously reported, can be performed either automatically, providing an algorithm that has the ability to automatically select the reference image is employed, or manually, assuming a human operator can nominate the image of best quality in the stack. A very important feature offered by the exact histogram specification and equalization is that all the images in the processed sequence have normalized histograms. This can lead to very effective results in the case of segmentation tasks, as the algorithms for thresholding and segmentation are based on mixtures of Gaussian probability density functions and optimal coding schemes are expected to be obtained if the image within the processed stack will have similar histograms. In the case when all images in the stack are considerably affected by the light attenuation, the methods based on histogram warping will provide better results than the method relying on histogram specification. However, these two methods may provide a result which can be radically different in aspect than the initial aspect of the images due to the possible over-enhancement. In the case of the method based on the exact specification of the reference frame's histogram, the histogram of one of the images in the stack (noted throughout the chapter as the reference image) is specified onto the other images in order to preserve an aspect close to original one. The reference image can be determined automatically taking into consideration the brightness, the standard deviation and the sharpness of the contours (edges) contained in the image. The proposed algorithm can provide the premises for the fast processing of the image sequence. However, when choosing to use this method one must limit to image stacks which contain images that represent optical sections of the same object; otherwise the contrast of the resulted images will be influenced not only by the light attenuation but also by the morphological structure of the objects contained in the image. In this case it would be useless specifying the histogram of an image that represents one object of a certain shape onto another image depicting an object with a completely different shape. The results in that case would be quite unpredictable. The proposed method based on the exact specification of the reference frame's histogram improves the contrast of the image in the case when images of good contrast are present in the stack, and in the same time preserves the initial aspect of the images. When the image content is not uniform throughout the stack the methods based on histogram warping may be regarded as better alternatives.

The techniques presented in this chapter do not restorate any high frequency degradation and, in the same time, cannot compensate the drawbacks that are related to the pinhole size that was used during image acquisition. These methods are simply meant to enhance the visual appearance of collected images that have a deficient aspect due to intensity attenuation, and to assist in segmentation tasks. Besides enhancement, histogram specification yields image normalization in respect to the average gray level, energy, entropy, etc.

6. Acknowledgments

The research presented in this paper has been supported by the National Program of Research, Development and Innovation PN-II-IDEI-PCE, UEFISCDI, in the framework of Research Projects 1566/2008 and 1882/2008.

7. References

Avanaki, A.N. (2009). Exact global histogram specification optimized for structural similarity, *Optical Review*, Volume 16, Number 6, pages 613-621.

Bevilacqua, P. Azzari, (2007). A High Performance Exact Histogram Specification Algorithm, ICIAP 2007, Image Analysis and Processing, pages 623-628.

Black, M.J., Sapiro, G., Marimont, D.H., Heeger, D. (1998). Robust anisotropic diffusion, *IEEE Transactions on Image Processing*, Volume 7, Issue 3, pages 421-32.

Capek, M., Janacek, J. and Kubinova, L., (2006), Methods for Compensation of the Light Attenuation with depth of Images Captured by a Confocal Microscope, *Microscopy Research and Technique*, Volume 69, Issue 8, pages 624 – 635.

Coltuc, D., Bolon, P., & Chassery, J.M., (2006), Exact Histogram Specification, *IEEE Transactions on Image Processing*, volume 15, issue 5 , p. 1143 – 1152

J. Cox, S. Rey, S. L. Hingorani, (1995). Dynamic Histogram Warping of Image Pairs for Constant Image Brightness, Proceedings of the IEEE Intl. Conf. on Image Processing, ICIP'95, vol. 2, p. 366- 369

Gonzales, R.C. & Woods, R.E., (2002). Digital Image Processing. Upper Saddle River, NJ: Prentice-Hall.

Minsky, M., Microscopy apparatus, 1961: US Patent No. 3013467, filed Nov. 7, 1957.

Nyul, L.G., Udupa, J.K. and Zhang, X. (2000). New variants of a method of MRI scale standardization. *IEEE Transactions on Medical Imaging*, volume 19, pages 143–150.

Osibote, O., Dendere, R., Krishnan, S. and Douglas, T. (2010). Automated focusing in bright-field microscopy for tuberculosis detection, *Journal of Microscopy*, Volume 240, Issue 2, pages 155–163.

Rigaut, J.P., Vassy, J., Herlin, P., Duigou, F., Masson, E., Briane, D., Foucrier, J., Carvajal-Gonzalez, S., Downs, A.M., Mandard, A.M. (1991) Three-dimensional DNA image cytometry by confocal scanning laser microscopy in thick tissue blocks, *Cytometry*, vol. 12, pp. 511-524

Rodriguez, A., Ehlenberger, D., Kelliher, K., Einstein, M., Henderson, S. C., Morrison, J. H., Hof, P. R., Wearne, S. L., Automated reconstruction of three-dimensional neuronal morphology from laser scanning microscopy images. *Methods* 30 (1), 2003, 94–105. , ISSN: 1046-2023

Sheppard, C.J.R., 15 years of scanning optical microscopy at Oxford. Proceedings Royal Microscopical Society, 1990. 25: p. 319-321

Sheppard, C.J.R., Hotton, D.M., Shotton, D. (1997). Confocal Laser Scanning Microscopy, ISBN 0387915141 ,Oxford

Stanciu, S.G. Friedmann, J., Compensating the effects of light attenuation in confocal microscopy by histogram modelling techniques, Proceedings of IEEE ICTON-MW 2008, pages 1-5

Stanciu, S.G., Stanciu G.A. and Coltuc, D. (2010). Automated compensation of light attenuation in confocal microscopy by exact histogram specification, Microscopy *Research and Technique*, Volume 73, Issue 3, pages 165–175, 2010

Stanciu, S.G., (2011) Image Fusion Methods for Confocal Scanning Laser Microscopy experimented on Images of Photonic Quantum Ring Laser Devices, in "Image Fusion" Ed. Osamu Ukimura, ISBN 978-953-7619-X-X, INTECH Open Access Publisher

Sugawara, Y., Kamioka, H., Honjo, T., Tezuka, K., Takano-Yamamoto, T., (2005) Three-dimensional reconstruction of chick calvarial osteocytes and their cell processes using confocal microscopy, *Bone*, 36, 5, Pages 877-883, ISSN 8756-3282

Sun, Y., Rajwa, B and Robinson, J.P., (2004), Adaptive Image-Processing Technique and Effective Visualization of Confocal Microscopy Images, *Microscopy Research and Technique*, volume 64, pages156-163

Wan, Y. and Shi, D. (2007). Joint Exact Histogram Specification and Image Enhancement through the Wavelet Transform, *IEEE Transactions on Image Processing*, volume 16, issue 9, pages 2245-2250

Semechko, A., Sudarsan, R., Bester, E., Dony, R. and Eberl, H. (2011) Influence of light attenuation on biofilm parameters evaluated from CLSM image data, *J. Med. Biol. Eng.*, volume 31, issue 2, pages 135-144.

Wilson, T. (2002). Confocal microscopy: Basic principles and architectures. In: Diaspro A, editor. Confocal and two-photon microscopy: Foundations, applications and advances, ISBN 0471409200, New York.

Permissions

The contributors of this book come from diverse backgrounds, making this book a truly international effort. This book will bring forth new frontiers with its revolutionizing research information and detailed analysis of the nascent developments around the world.

We would like to thank D.Eng. Stefan G. Stanciu, for lending his expertise to make the book truly unique. He has played a crucial role in the development of this book. Without his invaluable contribution this book wouldn't have been possible. He has made vital efforts to compile up to date information on the varied aspects of this subject to make this book a valuable addition to the collection of many professionals and students.

This book was conceptualized with the vision of imparting up-to-date information and advanced data in this field. To ensure the same, a matchless editorial board was set up. Every individual on the board went through rigorous rounds of assessment to prove their worth. After which they invested a large part of their time researching and compiling the most relevant data for our readers. Conferences and sessions were held from time to time between the editorial board and the contributing authors to present the data in the most comprehensible form. The editorial team has worked tirelessly to provide valuable and valid information to help people across the globe.

Every chapter published in this book has been scrutinized by our experts. Their significance has been extensively debated. The topics covered herein carry significant findings which will fuel the growth of the discipline. They may even be implemented as practical applications or may be referred to as a beginning point for another development. Chapters in this book were first published by InTech; hereby published with permission under the Creative Commons Attribution License or equivalent.

The editorial board has been involved in producing this book since its inception. They have spent rigorous hours researching and exploring the diverse topics which have resulted in the successful publishing of this book. They have passed on their knowledge of decades through this book. To expedite this challenging task, the publisher supported the team at every step. A small team of assistant editors was also appointed to further simplify the editing procedure and attain best results for the readers.

Our editorial team has been hand-picked from every corner of the world. Their multi-ethnicity adds dynamic inputs to the discussions which result in innovative outcomes. These outcomes are then further discussed with the researchers and contributors who give their valuable feedback and opinion regarding the same. The feedback is then collaborated with the researches and they are edited in a comprehensive manner to aid the understanding of the subject.

Apart from the editorial board, the designing team has also invested a significant amount of their time in understanding the subject and creating the most relevant covers. They scrutinized every image to scout for the most suitable representation of the subject and create an appropriate cover for the book.

The publishing team has been involved in this book since its early stages. They were actively engaged in every process, be it collecting the data, connecting with the contributors or procuring relevant information. The team has been an ardent support to the editorial, designing and production team. Their endless efforts to recruit the best for this project, has resulted in the accomplishment of this book. They are a veteran in the field of academics and their pool of knowledge is as vast as their experience in printing. Their expertise and guidance has proved useful at every step. Their uncompromising quality standards have made this book an exceptional effort. Their encouragement from time to time has been an inspiration for everyone.

The publisher and the editorial board hope that this book will prove to be a valuable piece of knowledge for researchers, students, practitioners and scholars across the globe.

List of Contributors

Alessandra Budillon and Gilda Schirinzi
Dipartimento per le Tecnologie - Università degli Studi di Napoli "Parthenope", Italy

Zhiyang Li
College of Physical Science and Technology, Central China Normal University, Hubei, Wuhan, P. R. China

Andon Lazarov
Burgas Free University, Bulgaria

Dilip K. Prasad
Nanyang Technological University, Singapore

Maylor K. H. Leung
Universiti Tunku Abdul Rahman (Kampar), Malaysia

Fábio Soares de Lima, Luiz Affonso Guedes and Diego R. Silva
Universidade Federal do Rio Grande do Norte – UFRN, Brazil

Ville Voipio, Heikki Huttunen and Heikki Forsvik
Department of Signal Processing, Tampere University of Technology, Finland

Faycal Kharfi, Omar Denden and Abdelkader Ali
Neutron Radiography Department/Nuclear Research Centre of Birine, Algeria

Juan F. Ramirez-Villegas and David F. Ramirez-Moreno
Computational Neuroscience, Department of Physics, Universidad Autonoma de Occidente, Colombia

Stefan G. Stanciu and George A. Stanciu
Center for Microscopy-Microanalysis and Information Processing, University "Politehnica" of Bucharest, Romania

Dinu Coltuc
University Valahia of Targoviste, Romania